T0320250

EUROPE'S NEXT STEP: ORGANISATIONAL INNOVATION, COMPETITION AND EMPLOYMENT

EUROPE'S NEXT STEP: ORGANISATIONAL INNOVATION, COMPETITION AND EMPLOYMENT

edited by

LARS ERIK ANDREASEN
BENJAMIN CORIAT
FRISO DEN HERTOG
RAPHAEL KAPLINSKY

FRANK CASS

First jointly published 1995 in Great Britain by
FRANK CASS AND COMPANY LIMITED
2 Park Square, Milton Park,
Abingdon, Oxon, OX14 4RN

and in the United States of America by
FRANK CASS
270 Madison Ave,
New York NY 10016

Transferred to Digital Printing 2005

British Library Cataloging in Publication Data:
A catalogue record for this book is available
from the British Library.

ISBN 0-7146-4630 X (hardback)
ISBN 0-7146-4151 0 (paperback)

Library of Congress Cataloging-in-Publication Data:

A catalog record for this book is available from the
Library of Congress

Typeset by Wendy Williams.

CONTENTS

CONTENTS (cont.)

CONTENTS (cont.)

THE CONTRIBUTORS

Lars Erik Andreasen is an economist working for the Directorate General for Employment and Social Affairs at the European Commission in Brussels.

Christian Berggren is a Senior Research Fellow at the Swedish Centre for Working Life in Stockholm and teaches in Industrial Management at the University of Linköping.

John Bessant works at the Centre of Business Research at the University of Brighton in Brighton.

Ronny Bianchi is a doctoral student and Research Assistant at the Universite Paris-Nord.

Benjamin Coriat teaches and researches at the Universite Paris-Nord.

Friso den Hertog is a researcher and Deputy Director of the Maastricht Economic Research Institute on Innovation and Technology (MERIT) at the University of Limburg in Maastricht.

Giovanni Dosi teaches and researches in the Dipartemento Di Scienze Economiche at the University of Rome (La Sapienza).

Alexis Jacquemin teaches and researches at the Department of Economics at the University of Louvain La Neuve.

Nathalie Lucchini is a research assistant at the Centre de Recherche en Economie Industrielle at the University of Paris 13.

*Bengt-Ake Lundva*l is Deputy Director of the Directorate for Science, Technology and Industry at the OECD.

Raphael Kaplinsky is a Fellow at the Institute of Development Studies at the University of Sussex.

Christophe Midler is a researcher at the Centre de Recherche en Gestion de l'Ecole Polytechnique in Paris.

Pascal Petit is Director of Research at CNRS-CEPREMAP in Paris.

Hanno Roberts teaches and researches at the Faculty of Economics at the University Carlos III in Madrid.

Nathan Rosenberg teaches and researches at the Department of Economics at Stanford University.

Klaus Semlinger teaches works at the FHTW in Berlin.

Ulbo de Sitter is an academic and consultant working in Nijmegen.

Luc Soete is Director of the Maastricht Economic Research Institute on Innovation and Technology (MERIT) at the University of Limburg in Maastricht.

Mieke van den Oetelaar is a consultant working with the KOERS Consultancy Group in Hertogenbosch.

Ed van Sluijs is a Research Fellow at the Maastricht Economic Research Institute on Innovation and Technology (MERIT) at the University of Limburg in Maastricht.

INTRODUCTION AND
ACKNOWLEDGEMENTS

Europe entered the decade of the 1980s with virtually stagnant growth (less than one per cent in 1981) and in an atmosphere of Euro-pessimism and Euro-sclerosis. Over the decade a number of major European initiatives were taken, including the Single Act and until the late 1980s, the growth-rate increased, investment revived, inflation was controlled and public deficit were maintained within manageable limits. At the same time, the structural funds were permitting a reduction of the gaps of level of development between regions within the community.

Nevertheless, at the turn of the decade, the positive cycle reversed and five years later, the negative signs have multiplied and have not been reversed. Levels of growth are very low, public deficits have suddenly inflated, the SMEs have regressed, and social tensions have arisen. Above all, Europe is experiencing a dramatically high level of unemployment. Although other regions of the world have also suffered from these trends, Europe has been particularly badly affected.

The Maastricht Treaty, which opened new possibilities for action in transforming the common market into an economic and monetary union, has not yet produced positive effects. The difficult process involved in resolving the differences between Member States and ratifying the Treaty took precedence over attempts to revive growth and reduce unemployment. It is within this context that the White Paper on Growth, Competitiveness and Employment, the Edinburgh Summit and other meetings (and the resulting recommendations) should be viewed. These initiatives marked the formalisation of efforts by the Member States to try to react to these negative tendencies and to stimulate the revival of growth and employment.

This volume focusing on the organisational challenge confronting European industry should be viewed in this framework. It provides clear indications of the route which is necessary to achieve these objectives. These conclusions are, however, confined to the microeconomic framework. They should not be seen as a substitute to the background analysis and policy prescriptions contained in the White Paper and other Community initiatives. Rather, their intent is to complement and enhance the macroeconomic policy prescriptions which are targeted on a revival of the European economy.

The notions presented here are deliberately chosen to focus on certain dimensions of competitiveness of the Union and its member States. These dimensions have only been sketched out in the White Book and, until now, have been underestimated and insufficiently considered. More precisely, the current study concerns the identification, promotion and diffusion of organisational innovations which lie at the heart of the productive activities of the Union and which provide the key for economic revival. It is the belief of the authors that over the past fifteen years a revolution has taken place in organisation which has been both powerful and pervasive. The authors also believe that if Europe ignores these organisational innovations, it will fall further behind, both in absolute terms and in comparison with our global rivals. Thus we believe that the systematic use of resources and the new opportunities opened by the organisational revolution present urgent and critical tasks for the economies of the Union. The central idea developed and illustrated in the present book is that the promotion of organisational innovations constitutes the 'missing link' in transforming large investments in research, technology and productive capacity into economic welfare and the revival of employment growth.

Part 1 of this book, considers the nature of Europe's competitive decline and identifies organisation as the missing link in its 'productivity paradox (Chapter 1). This is followed by an analysis of the organisational challenge confronting European industry, Europe's considerable expertise in this area, and the emergence of appropriate policy frameworks. Three spheres of organisational change in production are identified for both manufacturing and services, and these provide the structure for the individual case-studies. These three spheres are production, R&D and human resource management. The remainder of the book comprises a series of case-studies highlighting the progress made by leading European firms who have begun to innovate new forms of organisation. The intent of the case-studies is to both show the potential for change and to identify some of the policy levers which need to be pulled if the rate of diffusion is to be increased.

Part 2 focuses on organisational changes in the sphere of production, by examining the experiences of Swatch in Switzerland, Peugeot in France and a medium-sized silver-smithing company in the Netherlands. Part 3 addresses the experience of organisational change in R&D, by considering the performance of an Italian-French collaboration in the electronics industry (SGS Thomson) and Renault's development of its innovative Twingo small car. The third Part is devoted to issues of human resource management, and considers the personnel policies of four firms based in the Netherlands, a Dutch insurance firm, an employee-owned British company and a Danish firm which has developed a distinctive flexible division of labour amongst its staff.

Despite the large returns which arise from successful organisation, the pace of diffusion is slow. Therefore, Part 4 focuses on the policy environment. It considers the role of a local government and private sector scheme for assisting SMEs in Germany, and a similar government-private collaboration (with the active participation of the university sector) in the promotion of a network of firms experimenting with continuous improvement in the UK. It also includes a case-study of organisational change in a Swedish hospital to illustrate not only the relevance of organisational change to the service sector, but also to the task of increasing efficiency in the state sector itself.

To heighten the policy relevance of these case-studies, a number of commentaries have been included. These involve responses from prominent policy-related researchers in Europe and the USA.

The authors would like to acknowledge the help of a great many people in the preparation of this manuscript. Our primary gratitude of course goes to the many respondents who have made the research possible. We hope that there views have been reflected accurately and believe that we are able to participate together in an important initiative designed to revive European growth and employment. We would also like to thank the institutions which have made the research feasible - the Institute of Development Studies at Sussex University which coordinated the programme and provided supporting services, MERIT in the Netherlands and the University X111, Paris. In addition the European Commission provide financial assistance to cover some of the costs of the research.

One of the functions of the new forms of organisation considered in this book is to shrink the lead-time in delivering products to the final market. We are pleased to report that many of these organisational principles have been utilised in this book enabling a series of conference papers presented in late September to be revised and printed by early November. This could not have been possible without the hard work and initiative of a large number of people, of whom the following are particularly prominent. Frank Cass, Lydia Lindford and Daphna Weiss provided wonderful support in publication; Wendy Williams performed heroic acts in desk-top publishing; Annie Jamieson coordinated with fluid efficiency; Taraneh Azad worked beyond the call of duty and Corien Gijsbers, Antigone Lyberaki, Sam Macpherson, Asier Minondo and Maria Teresa Zappia provided critical backup. Our thanks to all, but as always the errors and misinterpretations are ours alone.

PART I:
EUROPE'S PROBLEM WITH COMPETITIVENESS

ORGANISATIONAL INNOVATIONS : THE MISSING LINK IN EUROPEAN COMPETITIVENESS

Benjamin Coriat

In order to establish the critical need for the European Union and its members countries to become deeply involved in the organisational revolution at present under way, this chapter opens with a preliminary assessment of European competitivity. This assessment is undertaken through the use of a series of simple yet essential indicators. As will be shown, there are many alarming signals, and the European economy is clearly going through a bad period (section I).

If we limit ourselves to the traditional indicators of economic performance, a more thorough examination shows nevertheless that in key domains which will be decisive for its future - such as Research and Development in information technology - Europe has made a considerable effort, and has to some extent caught up with the global leaders. It will therefore be shown that the real difficulties are to be found in the more qualitative dimension of competitivity: advancement in the field of innovative organisational systems, which are necessary to ensure that the efforts made thus far - as well as those in the future - produce the desired effects (section II). The last section will develop and illustrate this point, showing how organisational innovations are a crucial tool in support of competitivity and employment (section III).

I. THE EUROPEAN ECONOMY AND ITS COMPETITIVENESS: FIRST EVALUATIONS

Even if there exists no undisputed definition of the many-sided notion of competitivity, a consensus exists amongst economists working in this field that competitivity should be defined in terms of a series of questions concerning the health of a given economy, assessed in terms of its growth, employment and revenue on the one hand and, on the other, in terms of its ability to confront positively the global economy in which it finds itself. On the basis of such considerations different definitions of competitiveness have been put forward which are, in the final analysis, very similar, despite the fact that nuances - highlighting one or other aspect of competitivity - are given prominence according to the different definitions proposed.

For example, in one of its most recent issues, the journal *European Economy* proposes the following definition: 'the competitivity of an economy determines its capacity to increase its market share or to sustain a higher growth rate without deteriorating its balance of payments (*European Economy*, 1994, p.175). This first definition is reformulated more precisely, with a view to being more instrumental, by noting that: 'the degree of competitiveness of a country is measured by its capacity to sustain a share of export markets or to sustain a higher growth rate without a deterioration of the current account'. Here, the emphasis is placed on an implicit trade-off between internal growth and external balance, an economy being judged competitive if it can grow without harming, or indeed by improving the rate of cover of its imports by its exports.

This definition is very close to that of the Competitiveness Policy Council of the United States. This draws attention to two supplementary elements which are essential in the context of this discussion. According to this definition, competitiveness is understood to be 'the capacity to produce goods and services which respond to the demands of an international market, whilst at the same time allowing the citizens to enjoy a consistently rising standard of living in the long term' [*Competiteveness Productivity Council, 1992*]. Even though the same ideas are present, this definition draws attention to two further points: it includes in the notion of competitiveness the idea of the necessity of having a 'good' specialisation (that is, to produce at a given moment the goods in demand on international markets), and it stresses that the purpose of competitiveness, over and above the sole aim of growth, should be to improve the 'well-being' of citizens.

In the light of the above precision, a tentative assessment of the factors influencing the competitiveness of the European economy may be made. As we shall see by examining some key economic indicators, the situation at the present time is rather worrying.

Growth

If we consider the very first of these indicators, that related to the evolution of the Community's GDP, certain remarks are in order.

As Figure 1.1 shows, the Community's economy has passed through two distinct phases in the last fifteen years[1]. A first phase of uninterrupted growth between 1981 and 1988 saw the Community's GDP growth rate rise steadily to more than four per cent in 1988. It is clear here that the opportunities created by the Single Act played the role of an effective stimulant. Since 1989 however (starting with the Gulf War), the Community's economy has been in a strongly depressive cycle which, over the course of a long deceleration, has seen the GDP growth-rate fall from more than four per cent to less than one per cent. The gains acquired in the course of the earlier growth phase therefore seem to have been lost. Note also that although this deceleration of the rate of growth has also occurred in the global economy, it has been greater in the Community zone than in the other two regions in the Triad (Figure 1.2)

Figure 1.1. : Growth of GDP : The Dissipation of the Gains of the Eighties
(European Community including once 1995 new länders)

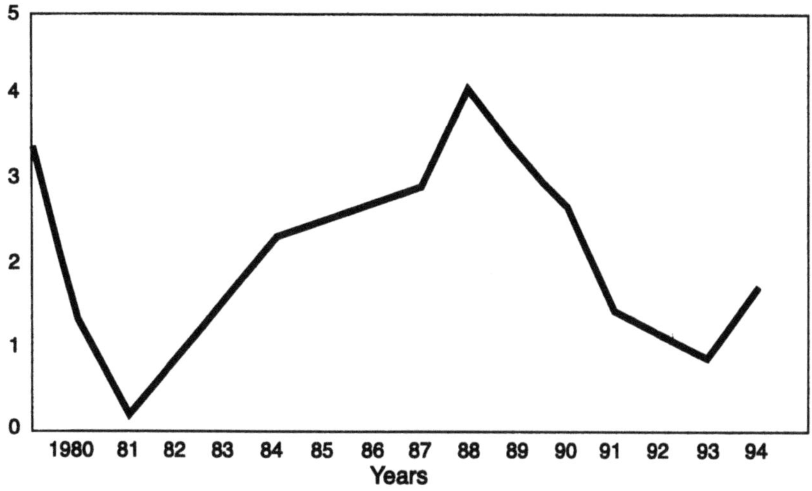

Source: European Economy n° 54, *[1993, p.4]*.

Thus, compared to the rest of the world, the Community's growth followed a very characteristic path over this recent period of fifteen years. GDP growth has been less strongly cyclical than that of the rest of the world and the recovery phases have been less rapid and less vigorous. On the other hand, the recessions have been less pronounced. It would appear that the number of institutional regulations which characterise the European Union (in relation to the rest of the world) protected it against severe recessions but, conversely, to some extent restrained the recovery phases. Nevertheless in the long growth phase of the 1980s and the early 1990s, the Community suffered from a relatively significant growth differential with the rest of the world.

5

Figure 1.2.: Growth in the European Community and in the Rest of the World

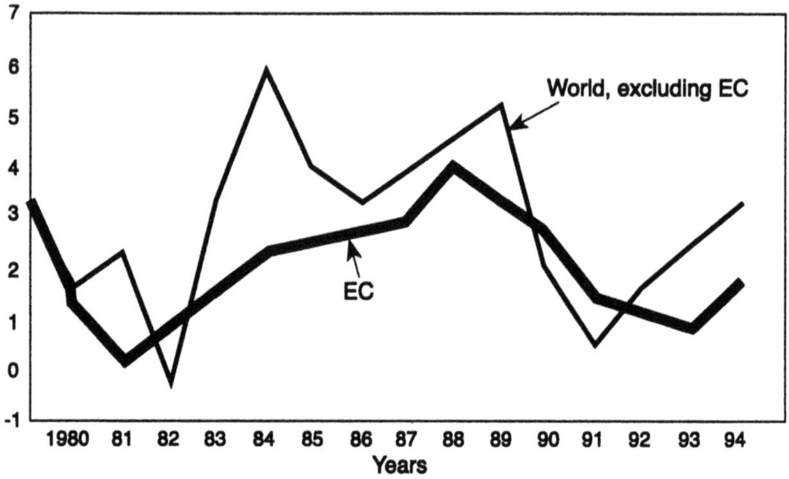

Source: European Economy n° 54, *[1993, p.12]*.

The role played by these institutional factors - both as a hindrance and a stabiliser of growth - is important, since it suggests that rather than suffering from an excessive number of 'institutions', what Europe requires is that these institutions be readjusted so as to conserve their role of cyclical dampness without however holding back the recovery cycles.

Investment and Profitability

These characteristics of the growth process are essentially the same as regards the trend in investment, although as is often the case, with a slight time lag. As Figure 1.3 clearly indicates, and following the trend in GDP, a long growth phase (1981-88) saw the negative level of investment at the beginning of the period increase steadily reaching approximately nine per cent of GDP in 1988. Since then, with the beginning of the recession phase, investment has fallen consistently, becoming negative again in 1993 and showing a slight recovery in 1994. Compared internationally (see Figure 1.4) and considered this time in relation to the share of investment in GDP, the European Community occupies a median position between the USA - which over the entire period made a smaller effort than the European Community - and Japan, which continues to perform remarkably (between 30 and 35 per cent of GDP over the period 1980-94, compared to 20 to 24 per cent for Europe).

6

Figure 1.3.: Investment in the European Community
(real rate of growth, excluding the five new Länders)

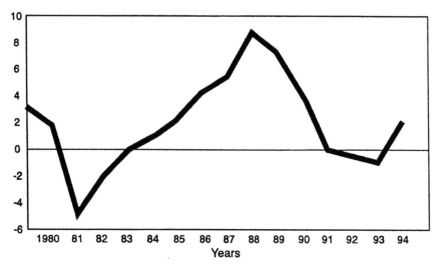

Source: European Economy n° 54, [*1993, p.7*].

Figure 1.4. : Share of the Investment in GDP : a Comparison between the European Community, USA, Japan

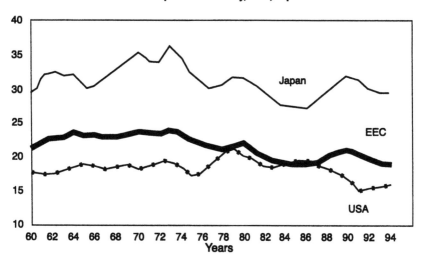

Source : European Commission [*1994, p.60*].

It should however be noted that European firms have performed well in two respects. On the one hand they have on the whole maintained their profit margins - even if this is truer of firms less exposed to foreign competition than the others. On the other hand they have managed to control their indebtedness, and in this respect have performed better than their Japanese and American rivals (*European Commission, 1994, p.62*).

Employment

It is in this field that Europe's performance has been disappointing and is a cause for considerable concern. Indeed, the situation in which Europe finds itself is characterised simultaneously by a strong, continuous rise in unemployment (excluding the period 1985-89 which saw a levelling-off of the rise) and by a very slow rate of employment creation which was insufficient to compensate for a rising labour force.

These European characteristics become clearer when the performances of member countries are compared to those of the USA and Japan. If we add other dimensions of European unemployment, more particularly the importance of long-term unemployment (which affects more than half of all the unemployed) and the relative numerical importance of unskilled workers, we can easily understand that the economies of the European Union are

Figure 1.5. : Unemployment in the European Community, the USA and Japan
(% of active population)

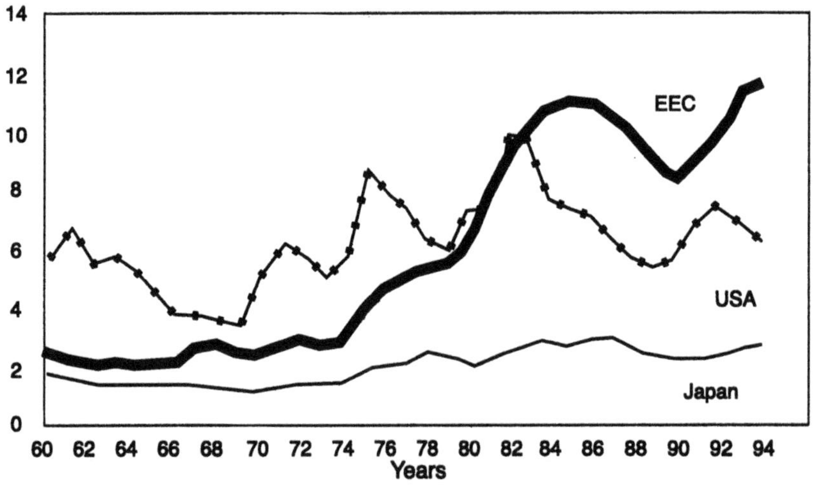

Source : European Commission *[1994, p.43]*.

Figure 1.6. : Job creation in the European Community, the USA and Japan

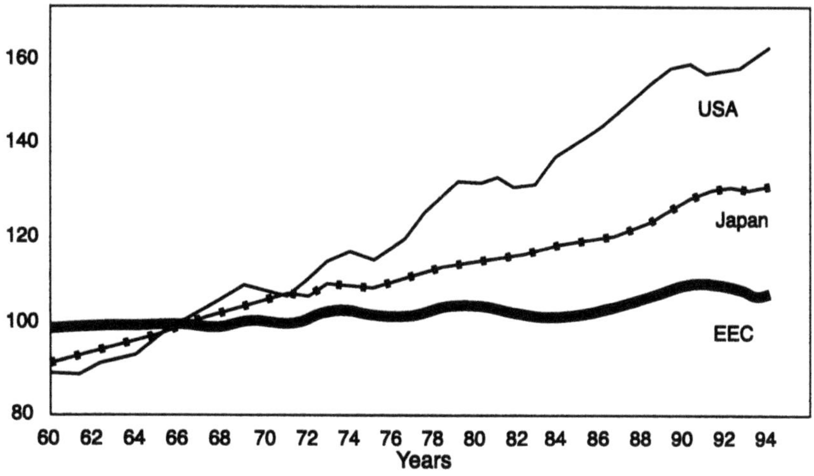

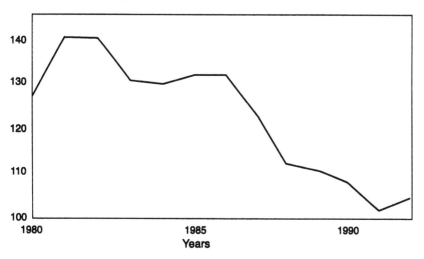

Source : European Commission *[1994, p.43]*.

Figure 1.7. : Coverage of Imports by Exports

Source : Eurostat, reprinted in European Commission *[1994, p.80]*.

9

going through a particularly difficult phase. Obviously a vigorous and carefully designed action is needed if present trends are to be reversed.

Foreign Trade: The Maintenance of a Positive Balance but at a Much Reduced Level

If we consider the foreign trade of the Community, things are hardly more encouraging. Since 1981 the foreign trade balance of the Community has been witnessing a continuous worsening. This occurred in two stages. From 1981 to 1986, which corresponds to a phase of acceleration in growth (the rate of growth of GDP rose from less than one per cent to more than four per cent - Figure 1.1) the rate of coverage dropped slightly. This constituted a satisfactory performance to the extent that the increase in growth, which is usually accompanied by a growth in imports, had little adverse effect on foreign trade which remained largely in surplus. On the other hand, the performance in the second phase (1989-94) was distinctly worse and very worrying to the extent that an uninterrupted decline in growth has been accompanied by a strong fall in the balance of external trade.

A breakdown of these aggregates confirms this pessimistic conclusion. For we can observe that while Europe has maintained and indeed even improved its position in slow-growing markets (such as rail equipment, textile machinery, tanning, slaughtering and meat packaging) its position has worsened considerably in high growth and high value added sectors (such as office automation, optical instruments, medical and surgical equipment). In fact, Europe seems to be caught in a pincer movement: on the one hand, it is unable to compete against the newly industrialised countries whose essential comparative advantage lies in labour costs, and on the other hand its poor performance in products based upon the electronic revolution. This places Europe in a very weak position in relation to Japan, the Southeast Asian Newly Industrialising Countries and even the USA, where in the last few years firms have caught up remarkably (for example, firms in the semiconductor field such as Intel and Motorola). As we will indicate below when we turn attention to information technologies, Europe's poor position is not a result of its performance in research or R&D. On this point, there is in fact a European paradox and it is this which the essay addresses.

If the above-mentioned results are related to the definition of competitiveness, the following conclusions may be drawn:

(1) In respect of the criteria which are widely accepted as useful indicators of competitiveness there is little doubt that Europe's' competitive position has worsened considerably over the past few years. Not only has Europe been unable to sustain growth at acceptable levels but the long phase of recession itself, which is not yet completely over, has been accompanied by a decline in the performance of its foreign trade. In

addition, these negative trends have been accompanied by an increase in the rate of unemployment which has grown from one cycle to the next. If being competitive means ensuring internal growth with a constant or improving foreign trade situation, in such a way as to improve the standard of living of the population, European performance has been far from the mark.

In assessing these results it is important to take into account at least two adverse factors which Europe has had to face. The first has been the sharp devaluation of the dollar since the beginning of the 1990s; this has exacerbated Europe's foreign trade difficulties. The second factor is the fall of the Berlin Wall and Germany's decision to merge as rapidly as possible with the East by borrowing internationally, thereby putting pressure on interest rates which were already high.

The double impact of these factors is certainly one element underlying Europe's current economic difficulties, particularly since the early 1990s. But clearly, too, even though the role of these destabilising factors should not be neglected, the data presented above also reveal European 'structural' difficulties as regards competitiveness.

(2) If we consider more detailed indicators, the loss of competitiveness experienced on a global level and indicated above, even if it is easier to explain, is no less worrying. For, as we have seen, the crux of the problem lies in the fact that Europe appears to be relatively badly placed in terms of product/market specialisation. For the products/sectors in which the relative advantage lies in labour costs, few if any changes can be expected. For products/sectors with a high value added, based on the utilisation of new technologies and/or where there is a rapidly-growing demand, the problem is more challenging, for it is clear that Europe's competitive potential lies here, when account is taken of its traditions and capabilities. Without strong positions taken by the European firms in the domains covering new and high added value products in both industry and services, it is impossible to ensure a durable increase in employment and standards of living to which Europe and its population aspire. And for the moment it is in these very sectors that the performance of the Community is worsening. But as we now propose to show, if we look more closely to the data, European firms find themselves in a paradoxical situation, which is not without its potential for improved performance.

The significance of this paradox - on which I now focus - is that its nature as well as the means to overcome it place us at the heart of the propositions made in the essay to improve overall European competitiveness.

II.   THE HEART OF THE DIFFICULTIES: THE PARADOX OF EUROPEAN RESEARCH

The argument I wish to present is basically very simple and may be briefly summarised in the following manner. Contrary to the received wisdom, Europe does not really lag behind in basic research or R&D. The effort devoted to scientific research, even if it can and should be increased in some domains, is in a satisfactory state and compares favourably with Asian and American competitors. Europe's weakness does not lie in this area, but elsewhere. The specific European weakness appears as soon as one examines the transformation of this research into innovations and, ultimately, into marketable goods. In other words, it is in the process from scientific discovery and invention to innovation, and from innovation to the market that Europe's' specific weakness lies.

This phenomenon is not necessarily unknown and some studies have clearly identified the existence of the problem. Characteristically in these cases, however, the solution offered has invariably set aside the diagnostic in order to recommend even more research or R&D.

This volume of case studies on leading European enterprises argues that the specific European difficulty - in the process of conversion of research into innovation and end products - should be treated directly by targeting the causes of the breakdown of this innovation cycle, for the lag under consideration has a clear identity: it is an organisational as well as an innovational one. From this perspective, Europe has not yet been able to break with the organisational models inherited from Fordism, whether it be those concerning the organisation of work inside the factory, or those concerning the management of R&D activities. As a consequence of this basic vision, this volume argues that parallel to efforts made within the framework of macroeconomic policy, specific long-term action must be undertaken to foster a programme of organisational reform. Such action must be based on a programme using the analytical tools adapted to the specific objective of promoting organisational innovation, or the fruits of the efforts made may well be lost. Worse, these efforts may fuel the progress of Europe's competitors.

From Table 1.1, which presents a comparison between the performance of different European countries, it can be seen that, contrary to the received wisdom, Europe does not lack winning cards.

Good Performances in Basic and Academic Research[2]

If we focus our attention firstly on a global level, some simple observations may be made.

TABLE 1.1
FROM RESEARCH TO INNOVATION PRINCIPAL ECONOMIC INDICATORS
CONCERNING EUROPEAN RESEARCH COMPARED TO THE USA AND JAPAN

	EEC	USA	JAPAN
Expenditure on Academic Research			
(1) % of GNP (1988)	0.38	0.29	0.18
(2) Millions $ billions (1988)	10.5	13.0	2.8
(3) Share of Triad (%)	39.9	51.2	10.8
% of Scientific Production			
(4) Of World	27.7	35.8	8.0
(5) Of Triad	387	50.1	11.2
Efficiency of the Expenses			
(6) (5) / (3)	0.97	0.98	1.04
(7) Scientific Impact (1981)	1,0	1,4	0,8
Research and Development			
(8) % of Industrial Production	2.3	3.2	2.7
(9) Volume $ billions (1989)	60.6	95.9	45.6
(10) % of Triad	30.0	47.5	22.5
Engineers and Researchers			
(11) % of the population	1.9	3.8	4.7
(12) Number (in thousands)	611.4	949.3	582.8
(13) % of Triad	28.5	44.3	27.2
% of patents in the US market (1991)			
(14) World weight	20.1	45.6	25.0
(15) % of Triad	22.2	50.3	27.5
In Europe			
(16) World weight	42.6	24.7	24.4
(17) % of Triad	46.5	26.9	26.6
Relative Efficiency			
(18) Researchers (15 / 13)	0.78	1.14	1.01
(19) R&D (15 / 10)	0.74	1.06	1.22

Source: Compiled by Amable and Boyer [*1993*]

An Effort Often Superior to That of Its Competitors in the Triad

It appears first of all that, as a percentage of its total GDP, Europe makes far and away the greatest effort (38 per cent), if we compare it to the USA (29 per cent) and that of Japan (18 per cent). In absolute terms (expenditure in

13

1988 at constant $ million), Europe's effort is important ($10.5bn), but is clearly lower than that of the USA ($13bn) whilst substantially higher than that of Japan (only $2.8bn).

This academic research appears to be highly diversified and Europe has no significant weaknesses in any major field, including information technology. On the contrary, it is often in the forefront. Similarly, the diffusion and international recognition of European science appears considerable. If we refer to the most traditional indicator in the field (the number of references made to European publications), it may be noted that even if European scientists have made a lesser impact than their American colleagues, this impact remains superior to that of the Japanese.

If we consider the relative specialisation of the different European countries, it is apparent that each major scientific discipline is represented in one or more of the member countries. There are often a number of advanced research centres situated within Europe. In this respect, three countries stand out: Germany, France and Great Britain, with the disparity with southern European countries (Spain, Greece and Portugal) remaining marked[3].

Industrial Research: A Greater Effort Than That of Japan

Europe's performance in basic research also compares favourably at a more applied level: that of industrial research (rows 8-13, Table 1.1). Even though Europe lags behind the USA in absolute terms ($60.6bn versus $95.5bn), it leads Japan ($45.6bn). In relative terms, if these figures are related to the respective GDP of the countries of the triad, Europe performs less well. With 2.3 per cent of its GDP devoted to R&D, Europe lags behind the USA (3.2 per cent) which is not surprising; but it also lags behind Japan. Only Germany performs as well as the USA and Japan. The two other European leaders in this field are France and Great Britain who have seen a marked decline in their performance.

Turning to sectoral data with regard to R&D spending, it is essential to highlight a little known but highly significant point: in the field in which Europe has such a large deficiency, that is to say in electronics and information technology, European spending on R&D outweighs that of Japan ($15bn compared to $12bn). In other words, Japan, which has a trade surplus with Europe in this respect, only spends four-fifths as much on R&D as the Europeans. I will return to the significance of these figures, since they epitomise the paradox I wish to highlight.

The result of this is that apart from certain specific sectors (primarily electronics), Europe is by and large self-sufficient and clearly has the potential to generate trade surpluses. Elsewhere, as in aeronautics and the aerospace industry, European players are making remarkable breakthroughs.

The Exclusion of a Very Weak Performance in the Field of Innovation

The relatively optimistic picture that has just been painted changes significantly, if we no longer consider performance in research as such, but in the transformation of this research into innovation. A primary indication in this regard is the number of applications made for patents (rows 14-17, Table 1.1). The figures speak for themselves. In the American market, which may be taken as a significant reference in this respect, Europe lags far behind the USA (20.1 per cent as against 45.6 per cent of all applications) and also behind Japan (25 per cent). This result is even more significant if it is remembered that Europe leads Japan significantly in basic as well as industrial research. This gives a clear illustration of the idea that the European problem lies not so much in the lack of research but in the 'transformation' of research results into innovation.

This weakness may also be appreciated if we look at the indicators of the 'yield' obtained by research in its conversion into innovation. On this point (rows 17-18, Table 1.1) the quantitative appreciations of the relative efficiency of European research in relation to that of its competitors in the triad are illuminating.

By relating the relative number of patent applications made in the USA by each of the members of the triad to the relative number of engineers and researchers for each country[4], it appears that the relative efficiency of European researchers is 0.78, as against 1.14 in the USA and 1.01 in Japan. Is this to say that European researchers have less training or fewer resources at their disposal than their American or Japanese counterpart? Or that they are less creative? The answer to these questions is negative taking into consideration the data already given above. The answer lies elsewhere: it is related to the European organisational model which is clearly unable to ensure the transformation of research results into innovation or, further, as will be seen in a moment, to orientate research from the very beginning towards innovation.

We may note in conclusion that the same mode of calculation (relating the data in row 15 to that of row 10) produces similar results that are even more unfavourable. If we consider the efficiency not of researchers but of R&D the efficiency of European R&D is 0.74, as against 1.6 for the USA and 1.32 for Japan. It is this which represents what I refer to as the 'European Paradox'. The loss of efficiency in the use of innovative resources becomes greater and greater the more one distances oneself from basic research and goes towards innovation. If information technology is considered, further conclusions may be drawn.

An Extreme Case of the Paradox: Information Technology

As we know, information technology is the Achilles' heel of European competitiveness. It is largely in this domain that the future will be decided, and it is here that Europe's performance is weakest. For these reasons a deeper exploration is fruitful.

Figures 1.8 and 1.9 show in a striking manner the extent of the accumulated lag of European firms as compared to American or Japanese one. The data in Figure 1.9 are alarming since they show that Europe has recorded deficits not only with all its developed competitors but also with the four Asian 'Tigers'.

**Figure 1.8. : European Total ICT Equipments
Imports/exports by regions, 1992
(Billion ECUs)**

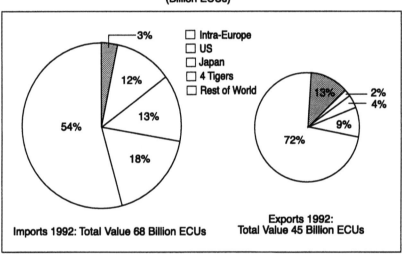

Imports 1992: Total Value 68 Billion ECUs

Exports 1992:
Total Value 45 Billion ECUs

Source : European Information Technology. Observatory

Those in Figure 1.8 are no less worrying since they reveal the discrepancy between Europe as a consumer of electronic equipment - where the market is vast, diversified and dynamic - and Europe as a supplier which it is increasingly incapable of meeting internal demand. If the results from numerous studies in this field (the assessments made within the framework of the preparation for the fourteenth programme for Community Research, is also considered, the works by Catinat [*1993*], and Mytelka [*1994*] being of special relevance here), it is clear that Europe's ability to supply is shrinking. The number of 'European firms' is declining, with former European firms disappearing or coming under foreign control (the take-over of

16

ICL by Fujitsu, the growing foreign stakes in Bull, etc.). In general, apart from some sectors (telecommunication being one of them), Europe faces grave danger in the sectors of electronics and information technology.

Figure 1.9. : Global Trade Flows 1992
(Billion ECUs)

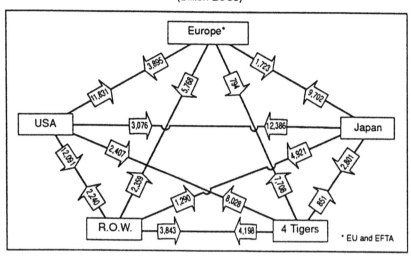

Source : European Information Technology. Observatory

If we bear in mind that European expenditures on R&D in this sector are significantly larger than those of Japan ($15bn as opposed to $12bn), it is clear that we have identified the core of a paradox that requires fuller explanation.

III. THE RESOLUTION OF THE PARADOX: ORGANISATIONAL INNOVATION AS THE MISSING LINK IN EUROPEAN COMPETITIVENESS

In order to interpret correctly the data presented above - which clearly shows the gap between research efforts and performances in innovation (measured either by patents or indirectly by trade in information technology), it is evident that Europe's difficulties are relatively recent. In practice, they coincide with changes in organisational forms which become necessary when markets change.

Europe one Step Behind in Organisational Models

If, indeed, we follow the development of the European economy since its inception (at the end of the 1950s) we find that in the early decades it performed well and benefited from its progressive consolidation. For the task at hand was simple: to catch up (with the USA in particular), and to adopt a specific mode of growth and development (that is, mass production) which had proved so successful in the USA. In this task of catching up, Europe performed brilliantly. It used the tried and tested techniques of the time: mass production technology with relative specialisation in middle and up-market goods in order to exploit its traditional strengths, a highly skilled labour force and an industrial know-how that was both specialised and diversified.

In the field of manufacturing and research, which may be considered to be of greatest priority, the essential vehicles of corporate competitiveness were the parallel exploitation of the economies arising from the division of tasks and functions, and specialisation in these tasks and functions.

However, generally speaking, universities and research centres were largely cut off from industry, and industry itself was distanced from the services necessary for its functioning. At other, more restricted levels, the principle of separation and specialisation were fully in evidence and there was little contact between basic and applied research, or that between applied and industrial research. In conformity with the principle of specialisation - which at that time was regarded as a fundamental principle of economic efficiency - these different tasks were compartmentalised and allocated to people with different specialisations in distinct, separate departments.

The final result was a simple, robust model characterised by a linear, sequential vision of the relationship between research and innovation. The underlying idea of such a model is that, in order to take advantage from specialisation, it is necessary to 'progress' from academic research to applied research and thereafter to industrial research, prototypes and innovation. The same principle or 'progressivity' applies to production itself: the pre-eminence and autonomy of the task of conception over that of manufacturing, and a clear separation between the one and the other, with each department (human resources, production, quality control, and so on) having its own management structure and its own regulations.

It is worth repeating that for a long time this system was efficient. However, with the benefit of hindsight it is possible to see that this efficiency was based on certain implicit conditions, one being a growing market for standardised and homogeneous products, and another being stable technological trajectories and long product life cycles. Under these conditions, competitive pricing and the ability to supply the mass market rapidly were

18

the key criteria of economic efficiency. This organisational model lying at the heart of the mass production system flourished.

As borne out by numerous studies, an important point in this discussion, is that these conditions no longer exist [*Dertouzos et al., 1989; Taddei and Coriat, 1993*]. With free trade and the increasing power of the newly-industrialised countries, the markets which were by and large 'demanders' have become suppliers. At the same time, the spread of the electronic revolution destabilised the directions taken by technological innovation both in the field of products and production techniques. A new series of parameters now held an increasingly central place in the relative competitiveness of firms and nations. In this manner, the time taken to bring a product on to the market and the capacity to modify and differentiate products so as to adapt them to different groups of existing or potential consumers had become key elements in competitiveness. Consequently what is now required is a new model of management of research and innovation if we wish to ensure the competitiveness of firms. The former model had manifested its limits, limits shown by the firms and nations which had not adopted the organisational changes required by the new times. Conversely, those countries which had the know-how to innovate in the organisational field were in a solid position which they could continually build upon by virtue of the interplay of accumulated advantages and the effects of learning [*Freeman et al., 1993; Coriat, 1990 and 1994*]

For Europe, which remained largely imprisoned in the old model, the lesson to be drawn from these transformations is that rather than trying to do 'more' within the old organisational framework, it would do better to do things 'differently'. What is at issue is nothing less than a need to change models.

We will return to this point in greater detail in Chapter 2. It suffices to conclude here that research and innovation may no longer be organised in a sequential manner, but rather in an iterative way, organising permanent exchanges of information between actors. Similarly, research may no longer be conceived and organised in ignorance of the demands and constraints of production or markets. In fact, it is often the imperatives of production that should guide conception. It is in this sense that new and more effective forms of the division of labour have become the cornerstone of change and the necessary condition for an improvement in competitiveness.

Several representations of the new model may be given. We ourselves will propose one which seems particularly well adapted to the specific problems Europe faces and has to resolve (Chapter 1.2). For the moment, and in order to make the argument more concrete, among all the different representations of organisational innovation in the field of management of R&D and innovation[5], the model proposed by Kline and Rosenberg [*1986*]

**Figure 1.10. : R&D and Innovation:
"The Chain Link Model"**

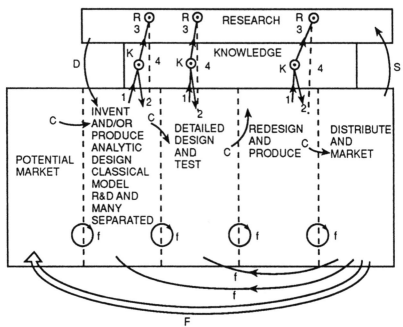

Elements of the "chain-link" model. Key: C = central chain of innovation, f = short feedback loops, F = long feedback loop, K-R = links through knowledge to research and return paths [If problem is solved at node K, link 3 to R is not activated. Return from research (link 4) is problematic – therefore dashed line.], D = direct link between research and problems in invention and design, S = support of scientific research.

Source : Kline and Rosenberg, [*1986, p.292*].

and partly developed by Aoki [*1988*] (Figure 1.10) merit our attention. As will be seen, taking its inspiration from the Japanese experience, it stresses certain key points of the new model whose introduction is so necessary. This model highlights some essential elements in Europe's difficulties, and clearly indicates the nature of the changes required. The main points it stresses are as follows:

(1) The main characteristic of such a model is that it is constructed from a 'central chain of innovation' around which two different series of 'feedback loops' can be identified: 'short' (if they concern activity such as commerce, design, manufacturing and so on) or 'long' (if the information needs to transit by research laboratories). In this way, the representation clearly highlights the gap between the classical model - of the sequential and linear type - and the new model. Contrary to the former, the new model is conceived of as a system of 'loops', established

from systematically constructed interactions within the 'central chain of innovation'.[6]

(2) These interactions link together all the functions essential to innovation, establishing different kind of interactions between the different manufacturing and research functions involved in the making of an innovation. Thanks to appropriate systems of information exchanges, these interactions introduce the principles of simultaneity (in the conduct of different functions implied by innovation) where the principle of sequentiality was the rule. In this way, even if the market remains the final goal of research and innovation, it also becomes the starting point and stimulus for research and innovation. Production and research take as their starting point, information about the behaviour and requirements of consumers. Innovation, therefore, is 'finalised' from the very outset. And all the more effectively to the extent that, in the course of production activity, the interactions between research on the one hand and the market (or the client) on the other, are managed, in such a way as to anticipate at each phase the problems which may arise, and to find the optimal solutions.

(3) Japanese firms are so efficient because they are particularly good at mastering the 'short loops' of the innovation chain. Aoki notes that in Japanese firms 'short loops' are created thanks to horizontal communication between adjacent units, and the fact that there is a flow of personnel between these unites' [*Aoki, 1988, p.269*]. More generally, all the Japanese innovations in production management which are based on decentralisation and sharing of information, as in team work, are elements which strongly encourage the circulation of information within the 'short loops' of the innovation chain.[7]

(4) If we look more closely at the innovation process described in the figure, we observe that a crucial element is the defining of the role and tasks allocated to the different categories of workers involved in the central chain. A key difference between the Japanese model and the traditional western model lies in the fact that in the Japanese model the central role is played by the 'divisional engineer', whereas in the western firm it is played by the 'researcher' in the central laboratory. The tasks of the divisional engineer are designed in such a way that he/she is both a production specialist and a researcher. More precisely, the tasks are to manage the interfaces between manufacturing and research.[8]

Although this discussion could be extended, for our purpose the above remarks will suffice since our aim is simply to show how innovations in organisation and product-management are essential elements of competitiveness and are capable of explaining much of the differences between European and Japanese performance. In answer to the question 'how can a smaller Japanese research effort be transformed into a better performance in terms of innovation?', we believe that this opposition between a 'sequential' and an 'iterative' model is an essential element of the solution, as well as indicating the future path to follow for the European economy (on this issue see Clark and Fujimoto [*1989*]).

Organisational Innovations, Competitiveness and Employment

In order to fully appreciate the necessity for Europe to undertake organisational reform, a brief return to the notion of competitiveness is in order. In this way, after having recalled the sources and determining factors of competitiveness, we will try to show 'why' and 'how', organisational innovations are so essential, not only for competitiveness but also for employment issues.

Organisational Innovations at the Meeting Point Between Price and Non-Price Competition

As it is well known, after having focused on only one dimension of competitiveness - the so-called 'price competitiveness' - economic theory has more recently attached greater and greater importance to another dimension: that of 'non-price competitiveness'. If such a distinction became necessary, it was because more and more statistical data indicated that, taking into account only the relative prices between trading partners, was not sufficient to explain in a satisfactory manner the evolution of trade between countries [*Helpman and Krugman, 1990; Asensio and Mazier, 1991; Lafay et al., 1991 and, Aglietta and Baulant, 1994*]. The quality of the products, differentiation, time to market, specialisation in products for which there is a rapidly-growing demand are among others element of 'non-price factors' which play an increasingly crucial role in determining changes in trade.

For our purposes, there are two essential points as regards 'non-price' advantages. The first is that they make it possible to benefit from 'monopolistic rents'[9] even partial and temporary. This is what permit the innovative firms, to liberate themselves from the constraints of price competition. For the products which present these advantages, the client - the professional user or ordinary consumer - is prepared to pay more than for a close substitute, since the latter's qualities are judged to be inferior. This point is evidently of great importance to the extent that it means that such a form of competitiveness may be attained without harming employment and salaries. On the contrary, the monopolistic rents enable the firm to maintain high or improved levels of employment and wages if the quality of the products enables the firm to benefit from profits that the consumer is willing to finance by buying the product.

The second point is that these advantages are the result of long and patients, conducted over the long-term. In such a strategy, continuous investment in organisation and human resources is required. Again, such a strategy is, in principle, strongly dependant on a policy oriented towards the building of a high level of skills and competences among the labour force which is required to be strongly involved in 'quality' issues. The strategy followed by Gemini during the 1980s gives a clear illustration of the potentialities offered by this systematic building of product-quality on the basis of skilled labour.

Each of these forms of competitiveness generate in this way a relative 'price' or 'non-price' advantage. And for a long time these two forms of competitiveness were thought to stem from a unique source - technical progress - either because certain technical combinations are more efficient in terms of factor utilisation (creating a price advantage), or because the innovation concerns the products and enables firms which introduce them to benefit from technological rents (creating a non-price advantage).[10] The critical point is that if this classical source of relative advantages is still active, and is experiencing a new vitality thanks to the current technological revolution, organisational innovations must now be analysed and considered as an independent, specific source of gains in competitiveness, ensuring its own relative advantages. A growing literature [*Leibenstien, 1982; Akerlof 1982; Menard, 1992*] has demonstrated the importance of the differences between 'allocative versus organisational efficiency'. Whether we consider the intra-firm aspect (just-in-time production techniques, project management groups and so on) or the inter-firm aspects (new forms of sub-contracting protocols involving co-operation and partnership between firms and so on) it appears that, just like technical progress, contemporary organisational innovations are indeed at the meeting point between the two forms of competitiveness we have defined. And, even if an assessment of their effects remains difficult[11], it is now fully accepted that the competitive relative advantages which can be obtained from efficient and innovative organisations is analogous to those coming from technical innovation. Just as technical progress gives rise to 'technological rents', 'organisational innovation' is the source of specific 'organisational rents', whether these originate from price factors (better global use of the factors arising from better organisation) or non-price factors: more efficient organisations enabling production cycles to be shortened, improvement in the quality of products, or production in differentiated series adapted to different demands and their variations [*Asanuma, 1987 and 1989*].

We can thus understand the crucial importance for the European economy of mastering and ensuring the diffusion within the Community of these ongoing organisational revolution.

ORGANISATIONAL INNOVATIONS, ORGANISATIONAL RENTS AND COMPETITIVENESS: DEFINITION AND CHARACTERISTICS

(1) Throughout this volume an organisational innovation is defined as any new technique of division of labour at intra- or inter-firm level which enables savings to be made in the use of resources, or a better adaptation of products to consumer needs and market variations. They are based on original and efficient methods in the management of information. The essential feature of an organisational innovation is that it focuses on new and more efficient way of managing the relations between tasks and functions along the production chain.

(2) The savings in the use of resources (which is the core of an organisational innovation) may concern 'global' time: that which separates the conception of a product from its launching, or it may concern a more 'localised' point in the conception-production-delivery cycle. In a similar way the best adaptation to clients' needs may lie in a simple 'quality effect', or may involve a 'differentiation effect' which would permit the supply of products with unique features. Therefore, as regards economic efficiency, organisational innovations involve price effects (savings in resources) as much as non-price effects (the quality and differentiation effects).

(3) In principle, organisational innovations do not necessarily imply the use of advanced information technologies, or more broadly speaking technical innovations. If innovating technologies are sometimes used or required, they do not condition the existence of organisational innovations. According to the context, organisational innovations either act as substitutes for, or complement, the technical innovations. Substitution occurs when organisational innovation is preferred to technical innovation. This is often the case when, even in mass production the quality of the products has to be carefully monitored. Complementarity occurs when organisational innovation accompanies technical innovation, adding to the yields obtained from the latter. (This in general is the case when automated or computerised technologies are set up, implying a new division of labour.) Finally, it is not unusual that an organizational innovation opens the way for technical innovation.

Organisational Innovations at the Heart of the New Virtuous Circles of Competitiveness and Employment.

Indeed, in the case of the European economy several factors militate strongly in favour of long-term actions in favour of organisational innovation. These factors are at least of three types.

(1) The general diagnosis: improve organisational efficiency in order to improve competitiveness.

We have seen above that if Europe is suffering, in most cases this is due less to insufficient quantitative efforts (measured in terms of investment or resources devoted to R&D, for example) than to an insufficiently judicious use of the resources invested. We have stressed this point by referring to information technology, the Achilles' heel of European competitiveness, and by recalling that what Europe lacks is an organisational model capable of generating innovation by converting R&D into marketable products. This diagnosis is true of almost all other fields. Thus the situation - of specialisation in 'wrong areas' can be redressed if - starting with existing products and know-how - a process of quality improvement and product differentiation (both horizontal and vertical)[12] enables Europe to focus on new, more promising markets. In view of their enormous potential, organisational innovations are a key element in the transformation and recovery required. This general orientation (product differentiation through continuous improvement), has been followed with remarkable success by the Japanese during the 1970s and the 1980s.

We should add that this kind of strategy, is all the more desirable as we are witnessing an increase in the relative importance of elements of non-price competitiveness, a domain in which organisational innovations - thanks to the quality effects they generate - appear to be especially suited. More generally, the increase in intra-trade industry requires ever-increasing specialisation, which in turn requires organisational forms capable of accompanying more and more unpredictable and demanding market changes.

(2) The safeguarding of European Social Welfare: realising productivity gains whilst at the same time favouring employment creation.

Another factor important for the Community lies in the obligation of member countries to preserve their social welfare systems, or even (in the case of those countries in the Union who are still lagging behind their more advanced partners) to improve them. In the face of competition from low-wage countries, Europe's only option lies in searching for gains in productivity by using methods of production and techniques which are not only more efficient but also maintain or raise the level of employment. Even if some adjustments are necessary here and there (in terms of relaxing certain regulations), Europe cannot compete, on the same ground, with countries which very low levels of regulation of their markets and social welfare systems. Therefore, faced with the difficult problem of achieving the productivity gains necessary to consolidate the competitiveness of the Union's members without allowing a deterioration in current levels of employment and wages, organisational innovations hold much promise. Indeed, in many cases they have led to significant gains in the utilisation of raw materials or energy, just as in that of fixed capital and stocks. In this manner they are a potential vehicle for an overall improvement in productivity which would not lead to reductions in employment, since savings would be realised and spread over the other resources used in production. To this, it should be added that by generating organisational rents, they create some additional revenues, part of which could be used to maintain and increase the number of jobs.

(3) The current phase (completion of the Single Market) is a favourable moment to initiate action to promote organisational efficiency.

The last, but not the least important factor, is more contextual in nature. As we know, the construction of the Single Market attempted to encourage a process of concentration and reinforcement of existing firms in the Community, the 'costs of the non Europe' (the Cecchini Report) being measured principally in terms of the costs of duplication, or the inability to profit from economies of scale in markets which were segmented by tariff barriers.

If this phase is not totally completed, it is nevertheless well advanced. Since the passage of the Single Act, we have witnessed a large number of mergers, company acquisitions and alliances of all types. In this way, the current period has also been one of consolidation and reorganisation of the different production structures acquired during the period of the general movement towards concentration which Europe has just experienced. This attempt at coherence signifies entry into a more qualitative phase [*Jaquemin, 1992 and 1994*]. What is now necessary is to set up within the suitable organisational models, efficient circuits for the flow of information between units and subsidiaries specialised in different fields and belonging to different national cultures and traditions. In this respect, it is a favourable moment to undertake action to improve organiaational efficiency. Such action fits in with reforms that firms have already begun to introduce from their own initiative.

26

IV. CONCLUSIONS

In spite of the grave difficulties which the Community's economy is facing today, there is a practical way out of the vicious circles of competitiveness and employment in which Europe seems to be captured. As it is suggested in the White Paper [*European Commision, 1994*], and parallel to macroeconomic measures which can and must be taken, resolute action is needed in non-material investment in order to revive Europe's capacity to innovate. By associating the benefits derived from quality and those derived from differentiation, this may strengthen the capacity for a revival of European competitiveness. From there on, the exploitation of Europe's traditional advantages, notably its skilled labour force and accumulated know-how in many sectors of industry and services, may serve as a basis for a solid recovery of its competitiveness and employment.

The chapters which follow explore the emergence of a European response to this crisis of competitiveness through the application of innovative forms of organisation. The policy responses required to address the market failures which arise in the diffusion of these organisational innovations are also outlined. But much remains to be done, both at the research and the policy level.

NOTES

1. In a recent assessment made for the EC lot of data on poor experiences in five critical technologies [*Narin and Albert, 1994*].
2. This paragraph is based largely on Amable and Boyer [1993]. Data and analysis on the information technology sector are presented in the European Information Technology Observatory (1994).
3. For more detailed analysis, see Amable and Boyer [*1993*].
4. In practice, this index is obtained by relating the figures in row 15 to those of row 13 in Table 1.1.
5. Among the recent models proposed, see Roos [*1991*].
6. On this basis, within the central chain of innovation, another distinction is made between two types of innovations:

    - those concerning the development of existing products (product improvement) or those which derive from an effort of analytical conception which consists of gathering existing procedures in order to create new products (product development) (pp. 266-267);
    - those which concern inventions themselves, that is to say which imply operations which have no link with the past; contrary to the case of product development, these innovations concern new products.

    Even if these two series of innovations, based respectively on short and long 'loops' do not use the same circuits for exchanging information, they nevertheless have in common the need for a division and coordination of tasks (which are different from those of the linear model)

7. The Japanese model is itself not without weaknesses. Its weakness lies in relation to 'invention' for 'radically new' products. In this case, the central research laboratory plays a crucial role and multi-disciplinary knowledge is necessary but is not available inside the firm. In such a situation, innovation depends on the good management of what we have called 'long feedback loops', an area in which the Japanese method performs less well.

   Regarding this limited efficiency in the 'long loops', two types of motives may be advanced:

   - the fact, as we have seen, that in basic research Japan has made less of an effort than the USA or Europe, means that the available potential remains limited. The Japanese 'reserves' in research are lower than those for Europe or America

   - the fact that 'external' transiting, that is to say, outside the firm, is always relatively complex in Japan: the existence of multiple contractual relations of 'Keiretsu' types make the acquisition of know-how not available within a 'Keiretsu' very difficult. For similar reasons, it is difficult to acquire skills or know-how which is not already available inside: neither individually (since dismissal is strongly discouraged by the life employment system, salary based on seniority and other incentives which make the Japanese efficient in product improvement and development), nor by mergers and acquisitions, which for institutional reasons are debarred in Japan.

   With a view to European organizational reform, which needs to draw on Japanese innovations whilst at the same time looking for specific European advantages, these remarks are important. We will return to this at a later stage (Chapter 2).

8. Even if (still according to Aoki) the exchange is more efficient in the direction divisional engineer/manufacturing than in the direction central laboratory/manufacturing.

9. Here it is indeed question of 'monopolistic rents' in Chamberlain's definition of the term (linked to temporary, mini 'monopolies' based principally on differentiation of product characteristics) and not of monopoly profits in the sense of the oligopoly theory [*Chamberlain, 1933*]. For a general review of the thesis on competition and differentiation, see Tirole [*1989*].

10. Note that in the case of price competitiveness, all else being equal, decreases in salary may also create an advantage. This hypothesis will not be examined here since it is not a serious long term option for the future in Europe.

11. Several attempts at quantification have been made. The well-known World Automobile Project of MIT [*Womack et al., 1990*] based itself on the work of Clark and Fujimoto [*1989*] draws up a table of the gains which can be ascribed to the methods used by the Japanese groups.

12. 'Horizontal' differentiation consists of proposing the same product with slightly different features between them, but targeting the same group of incomes and

consumers, whilst 'vertical' differentiation consists of proposing products for different income levels, and therefore different consumer preferences.

REFERENCES

Aglietta, M. and C. Baulant (1994), 'Contrainte Extérieure et Compétitivité dans la transition vers l'Union et Monétaire', *OFCE Revue, No. 48, Janvier.*

Akerlof, G. (1982), 'Labor Contracts as Partial Gift Exchange', *The Quarterly Journal of Economics*, Vol. XCII, No. 4, pp. 543-569.

Amable, B. and R. Boyer (1993), 'L'Europe est-elle en retard d'un modèle technologique', *Economie Internationale, Revue du CEPII*, No. 56, 4iéme trimestre, La Documentation Française.

Aoki, M. (1988), 'Information, Incentives and Bargaining Structure in the Japanese Economy', Cambridge: Cambridge University Press.

Asanuma, B. (1987), 'Transactional Structure of Parts Supply in the Japanese Automobile and Electric Machinery Industries: A Comparative Analysis', *Working Paper*, Kyoto: Kyoto University.

Asanuma, B. (1989), 'Manufacturer-Supplier Relationships in Japan and the Concept of Relation Specific Skill', *Journal of the Japanese and International Economy*, March 3(1), pp. 1-30.

Asensio, A. and J. Mazier (1991) 'Compétitivité, Avantages coûts et horscoûts, et Spécialisation', *Revue d'Economie Industrielle*, No. 55, 1er trimestre.

Catinat, M. (1993), 'Les industries des technologies de l'information', in Coriat, B. and D. Taddei.

Chamberlain, E.H. (1933), *The Theory of Monopolistic Competition*, Boston: Harvard University Press.

Clark, K.B. and T. Fujimoto (1989), 'Product Development and Competitiveness', Paper presented to the International Seminar on Science, Technology and Growth, OECD, April.

Competitiveness Policy Council (1992) *Report*, Washington, DC: Competitiveness Policy Council.

Coriat, B. (1990-1994), 'L'Atelier et le Robot - Essai sur le Fordisme et la Production de Masse à l'Age de l'Electronique, in C. Bourgeois (ed), Paris.

Coriat, B. (1991-1994), 'Penser à l'Envers, Travail et Organisation dans l'Enterprise Japonaise', in C. Bourbois (ed), Paris.

Coriat, B. and D. Taddei (1993), *Entreprise France - Made in France 2*, Hachette: Le Livre de Poche.

Dertouzos, M.L., R.K. Lester and R.M. Solow (1989), *Made in America*, Cambridge, MA: MIT Press.

European Commission (1994), *White Paper on Growth, Competitiveness and Employment*, Brussels-Luxembourg: ECSC-EC-EAEC.

European Economy (1993), *Annual Economic Report for 1993*, No. 54, Brussels: The European Commission.

European Information Technology (1994), *Observatory 1994*, Frankfurt/Main: EITO (European Information Technology Observatory) and EEIG (European Interest Grouping).

Freeman, C. and L. Soete (1993), 'Macro-Economic and Sectorial Analysis of Future Employment and Training Perspectives in the New Information Technologies in the European Community', Report for the Commission of the European Community, Brussels.

Greenan, N., D. Guellec, G. Broussaudier, and L. Miotti (1993), 'Innovation organisationnelle, dynamique technologique et performance des enterprises', Document de Travail, Direction des Etudes et de la Statistique, Paris: Institut National de la Statistique et des Etudes Economiques.

Helpman, E. and P.R. Krugman (1986), *Market Structure and Foreign Trade*, Cambridge, MA: The MIT Press.

Jacquemin, A. et al. (1992), 'Merger and Competition Policy in the European Community', ed P. H. Admiraal, Oxford: Basil Blackwell.

Jacquemin, A. (1994, forthcoming), 'Capitalism, Competition, Cooperation', Inaugural Francqui Lecture, Université Libre de Louvain, *De Economist*.

Kline, S.J. and N. Rosenberg (1986), 'An Overview of Innovation', in Landau and Rosenberg.

Lafay, G. and C. Herzog (1989), 'Commerce International: La fin des avantages acquis', Paris: *Economica*.

Landau, R. and N. Rosenberg (eds.) (1986), *The Positive Sum Strategy*, Academy of Engineering Press.

Leibenstein, H. (1982), 'The Prisoner's Dilemma and the Invisible Hand: An Analysis of Intra-Firm Productivity, *The American Economic Review*, Vol. 72, No. 2, pp. 92-97.

Menard, C. (1992) *L'Economie des Organisations*, Paris: Le Découverte.

Mytelka, L.K. (1991), *Strategic Partnerships and the World Economy*, London: Pinter Publishers.

Narin, F. and M.B. Albert (1994), *Assessment of Critical Technologies in Europe in Selected Fields Covered by the EC Research Programmes*, Brussels: European Commission.

Roos, D. (1991), 'The Importance of Organisational Structure and Production System Design in Development of New Technology', in *OECD/TEP*, Paris: OECD.

Taddei, D. and B. Coriat (ed.) (1993), 'Made in France - L'Industrie française dans le compétition mondiale', Hachette: Le Livre de Poche.

Triole, J. (1989), *The Theory of Industrial Organisation*, Cambridge, MA: The MIT Press.

Womack, J.P., D.T. Jones and D. Roos (1990), *The Machine that Changed the World*, Cambridge, MA: The MIT Press.

2

FLEXIBLE ORGANISATION: EUROPEAN INDUSTRY AND SERVICES IN TRANSITION

Lars Andreasen, Benjamin Coriat, Friso den Hertog, Raphael Kaplinsky

I.   INTRODUCTION

As we have seen in Chapter 1, the EU is confronted by a series of major challenges which threaten both the sustainability of economic growth and the social and political cohesion of its member states. In the context of an increasingly open global trading system, it is thus imperative that the European economy is able to sustain the competitiveness of its tradable sectors, as well as to deliver non-tradable services to its population with maximum effect and at minimum resource-cost. In an earlier era, it was thought that these objectives could be attained through the adoption of the most modern and complex technologies, and for this reason both the EU and individual member states invested significant resources into R&D and the adoption of advanced embodied technologies. However, the returns to this innovation effort have been low and it has become apparent that a new approach is required.

Attention to the performance of successful innovators throughout the global economy indicates that the precondition for the successful utilisation of inventive resources and new embodied technologies is the adoption of new forms of organisation, within firms, between firms and in the relationship between the corporate sector and wider societal institutions. Individual actors in the innovative process must thus not only operate in new modalities, but also in a less isolated context. The restructuring which is required to regain competitiveness will in part be driven forward by market forces, but there are critical areas of market failure which are demanding of a concerted policy response, at the local, national and European levels (as appropriate).

The case studies which are presented in this volume indicate both the steps taken by leading European innovators - in both the manufacturing and services sectors - and the role for public policy. This chapter aims to briefly set these case studies in context, indicating the historical significance of the challenge confronting the European economy and the specific organisational expertise available to support a programme of organisational restructuring. The following chapters include case studies exploring the systemic application of organisational change in the spheres of production, human resource development and R&D. In addition case studies are presented of policy experience in the furthering of organisational reform.

II.   THE CHANGING BASIS OF COMPETITION

From Internationalisation to Globalisation

The challenge confronting post-war Europe was to catch up with the future and not to invent it. This meant adopting a particular pattern of industrial production that had been developed in the United States and then been transferred to other parts of the world, in part through the operations of American multinationals. This process of diffusion was one of 'internationalisation', a period in which a single dominant mode of Fordist mass production came to be widely replicated, involving not only the adoption of particular organisational structures and technologies by firms, but also the construction of supporting physical and institutional infrastructures by governments.

In recent years we have begun to move from this era of internationalisation (in which a single production structure was paramount) to an era of 'globalisation'. This is a much more uncertain and complex world in which competition has become multidimensional and multipolar. This complexity of competitive response and the tensions between global and local production span virtually all industrial sectors, as well as service sectors as banking, insurance, distribution and accounting. It has meant that there is no longer a single dominant 'best way' of doing things - globalisation implies a multiplicity of innovation trajectories with rival innovators from all corners of the world.

Changing Norms of Competition

In the Fordist era of production competitive requirements were both stable and limited. Subject to 'acceptable' levels of quality, market dominance was achieved through price competition and it was widely believed that enhanced levels of quality and product differentiation and innovation would have to be traded-off with higher production costs. By the beginning of the 1980s, American and European producers were confronting a new form of competition emanating from Japan. This is one in which price competitiveness was complemented by an ability to shorten product innovation cycles, and to produce to higher levels of quality and with greater differentiation. These new competitors also proved themselves to be considerably more adept at adjusting their production to meet fluctuating markets, as well as the particular characteristics of different final markets.

Initially many European and American firms thought that they could match this performance by introducing new automation technologies based upon the use of information and communication technologies, but when introduced into Fordist forms of organisation, these radical new process technologies had limited impact. As the 1980s progressed, it rapidly became clear that this superior Japanese performance arose more from the introduction of different modes of organisation than from the introduction of new process technologies [*Jaikumar, 1986; Kaplinsky, 1994*]. Thus the initial response of non-Japanese competitors was to adopt some of these organisational elements, such as quality circles, JIT production and the adoption of American style programmes for cultural change. In many cases the piecemeal adoption of these organisational techniques did improve competitive performance but it has become clear that when these organisational changes are adopted in isolation, the competitive rewards are limited and are often only of limited duration. An integrated approach to reforming the organisation of production is therefore essential. For example, quality has to be built into the whole innovation chain, from the development laboratory, through detailed design and process engineering to production itself and then to distribution. Similarly, JIT is not only delivered through reorganising production scheduling, but also requires altered relations with suppliers and customers. And rapid and effective product innovation cannot be achieved through the adoption of CAD technology or through the reorganisation of the design department within a firm, but only when the relations between the design, production and marketing departments are altered, and when new relations are organised with suppliers and customers.

The message is very clear, and consists of two linked issues. First, the basis of competition has been changing in many markets and many sectors, and price attributes are no longer adequate. And, second, these new competitive attributes cannot be achieved through introducing new process technologies alone. The very basis of productive organisation has to be altered, and this has to occur within an integrated framework that includes relationships with parties outside of the individual enterprise.

Commitment and Trust: The Challenge to Industrial Relations

A particularly critical component of the new organisational challenge lies in the sphere of industrial relations in which the structures of mass production organisation remain deeply rooted. Even those firms that are struggling to come to terms with these new forms of organisation find themselves constrained by the inheritance of past attitudes. In this mass production perspective, the dominant thrust has been to enforce compliance rather than to see shopfloor workers as agents of improvement and change. The result has been a form of work organisation that is based upon the specialisation of tasks and skills, the separation of conception from production, and the development of industrial relations that are informed more by the spirit of mistrust and hostility than by cooperation and common interest.

But the new competition demands a fundamental change to this inherited pattern of work organisation and industrial relations. This involves a number of changes - a greater investment in the labour force, new forms of work design, and enhanced working conditions. The likely consequence of these changes is that both management and labour will have a vested interest in the greater stability of employment.

Thus, continuous and sustained quality improvement requires high quality working environments. It also requires group work, dialogue between workers and management and greater participation by all employees since quality can no longer be seen as being the sole responsibility of specialised 'quality control' workers. Process innovations also require new norms of labour relations. The diffusion of the building blocks for computer integrated manufacturing (CIM) has meant that production has become increasingly capital-intensive, so productivity has become correspondingly reliant on machine reliability. It is also an environment in which unpredictability and breakdown can pose severe penalties and where responsible and autonomous responses by the labour force are an essential component of efficient production. Moreover, the complexity of much of this process technology has meant that the workforce is required to perform tasks that demand a technical grasp of the production process and of much of the technology. Hence, in all these respects the efficient use of process innovations requires a workforce that is flexible and multi-skilled, and actively participates in meeting the challenges posed by production.

Similar observations apply to the development of product technology. The continuous and incremental improvement in products requires close interaction between all employees and cannot be the purview of specialised research workers alone. More particularly, to be successful, blue-collar workers are required to become active participants in the process of change. But even the process of developing wholly new products requires new patterns of interaction and a new willingness to participate beyond the narrow horizons of the R&D department.

In all these respects new forms of social process are critical. New attitudes are required by both management and the labour force and this often translates into the requirement for new forms of industrial relations. In both cases, efficient production requires enhanced levels of both trust and commitment, from all the relevant social parties. The evolution of industrial relations in countries such as Germany and Sweden shows that this trust and commitment can be effectively combined with sound formal contractual agreements.

Lean Production and Beyond

For many years the Americans set the standards for modern production management. Their textbooks, journals and manuals on production and distribution management were widely distributed and implemented. But it is increasingly clear - for the reasons noted above - that the new organisational orthodoxy derives from an agenda set by the Japanese. Concepts such as Total Quality Management, JIT and *kaizen* (continuous improvement) are diffusing rapidly throughout Europe and elsewhere, for example, under the lean production rubric popularised by the MIT research programme on the auto industry [*Womack et al. 1990*].

This set of organisational techniques represents an accumulated body of organisational practice that has been developed and refined over a 30 year period and is clearly of relevance to a large number of sectors and countries. It is useful for European producers in that it provides the key to reopen the door of productivity growth through:

- slimming complex and bureaucratic corporate managerial structures;
- integrating the processes of conception and execution, and thereby making the design cycle more effective and more rapid;
- introducing 'design for manufacture' techniques to facilitate the organisation of the operations in production and services;
- eliminating wasteful activities in manufacturing and services areas, thereby improving quality, shortening delivery cycles and cutting costs;
- making production and services more flexible, and by doing so, allowing firms to meet the more varied needs evident in rapidly changing global markets;
- establishing long-term relationships with suppliers and customers and hence speeding up innovation, cutting costs and allowing for the customisation of production and services for individual market requirements; and
- providing a sharper focus in final markets regarding delivery, quality, customisation and service.

In pursuit of these competitive objectives, European firms have largely been drawn to this Japanese organisational agenda since it has been evident that this has been the source of Japanese competitive advantage.

However, it is appropriate that a more critical approach be adopted if European industry is to successfully adopt the new forms of organisation that will be most appropriate for competitive production in the 1990s and beyond. First, many of the ideas behind the concept of lean production are remarkably close to models and approaches developed in both Europe and the United States. For example, many European firms have used multifunctional workers and team-work; other European firms have avoided the strict division of labour between blue- and white-collar workers and have had some measure of integration of different functional divisions. Concepst such as 'the focused factory' [*Skinner, 1974*], 'the factory of the future' [*Agurèn and Edström, 1980*] and 'flow-oriented production' [*De Sitter, 1981*] are not new. They have been the subject of discussion and experimentation for almost two decades. It is also worth bearing in mind that the total quality approach (which the Japanese have used to such effect) was initially developed in the USA in the 1930s. Therefore it would seem that European industry is not so much lacking in ideas or in resources but that it has under-performed in the systematic application of these ideas to ensure long-term continuous improvement and innovation, that is the growth of a 'learning culture'. In these circumstances it is important to note that there is no short-cut panacea to achieving competitive production to be achieved through the uncritical adoption of the prescriptions of lean production or other 'cookbooks' purporting to provide a quick an easy route to Japanese competitiveness.

Second, lean production has been most clearly identified with successful attempts to promote incremental innovations through the use of available and proven technologies and knowledge. The success of Japanese organisational techniques is most clearly reflected in that country's 'rapid follower' status. But, hitherto, Japan's strength has not lain in the realm of invention and radical innovation in which much of European industry and science and technology has excelled. In this sense Europe can be seen as having the ability to more than hold its own against Japanese innovation. But where European industry has fallen down and where the requirements for new organisational practices are most apparent has been in the ability to rapidly turn these invention into successfully marketed products. The experience of Philips with its technically superior VCR2000 technology is a case in point.

Thirdly, Japan itself is undergoing a process of social change that suggests that parts of its past organisational strengths and its structure of social relations (including its labour market) may no longer be optimal for the emerging competitive environment. Rising levels of education and intensified global cultural interchange have altered the view of many Japanese towards the worlds of work and the family, and towards the power relationships inside and outside the firm; even in Japan unemployment has become

38

a 'normal' phenomenon. The 'heavy' industries are increasingly finding difficulty in recruiting blue-collar workers, many educated young job-seekers are sceptical about the attractions of lifetime employment, and female workers are growing resistant to their partial access to professional careers.

And, fourth, Japan may have managed to develop a pattern of production that allows its industry to compete effectively in global markets. But the social relations that underlie this particular structure of organisation are not only based upon its own individual political and cultural traditions, but also embody characteristics that may not be appropriate or desirable in Europe short cycle times in production, weak trade unions and long working hours hold little attraction for European structures of democracy and family life. Consequently, even if current Japanese organisational structures could be effectively utilised to meet the competitive challenges of the future, this may not provide an adequate role-model for European industry and society.

For these reasons, it is clear that whilst European industry has much to learn from organisational innovations arising from Japan and elsewhere, these can not, and should not, be adopted uncritically. Not only may many of these techniques need to be changed to meet the evolving competitive environment of the 1990s and beyond, but since they are inherently social in nature they will have to be fashioned to reflect the particular traditions to be found in Europe. Moreover, as will be seen in the following section, Europe has begun to develop its own organisational capabilities and these provide a springboard for a concerted programme of support for organisational innovation in Europe.

III. THE ORGANISATIONAL CHALLENGE

In Fordism the innovation process had been characterised by specialisation and separation. Similar skills, professions and processes were grouped together within the boundaries of functional departments and were confined within individual firms. Innovation in this context was viewed as a linear and sequential process in which different stages of design were handed on to the next department as batons in a relay race. Innovation was compartmentalised into smaller problems, each of which became the responsibility of a particular sub-unit. At the end of this process these partial solutions had to be put together again, in the hope that the final result would fit together in the intended manner. Consequently, innovation became bogged down in a bureaucratic web. The result was not only a costly process, but one that frustrated the creativity of its participants, and led to sub-optimal designs that reached the market too late to provide the anticipated rewards.

But, as we have observed, the result of this innovation trajectory has been that European competitiveness has suffered. Thus new organisational procedures are required, particularly those which recognise the systemic components of production and innovation. In exploring the policy relevance of this requirement for organisational restructuring, it is necessary to distinguish three spheres of industrial activity (Figure 2.1) - production,[1] R&D and human resource management; it is also necessary to distinguish three key levels of integrative activity. We begin with the three levels of integration.

Figure 2.1.: The Integration and Organisational Change

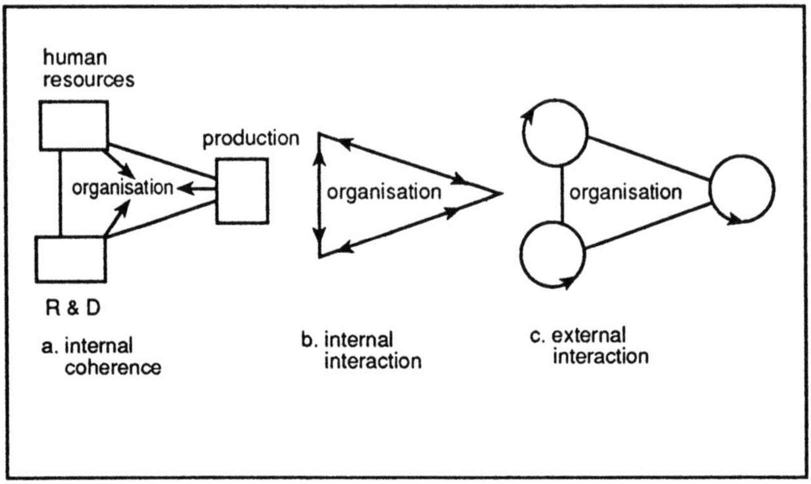

Three Levels of Integration

The first level of integration is that within each of the three major spheres of the firm (that is, production, R&D and human resources - see below). Organisational innovations are required in each. For example, new specific organisational procedures such as group work, flow-oriented production and quality management are relevant in production; inter-functional design groups, the decentralisation of support staff to production units in R&D; and an integrated approach needs to be developed towards human resource management.

The second level of integration refers to that between these three functions within the firm. This involves closer links and the dissolution of many of the functional divisions between, for example, R&D and production activities, and between human resource management and R&D activities.

The third and final level of integration arises between the firm and its external environment. This requires closer integration between manufacturers and suppliers and customers (vertical integration), and closer co-operation between partner firms in the same sector (horizontal integration).

Three Spheres of Industrial Activity

The three spheres of industrial activity - production, R&D and human resource management - represent the core of competitive production.

Production

In the past the organisational challenge in production has been oriented towards improving the quality of working life, the quality of final product and the flexibility of production. But new challenges now confront work system design as a consequence of the need to deepen the process of integration within this sphere. European firms have to learn, and to date they have to a large extent learnt to absorb the systemic changes required for the successful adoption of the JIT and TQM procedures emanating from Japan. However, more is required than the introduction of procedures and techniques. The challenge is now to integrate these techniques into a new organisational order which embraces all aspects of production. This requires a holistic approach to production, affecting synergistic changes in plant layout (cellular manufacturing), flow-oriented production and work organisation. It also requires a changing organisational culture in which members of the organisation do not regard work organisation as a steady state, but as a process requiring continual improvement (*kaizen*). At the same time, industry and the service sector have to confront the challenge of successfully introducing information and communication technologies in all areas of production. These are complex and costly technologies and it is clear that their systemic potential (arising through their common use of electronic control systems) cannot be reaped if introduced in traditional segmented organisational structures.

Linking production with R&D is an important objective with respect to the second level of integration (that between the three activities in the firm). A key perspective here is in respect of 'design for manufacture'. This involves two-way communication between product and process development in order to reduce production costs, improve product quality and to speed-up the innovation cycle. Similarly, the introduction of cellular production, which is an important component of flexible production and JIT, requires the availability of multi-skilled workers and the introduction of quality assurance procedures and hence affects human resource management.

With regard to the third level of integration - between the enterprise and the external world - closer coordination of production with suppliers and customers is required. The growing complexity and variety of production has led many firms to concentrate on their core competence [*Prahalad and Hamel, 1990*], and this has led to greater levels of subcontracting. To be managed successfully, it is clear that production scheduling between these related enterprises needs to be carefully coordinated. Similarly, to be fully effective, intra-plant JIT needs to be complemented by inter-plant JIT deliveries and this too, requires high levels of productive coordination. It is here that the Japanese are particularly well advanced. As in the case of intra-firm integration, this co-operation only becomes viable on the basis of competence, communication and trust and requires the establishment of long-term ties between these linked enterprises.

Research and Development

The specialisation of functions within R&D has become highly specialised and professionalised as technology has become increasingly complex, such that in the organisational literature this environment has come to be termed the 'professional bureaucracy' [*Mintzberg, 1979*]. But the effectiveness of these compartmentalised organisational structures has increasingly been found to be wanting in the new competitive environment, with respect to quality, costs and speed. Many organisational innovations are thus emerging in this sphere of activity such as 'inter-functional heavyweight product development groups [*Clark and Fujimoto, 1991*], 'skunk works' [*Peters, 1983*] and 'self-organising groups' [*Florida and Kenney, 1990*]. The function of these organisational innovations is to try and break down traditional professional barriers and thereby to increase the level of integration within this key area of activity.

Integrating R&D with the other major functions of the firm represents the second level of integration. The isolation of R&D in many firms is the consequence of the same principle of functional specialisation and has been standard organisational practice since the establishment of Fordism. But in the context of new competitive pressures, linking R&D more closely to business strategy as well as to production and to human resources has become a high priority. This often results in tension with entrenched professional attitudes, and sometimes leads to an overemphasis on short-term goals and a loss of synergies. The response has been the development of a new corporate activity designed to promote integration without paying the penalties of loss of specialisation - technology management. This involves adopting a portfolio approach to link corporate and business related R&D and to monitor horizontal exchange and cooperation between different areas of corporate activity.

The third level of integration of the R&D functions refers to links with the extra-corporate world - both with other firms and with the science and technological infrastructure. Europe has a strong tradition of academic research, far stronger than, for example, to that in Japan. Yet its links with the productive system has been weak and many European inventions have been commercially exploited elsewhere [*Amable and Boyer, 1992*]. EU

R&D programmes have also experienced some problems in this regard and although it has funded a considerable body of collaborative research, there are some doubts as to whether these research results have been adequately reflected in innovation in European industry.

Although substantial progress has been made in the integration of R&D functions in European industry, both within firms and with their external environments, the shortfall of integration with respect to all three levels of integration in R&D represents a considerable competitive weakness. It is a challenge that may potentially have a particularly negative impact upon the operations of SMEs. The inherent flexibility of these firms is often based upon their internal integration, including of R&D. But this may be undermined by their lack of resources to fund R&D in an increasingly technologically complex environment, and for these firms R&D networks are likely be an important component of competitive survival.

Human Resources

Human resources are of increasing importance as production becomes more knowledge intensive. Thus the development, integration, transfer and use of knowledge have become a core component in successful business practice. However, personnel management has become a victim of the same functional specialisation that has bedeviled the effectiveness of production and R&D. This has been exacerbated over the past two decades as personnel management has become professionalised [*Van Sluijs et al., 1991*]. Activities such as recruitment, training, career development, wage policy, the design of working conditions and industrial relations have become distinct specialisms.

Human resources management has reacted to this compartmentalisation by focusing on the need to integrate these different elements of organising human resources. It concentrates on developing an holistic perspective in which these formerly specialised concerns are coordinated within a single, integrated overview of human resource management within the firm. But human resources management also addresses the requirement of integrating personnel policy more closely with the spheres of production and R&D. Thus barriers between conceptual ('white collar') and executing ('blue collar') work are being broken down. Continuous change in production, flexibility and high quality output require continuous upgrading of worker skills, the development of multiskills in the labour force and high levels of trust and commitment between management and labour; these are the purview of an integrated strategy towards human resources. So, too, is the management of career development in the sphere of R&D which in the past this has been overly focused on recruitment (entry) and transfer to other business divisions and retirement (exit). What is also required, however, are explicit strategies to cope with career development within the R&D function so that these human resources are utilised most effectively. The development of adequate tools to facilitate this approach is still in its infancy [*Van Assen, 1992; Van Diepen, 1993*].

The need to manage the integration of human resources with the external environment is receiving greater recognition. Thus policy makers have placed great attention on the quality of the institutional infrastructure in the formal education and training systems, as well as with its links to internal systems of training and knowledge acquisition. The well-known 'dual system' in Germany has long been admired, as has the French system of DUT and BTS which provide the material on which internal training systems can be constructed. But there is no cause for complacency. For example, the German craft-system may not fit easily with the need to demote specialisms and to provide all of the workforce with a mix of skills. Similarly, traditional policies towards training have not adequately recognised the requirement to promote continuous change and hence encourage promote continuous learning adequately.

The integration of human resources policies with the external environment is not confined to issues of training and personnel development. It also relates to employment relations, health and safety at work, concerns with gender and minority groups, and wage systems. One important change is the development of closer dialogue between the industrial actors on the basis of greater trust and commitment. Another important change is that human resource management that includes enhanced working conditions, is rapidly becoming a necessary component for competitive production. In this key regard it represents a sharp disjuncture with past perspectives in which it was believed that enhanced working conditions could only be delivered once competitive production was attained.

IV. EUROPEAN PERSPECTIVES ON ORGANISATIONAL INNOVATION

Theory and Policy

Over the past decade Europe has been inundated with organisational models, instruments and routines emanating from Japan and the United States. 'Zero defects', 'Just in Time', 'Corporate Excellence', 'High Performance Groups', and the more recent 'Lean Production' and 'Business Process Re-engineering' have become familiar phrases in current European management terminology. It would seem that Europe is not only in danger of becoming dependent on imported technology, but also on a foreign management culture.

This is not to say that European management has nothing to learn from the experience of other countries. But it is important to bear in mind that there is no need for excessive dependence on external managerial ideas, since a wealth of knowledge and experience has been accumulated within Europe which is directly related to the organisational practices which are so important to contemporary competitiveness. They are to be found in a broad range of disciplines and techniques in production engineering, psychology, sociology, business administration, operations research, accounting, marketing and business informatics. Indeed, much of contemporary thinking in organisational sciences derives from the work of European scholars. They laid the foundations for many areas of organisation design and organisational innovation. After the Second World War they showed new ways that went beyond the American Human Relations approaches. The pioneering work of the Tavistock Institute [*Bamforth and Trist, 1951*] led to the discovery of the 'self-managing groups' as essential building blocks of organisation design. The classical study of Burns and Stalker [*1961*] inspired a whole generation of researchers in the search for organisational regimes that foster innovation. The early Scandinavian experiments in job design opened a new perspective on the translation of democratic values in practical organisational concepts and Dahrendorf [*1958*], Crozier [*1964*] and Emery and Thorsrud [*1976*] shed new light on power and decision making within organisations.

One remarkable difference with American theoretical discourse in this area is that the European research agenda has been more concerned with social questions and has been less data driven. In general it has attempted to both understand and implement organisational structures that stimulate and support innovation. Although there is considerable diversity in this research tradition, a number of common relevant themes have emerged:

- It is in the nature of organisational structures and organisational change that there is no 'one best way' ('best practice') in organisation and job design. Organisations are created to serve a variety of functions in various social and economic contexts, and at different periods of time. The task therefore is to continually search for what might be called 'better practice'.

- Individual organisational disciplines offer only partial views on organisation and a multi-disciplinary approach towards organisational design is thus required.

- Organisational structures developed for specific contexts cannot be replicated elsewhere, but need to be modified; moreover, they also need to be continually changed if the firm is to maintain its competitive edge.

- The competence of our services and industries to innovate is primarily based on the qualifications of workers throughout the organisation. Qualifications can only be maintained and developed in a challenging work environment. The quality of work and the qualifications of the workers are, in this sense, two sides of one coin.
- The enhancement of the firms flexibility can only be achieved by changing from a complex functional organisation with simple jobs, to a more flow-oriented simplified organisation with challenging and more complex jobs. Thus it is imperative that work redesign and organisation redesign go hand in hand.
- An active and early involvement of the operators and users of new product and process technology is an essential condition for organisational effectiveness.

But despite the wealth of European research expertise in these areas and the very obvious organisational innovations made by large and small firms alike (as is shown, for example, in the case-studies which follow), market failure in organisational restructuring is endemic. To some extent these policy issues have been raised tangentially in a variety of related policy areas, such as:

- Labour policy, for example, safeguarding qualifications and improving the Quality of Working Life by early participation in decision making by workers. These objectives can be found in laws on working conditions and worker participation in government-sponsored programmes in Germany, the Netherlands, Norway and Sweden.
- Regional policy, for example, in programmes designed to strengthen the social and technical infrastructure of problem areas, as in the German Work and Technologies Programme of the land of Nordhrhein-Westfalen and the city of Bremen (ITB).
- Technology policy, for example, in attempts to increase the effectiveness of technological development programmes by incorporating work and organisational design criteria and in the German technology programme (Feritgungsprogramm)
- Science policy, for example, the desire to reinforce scientific infrastructure in the Dutch TAO programme, and the British PICT programme, and
- Business policy, through contributing to business development by integrating technological and organisational innovation as in the UK MAP programme.

Some of these policy responses have also been found at the European level, through EU programmes and institutions such as FAST-MONITOR, CIRP and ESPRIT, EFILWC and EUROTECHNET.

However, examples of comprehensive policy responses can be found in Norway, Sweden and Germany [*Den Hertog and Schröder, 1989*]. The Norwegian tradition of work reform programmes which started in 1964 with the Industrial Democracy Programme [*Thorsrud and Emery, 1967*] has the longest history. This programme was followed by a number of programmes such as HABUT and SBA. Recently, a new programme has been formulated which is meant to support the competitive advantage of Norwegian firms from the perspective of their technologies, their organisation and their markets. A parallel development can be observed in Sweden, which has a long history of research, development and action programmes focusing on organisational reform such as the Development Programme, MDA, OM and (presently) the Programme for Learning Organisations. The largest current programme in Europe is probably the German federal Programme on Work and Technology, which was launched in 1974 as the Programme for the Humanisation of Working Life. These publicly-funded programmes tends to focus on medium- and long-term support, are generally multi-disciplinary and include representatives of the various industrial actors. But as yet they are still largely confined to the production organisation of individual firms, although there is a trend to begin to work with networks of firms.

This agenda of emerging research and policy reflects an important shift in perspective. First, the focus has moved from particular organisational problems (within individual activities) to those of a more general and related nature. A second significant trend has been the growing attention paid to the organisation of the whole chain of process and product innovation. This begins with research, passes through development, design, production, distribution and after sales support. Initially, research in this area focused on the downstream implications of upstream design choices with the idea of 'selecting out' negative impacts at the design stage. More recently there has been a subtle, but important shift towards a more proactive approach, one that attempts to 'design in' (rather than to 'select out') particular attributes. This has required a more holistic focus on the innovation chain so that the strengthening of the organisation of these interconnections becomes a critical focus of research and innovation policy. In many sectors the complexity of this innovation cycle has made it necessary to focus both on inter-firm relations and on relations between firms and the science and technology infrastructure.

V. THE DIFFUSION OF NEW FORMS OF ORGANISATION IN PRODUCTION

There have been an increasing number attempts to introduce new forms of organisational design within and between European industry and the related institutional infrastructure, both within small and medium-sized enterprises (SMEs) and large firms. In the former category, efforts have been directed at improving the quality of work, raising the qualifications of the workforce through training and retraining, enhancing flexibility and improving product quality. The long tradition of craft labour in Europe has contributed to the success of this continual updating of work organisation, for example in the Scandinavian development programmes and the German qualification process [*Altman, 1992*], and the socio-technical redesign projects in firms throughout Europe [*Van Eijnatten, 1993*]. Multiskilling, autonomous work teams and the reintegration of the processes of conception and execution ('thinking and doing') can be regarded as basic elements of this programme.

Similar developments have occurred in the large scale sector, for example, in the recent attempts to imbed JIT organisation within the European tradition of autonomous work teams. The recent experience of Rover (absorbing and adapting principles learnt form its joint venture with Honda) and Renault and Volkswagen (with the introduction of '. und Jetzt-In-Teams') are examples of this process of learning and adaptation. It is significant that a basic condition for this process of organisational learning with respect to work organisation is that these have been imbedded in systems that strive towards single-unit flow production, that is by adopting JIT principles and (where relevant) cellular manufacturing organisation.

Experience with inter-firm networking also confirms the existence and importance of programmes of continual learning, and here Europe would appear to have particularly strong capabilities. This is evident in regard to the large firms sector, to SMEs and to the links between large firms and SMEs. For example, in the aerospace sector, co-operation between large firms has placed European industry at the forefront of global competition, both in the Ariane launcher programme and in the civilian aircraft sector. Similar processes of networking between large firms that embody processes of advanced innovation and continual learning are to be found in the electronics (Thompson and Philips) and auto (Renault and Volvo) industries. With respect to networking between SMEs, in both Denmark and the Netherlands, many of the smaller firms have shown remarkable creativity. In Italy, small firms have notably clustered in industrial districts and have shared a variety of indirect scaling costs (such as in design and marketing) to become dominant in their sectors in the global economy.

European firms have also displayed the capacity to develop organisational structures which enable them to learn how to use new information technologies. In the banking sector, telematic networks have enabled the Visa system to successfully challenge the dominance of the large American networks on the basis of the quality, the security and the continual modernisation of the services offered. Similar examples concerning the use of telematic networks to link production and distribution are to be found in the automotive, steel and textile industries [*Bar, Borrus and Coriat, 1989*]. In relation to industrial automation, flexible manufacturing systems and automated transfer lines produced by firms such as Comau and Fiat have been widely used throughout the world; in telecommunications, Ericsson and Alcatel have remained at the technological frontier and have been gaining in global market share. Once again, the basis of success has been the ability of these firms to continually update their products.

Thus there is widespread evidence of the ability of many European firms to institute processes to ensure continual learning and renewal, with regard to work-organisation, inter-firm networking and the use of information technology. Yet there are grounds for concern in relation to the extent to which these capabilities are adequately spread through individual sectors and individual countries. Moreover, even in those sectors where European industry has performed well, their competitors show the ability to consolidate their own learning capabilities as the networks of small Italian footwear firms have found to their recent cost as Taiwanese, Brazilian and Korean competitors have moved into the upper-end of the market that had previously been the strength of these European firms.

But, most importantly, our knowledge of the detailed social processes underlying these successful (and indeed unsuccessful) cases of organisational reform is weak. The strategic challenge is thus to understand the barriers to endogenising processes of continual learning in European industry and to assess the extent and the processes whereby these capabilities can be enhanced by learning from the experience of successful firms in Europe and elsewhere. It is hoped that the case-studies which follow provide important insights on which a successful programme of policy support can be based, at the local, national and European-wide levels.

NOTE

1. Throughout this chapter, the word 'production' is meant to cover both the manufacturing process and the delivery of services.

REFERENCES

Agurèn, S. and J. Edström (1980), *New Factories: Job Design Through Factory Planning in Sweden*, Stockholm: SAF.

Altmann, N., Ch. Köhler, and P. Meil, (Eds.) (1992), *Technology and Work in German industry*, London: Routledge.

Amable, B. and R. Boyer (1992), 'The R&D Productivity Relationship in the Context of New Growth Theories: Some Recent Applied Research', paper presented at the seminar on 'Quantitative Assessment of Technological Change', Brussels, January 23 24, 1992.

Assen, A van (1990), 'Obsoletie en loopbaankenmerklen can R&D-medewerkers: Resultaten van een pilot-studie', *Gedrag & Gezondheid*, Vol. 17, No.4., pp. 162-166.

Bar, F., M. Borrus and B. Coriat (1989), *Information Network and Competitive Advantages: The Issue for Government and Corporate Strategy (Working Document)*, Paris: OECD-BRIE.

Burns, T. and G. M. Stalker (1961), *The Management of Innovation*, London: Tavistock.

Clark, K. B. and T. Fujimoto (1991), 'The Power of Product Integrity', *Harvard Business Review*, vol. 68, no. 6, pp. 107 118.

Crozier, M. (1964), *The Bureaucratic Phenomenon*, London: Tavistock.

Dahrendorf, R. (1958), 'Out of Utopia: Towards Reorientation of Sociological Analysis', *American Journal of Sociology*, Vol. LXIV, pp. 115-127.

Diepen, B. van (1993), *Patterns of Competence Development Among Personnel*, Maastricht: MERIT.

Eijnatten, F. M. (1993), *The Paradigm That Changed the Work Place*, Assen: Van Gorcum.

Emery, F. and E. Thorsrud (1976), *Democracy at Work*, Leiden: Nijhoff.

Florida, R. and M. Kenney (1990), *The breakthrough Illusion: Corporate America's Failure to Move from Innovation to Production*, New York: Basic Books.

Hertog, J. F. den and P. Schröder (1989), *Social Research for Change*, Maastricht: MERIT.

Jaikumar, R. (1986), 'Post-Industrial Manufacturing', *Harvard Business Review*, Nov. Dec., pp. 69 76.

Kaplinsky, R. (1994), *Easternisation: The Spread of Japanese Management Techniques to Developing Countries*, London: Frank Cass.

Mintzberg, H. (1979), *The Structuring of Organizations*, Englewood Cliffs, NJ: Prentice-Hall.

Peters, T. (1983), 'The Mythology of Innovation, or a Skunkworks Tale, Part II', *The Stanford Magazine*.

Pralahad, C,. K. and G. Hamel (1990), 'The Core Competencies of the Firm', *Harvard Business Review*, Vol. 68, No. 3, pp. 79-91.

Rothwell, R. (1992), 'Successful Industrial Innovation: Critical Factors for the 1990s', *R&D Management*, Vol. 22, No. 3, pp. 221-238.

Sitter, L. U. de (1981), *Nieuwe kantoren en fabrieken*, Deventer: Kluwer.

Skinner, W. (1974), 'The Focused Factory', *Harvard Business Review*, Vol. 52, No. 3, pp. 113-121.

Sluijs, E van, Assen, A. and J. F. den Hertog (1991), Personnel Management and Organizational Change: A Sociotechnical Perspective, *European Work and Organizational Psychologist*, Vol. 1, No. 1, pp. 27-51.

Thorsrud, E. and F. Emery (1967), *Form and Content of Industrial Democracy*, London: Tavistock.

Trist, E.L. and K.W. Bamforth (1951), 'Some Social and Psychological Consequences of the Longwall Method of Coal-Getting', *Human Relations*, Vol 4, No. 1, pp. 3-38.

Womack, J.P., Jones, D.T. and D. Roos (1990), *The Machine that Changed the World*, New York: Rawson Associates.

3

EUROPE'S PROBLEM WITH COMPETITIVENESS: A COMMENTARY

Alexis Jacquemin

These two introductory chapters are very useful for understanding a paradox for European Competitiveness. On the one hand, European advantages are still important, especially in R&D, but, on the other hand, performances are not impressive. It is then argued that a central explanation relies on the insufficient capacity of European industry to meet the organisational challenge of the 1990s and beyond. New organisational procedures are required 'particularly those which recognise the systematic components of production and innovation'.

The main messages of the authors are convincing and confirm the message of the EC White Paper on *Growth, Competitiveness, Employment*. The key elements for competitiveness which are now of great importance are no longer confined to the relative level of the direct costs of the various factors of production. They include, in particular, the quality of education and training, the efficiency of corporate organisation, the capacity to make continuous improvement in production processes, the intensity of R&D and its industrial exploitation. Even more crucial is the capacity to incorporate all of these elements into coherent strategies. Between 75 per cent and 95 per cent of firms' total wage and salary bill is now accounted for, by functions linked to organisation rather than to direct production, for example information technology, engineering , training, accounting, marketing and research. Organisational capacity is thus one of the key components of a firm's competitiveness. I do not think that this argument is an issue only for corporations. Today, global interdependence does not automatically produce order and, in search for the public interest, it is necessary to have some forms of corporation at each level of competitive areas. In relations between firms, between nations, between regional groupings and between socio-cultural systems, there is everywhere a need for forums of exchange, cooperation and organisations, to generate a degree of trust and consensus that is superior to what can be expected from the different forms of capitalism.

My view is that the analysis made by the authors could usefully be presented in this broader context, as part of the more general problems for our societies. In what follows, I should like to make some specific comments, first on the use of indicators of competitiveness, and secondly on the role of organisations.

Concerning the global indicators used in the chapters, many of them are ambiguous and it is not easy to relate them to the role of corporate organisation. We know very well that the trade dimension is not very relevant and that competitiveness is mainly determined by domestic factors. Comparing the situation of employment in the US and the EC is also tricky. In Europe, adjustment is essentially made in quantity, that is the level of employment, given the rigidity of prices/wages. In the US, adjustment is primarily in the level of wages. It is hard to make a judgement as to which system works best. America's labour market delivers more employment, but the cost is increased in poverty and out of work, and greater economic insecurity.

Another type of indicator used in the chapters concerns the poor ability of Europe to transform its substantial R&D efforts into new innovations, products, processes and patents. Such an inefficient 'transformation function' is attributed, by the authors, to bad organisations. I agree with the view that this is indeed a major explanation, but it would be wise to take into account the role of other factors, such as the lack of coordination between national programmes and initiatives in the domain of R&D (in spite of the efforts made by the Commission), the bias of public policies in favour of producers, at the expense of users, and the support of 'national' or 'European' champions, at the expense of SMEs. From that point of view, it would be useful to put the role of corporate organisation in the context of the science and technological infrastructure, as well as in the policy context.

Concerning the links between organisation and employment, my feeling is that the main connections are in terms of improving human resources, training and personnel development, and not so much in terms of increasing the level of employment. The view according to which monopolistic rents extracted from a more efficient form of organisation could help in maintaining or expanding employment is dubious. Today, the general tendency of corporations is to use additional rents or incomes for restructuring, acquiring competitors, and consolidating their positions. These strategies will not be favourable to employment.

What would be a better track for the improvement of employment, due to better corporate organisation, is what we call, in the White Paper, 'internal flexibility'. Internal flexibility is the result of the optimum management of a company's human resources. The aim is to adjust the work-force without making people redundant wherever this can be avoided. Focusing on the continuity of the link between the company and the worker it maximises the investment in human resources and staff involvement. It is up to individual companies to improve internal flexibility by means of more polyvalent training, staff mobility, the integrated organisation of work, flexible working hours, and performance-related pay. Tailored to the European company model, it is should be central to negotiations within the company.

My last comment concerns the link between the corporate choice of organisational structures and its use to control the market, a link that is not explored in the chapters. The main point is that even if a given organisational form is able to achieve efficiency, more complex and costly modes could prevail in response to a quest for controlling the markets, as long as they have a net positive effect on profits [*Jacquemin, 1987, Chapter 5*].

In the same way that market structures are not totally exogenous and are partially manipulated by players in order to improve their market power, organisational structures of the firm constitute a decision variable allowing for the setting up and reinforcement of market control. For example, one can imagine situations in which a simple contract between suppliers and distributors would have realised the proposed transaction at minimum transaction costs; however, the firm could resort to a more costly form of organisation, for instance, a legal merger or control of shareholding in order to set up a barrier vis-à-vis existing rivals or potential entrants. There are many ways in which a firm may obtain monopoly rent by adopting costly organisational structures that restrict its rivals' choices. So, in the selection of their organisational structures, firms attempt to improve simultaneously their efficiency and their market power.

To conclude, I wish to underline the importance of this research on organisational structures and organisational change. Understanding the dynamics of organisation is especially crucial. This requires a broad interdisciplinary approach where history and cultural patterns play a central role.

REFERENCE

Jacquemin, a. (1987), *The New Industrial Organisation,* Oxford: Oxford University Press.

PART II:
ORGANISATION AND INTEGRATION IN PRODUCTION

As we have seen in Part I, the primary explanation for the failure of the European economy to maintain its competitive position despite investing comparatively large resources in technology and research is the commitment to outdated forms of industrial organisation. The challenge is now twofold - to introduce new techniques of organisation in three spheres (production, R&D and human resource management), and to move to deeper forms of integration within each of these spheres, between these three spheres, and between the enterprise and the external world.

The three case studies in Part 2 - Swatch, Peugeot and Zilverstad - reflect this process of restructuring in the sphere of production. Swatch was able to recover the dominant position of the Swedish watch industry through an innovative approach to the new quartz technology. Through a commitment to design and variety, and a purposeful programme of design-for-manufacture, it was able to dominate the low end of the market with innovative and constantly changing designs, offered at low prices. Peugeot has consolidated its growing position in the European auto industry through the effective adoption of just-in-time manufacture; this involved significant changes to production organisation and a major alteration of its relationships with its suppliers. As in the case of Swatch, Zilverstad was able to beat back far eastern competition through the introduction of new forms of production and work organisation.

In each of these cases not only were a variety of new organisational techniques introduced into production, but the firms were also linking production organisation with the two other spheres - R&D and human resource management - as well as restructuring their relationships with external suppliers and customers.

4

SWATCH: A EUROPEAN RESPONSE TO THE JAPANESE CHALLENGE

Benjamin Coriat and Ronny Bianchi

I.   INTRODUCTION

The case of the Swatch industry we are presenting a model in more ways than one. It is an illustration of one of those rare experiences of a European business at this level which has been able to resist and to take an initiative against the offensive launched by the countries of the Far East (Hong Kong and Japan in the lead). Swatch has not only succeeded in winning back lost markets but also in regaining Swiss market dominance.

The first section presents the conditions in which the crisis in the Swiss watch industry developed in the 1970, a time of intense technical change (the introduction of quartz) and of the beginnings of the Far East offensive. The second section is dedicated to the analysis of the counter-offensive launched with Swatch products by the SMH group. The emphasis is placed on the joint revolution in product and process that assured its success by promoting a new watch concept on the world market. The third section completes this view by bringing out the technical/organisational dimensions of the change and their links with the changes in the division of work within the industry.

II.   THE 1970s: THE CRISIS IN THE SWISS WATCH INDUSTRY AND THE RISE OF FAR EAST COMPETITION

Contrary to the image often portrayed, the watch industry is very complex and includes a wide range of skilled jobs which bring into play the finer processes of co-operation between businesses. It must be added that, since at least the middle of the 1970s, the sector has developed rapidly. This has been influenced in particular by a major technical progress: the introduction of the quartz technologies. Finally, an element that makes for complexity - the sector has always covered a large range of products. At the two extremes one can find, on the one hand, on the side of tradition, the up-market watch, almost exclusively Swiss, produced in small quantities and following methods that are very close to those of the craft industry. If the demand is sensitive to the price, this type of watch nevertheless remains an object of 'distinction', being the owner of a Rolex or even better, a Patek Philippe means the owner has deliberately looked for outward social signs of distinction and recognition. The quality, image, and reputation attached to the product - and to its owner - are in this case a key element of the firm's success. On the other hand, there is the utilitarian watch, the 'cheap' watch. In this case the price is a determining element and cannot exceed certain limits (from SF50 for most down-market watch and up to SF1,000 for more sophisticated items). Any innovation that permits a reduction in the price here is eagerly sought. It is in this segment of the market, which is particularly exposed to competition, that Swatch positioned itself. Notwithstanding, a key factor to the success of Swatch is that the Swiss company entered the market by using the key elements of its tradition of quality and prestige, accumulated over time by Swiss watch-makers.

However, regardless of whether it was 'up' or 'down' market, at the beginning of the 1970s, the whole of the Swiss watch industry entered a severe and deep crisis. The determining factor in the crisis was the introduction of a new product (the quartz watch) which, in turn, brought new rivals (Hong Kong and Japan). Other elements also played an important role in sparking off and deepening the crisis. At least three elements must be kept in mind.

Monetary Instability During the 1970s and the Strong Appreciation of the Swiss Franc Heavily Penalised the Swiss Watch Industry

In 1971, the unilateral declaration which put an end to the convertibility of the dollar into gold and, at the same time, to the Bretton Woods system, marked the beginning of a period of monetary turbulence and significant modifications to the relative parities of national currencies. In this context, the relative value of the Swiss franc soared. From 1971 to 1979, this assessment was 60 per cent in real value (125 per cent in nominal value). The consequences for the watch sector were very severe because virtually the entire production was destined for the export market (in 1970 more than 71 million items out of 75 million produced by the Swiss manufacturers were exported). The result was a drastic effect on the Swiss industry which contracted spectacularly: production fell from 94 million items in 1974 to 45 million items in 1983.

The combined effects of the world crisis (after 1973) and of the value of the national currency was even more important than expected, since one of the distinctive traits of the Swiss watch industry was that it was centred upon 'up' and 'middle' market products. These products are by their nature more sensitive to economic variations and monetary parities. Even if it is difficult to evaluate precisely the impact of these variables on the watch crisis, it is certain that these elements contributed significantly to the weakening of the watch industry as a whole.

Switzerland and the Entry of New Far-Eastern Competitors

Table 4.1 clearly shows the speed and extent of the rise in power of the new competitors to the Swiss industry.

The data presented in this chart show the strong relative growth of Japan in the watch production industry, by items and by value, and the spectacular rise of Hong Kong which, within ten years, had a production of nearly 100 million items.

Switzerland has maintained its supremacy where the value of production is concerned (with a turnover of SF40 bn in 1985). This is, however, due to 'up-market' production, which is a segment of the industry that has remained almost entirely in Swiss hands. However, it must be noted that since this period (as shown in the partial data of 1989), Swatch has recorded a remarkable number of successes and contributed largely to maintaining Swiss supremacy.

In fact, a very important transformation began during the 1970s and the 1980s: the world watch production centre had taken itself to the Far East. This was accompanied by a depression in the watch sector in industrialised countries such as in France and the United States. Switzerland was also deeply affected and threatened, as we have already seen. The reasons for this change were twofold: the relative cost of labour (much lower in Japan and even lower in Hong Kong) and the development of new technologies which allowed firms without a tradition of watch making to enter the market. These new technologies brought about a 'technical leap' strategy in the conception of the products.

The Swiss watch industry is the only western watch industry that eventually managed to reverse the negative tendency that had marked all western watch industries over recent years. The dual revolution in both the Swatch 'down-market' products and the successful renovation of 'up-market' products was at the origin of this come-back. However, this could not have been foreseen simply by looking at the conditions of the watch industry in Switzerland at the time. It had been damaged by the dispersion of the firms and of savoir-faire and was dominated by two large holdings whose own structures were not solid. They seemed quite unprepared to meet the dynamism of the new challengers from the Far East[1].

Different studies on the industry were carried out by research departments and were financed notably by the watch industry's syndicate and the bank consortium which had been made responsible for the restructuring during

TABLE 4.1
GLOBAL WATCH PRODUCTION

Years	Switzerland				Japan				Hong Kong		USSR		USA	
	Volume		*Value*		*Volume*		*Value*		*Volume*		*Volume*		*Volume*	
	Units (m)	% of Global output	SF(bn)	% of Global output	Units (m)	% of Global output	SF(bn)	% of Global output	Units (m)	% of Global output	Units (m)	% of Global output	Units (m)	% of Global output
1950		52			0.7	1					2	4	10	21
1960	42	42				7					17	17	10	10
1970	76	44	2.3		24	14	0.7				22	13	20	12
1974	94	43	3.5		32	15	1.5		5	2	28	13	26	12
1975	75	34	3.0	36	90	14	1.5	38	6	3	30	14	27	12
1980	88	29	3.3	35	88	29	2.9	31	59	20	38	13	12	4
1985	60	13	4.1	40	177	38	3.8	33	95	20	44	9	2	0.4
1989	89	13		48										

Source: Poitet [1988]

the serious crisis of the 1970s. In their diagnoses, all the analyses converged on a few elements of the weaknesses of the industry (see Box 4.1).

Box 4. 1
The structural weaknesses of the Swiss watch industry in the 1970s

* Too many firms whose business concentrated on production in small series and often subcontracted to larger firms; were thus incapable of taking the initiative required to diversify and modify their traditional methods of production.

* Difficulty for the actors in the industry to get a global view of the production cycle; the 'horizontal' organisation which characterised the industry prevented a rational division of labour; suppliers and sub-contractors are too dependent on final assemblers.

* High production costs due to more expensive labour costs in comparison with competing countries and to outdated production systems and methods.

* A too narrow financial basis (taking into account the weak turnover and profit margins), which did not allow the necessary investment in R&D or the modernisation of production tools.

* Antiquated management methods (both paternalistic and bureaucratic) which blocked the rapid decision making necessary in the face of the competition from the Far-East.

Source: The Swiss Watch Syndicate

The challenge that had to be confronted from 1980 to 1984 was reflected in the fact that the average cost of a Swiss watch doubled, whereas that of the Japanese watch dropped by 30 per cent and that of the Hong Kong watch by 50 per cent [*Crevoiser, 1990*].

The Quartz Revolution and its Multiple Effects

It is within this context that the quartz watch revolutionised the industry and opened a gap through which the Far Eastern competitors could enter. It is remarkable to note here that in 1967 the Swiss were the first to develop the technology of the quartz watch. However, after a low-key and almost experimental show on the market, this technology was abandoned by the

Swiss producers. It was only really put into production from 1974 and then by foreign competitors[2].

Quartz technology rapidly revolutionised the industry as its precision and reliability are extremely high and its costs are much lower than for a traditional watch. It was first applied to 'down-market' products, but it had a considerable impact on the entire industry. Quartz watch production on the world market started in 1974 with five million items and rapidly increased by 340 items in 1984 and to 690 in 1989 covering more than 80 per cent of world watch production. For the most part, it was the producers from the Far East who ensured the rise to dominance of this technology and which, at the same time, set up a redivision of the market in their favour.

Almost all Swiss firms proved to be incapable of reacting to this change. Apart from the structural changes already mentioned briefly, the main reason was that they could not incorporate quartz watch-making techniques into their traditional structure of production. By promoting the change-over to electronics and micro-electronics, the introduction of the quartz watch also involved the rise of a series of savoir-faire and new techniques: knowledge of integrated circuits, quartz resonators, micromotors and LCD displays. Such trades and savoir-faire were at an embryonic stage in Switzerland. Thus, this change favoured the countries of the Far East which could take on these technologies and develop them. However, as will be seen, an essential component of this change is that it also enabled firms operating in different sectors and interested in diversifying their activities to progressively enter the market. Thus, for the established Swiss watch firms this meant new foreign competitors (Japan and Hong Kong in particular) but also competition at home with Swiss firms which had previously operated in different sectors. By bringing a certain savoir-faire from other areas into the watch industry, quartz technology also modified the roles and the respective place occupied by the different actors in the industry.

The revolution introduced by quartz did not stop there. By shaking up the technologies and production conditions, quartz technology also shook up the market and marketing conditions. The possibilities opened by the new products and new techniques also demanded the reorganisation of distribution networks, of marketing and of management, linked to the possibilities offered by the mass production of watches. Thus over several decades this case confirms the pattern described by Chandler in his classic works [*1962; 1977*], concerning the way in which advances in mass production necessarily bring about a shake-up in marketing and distribution networks.

To begin with, the crisis that followed these changes was severe for all actors in the industry. The two main groups present on the market were particularly affected. This necessitated the intervention of the large Swiss banks. The banks provided more than SF1 bn to the firms during a complex restructuring period. The support was not only financial. It also concerned the industry's productive and organisational dimensions and involved introducing and developing new technologies. Finally, the intervention from the banks lead to the fusion, in 1985, of ASUAG and SSIH in the SMH SA group (Société Suisse de Micro-électronique et d'Horlogerie). This group (briefly presented in Box 4.2 below) is important because this is where the concept and the Swatch line of products was developed. It was in this context that the Swatch watch, an advance in itself in the concept, entered the market.

Box 4. 2
The SMH group (Société Suisse de Micro-électronique et d'Horlogerie)

Main information for 1993
-15,039 employees
-SF2,865m turnover
-SF441m profit
-SF559m cash flow
-SF100-140m invested in R & D

SMH is a vertically integrated group :
.Deluxe watches : Blancpain
.Luxury watches : Omega, Longines, Rado
.Middle market : Tissot, Certina, Mido, Hammilton, Pierre Balmain
.Down market : Swatch, Flik Flack, Enduro
.Watch production, clock working, components and precision pieces: 5 firms
.Micro-electronics, components and telecommunication systems: 5 firms
.Production system : 2 firms
.Services, research, patents, real estate, etc.: 7 firms

Swatch watches are produced in 5 factories and the company employs in all between 500 and 600 persons. In 1987, production amounted to 15,000 million watches. This enabled SMH to become the leader in world watch production.

III.   BETWEEN TRADITION AND REVOLUTION : THE SWATCH CONCEPT

To fully understand the Swatch concept it is necessary to overview several key innovations which highlight the novelty of the concept.

A 'Down-Market 'Product but Differentiated and Supported by the 'Swiss Made' Label

One of the first particularities of Swatch was to position itself in the 'down-market' segment where the industry was most vulnerable. At the beginning of the 1980s, this segment was virtually entirely dominated by the Asians. It must be noted that in 1982-83 as the first Swatch watches appeared on the market this appeared to be an almost impossible challenge for the Swiss watch manufacturers.

Box 4. 3
The role of the 'Swiss Made' label

In 1979, Hayek Engineering was consulted to evaluate the watch sector. They carried out a commercial test on the American market. Consumers were offered three identical watches - the first was made in Switzerland, the second in Japan and the third in Hong Kong. The first was sold at a price equivalent to SF107, the second at a price of SF100 and the third at SF95. The consumers' reaction was clear: 82 per cent preferred the watch made in Switzerland even if it was more expensive, 15 per cent would have bought the Japanese watch and only three per cent of the people tested would have bought the watch made in Hong Kong.

Mr. Hayek subsequently became the director and principal shareholder of the SMH Group.

Source: Chevalie and Gremont [*1988*]

In fact, if Swatch has succeeded it was because its response was not 'passive'. It did not align itself with the Japanese or the Hong Kong concepts. Its strength lay in modifying the nature of the 'down-market' product itself and in confronting its competitors on home ground, where the rules of the game were set up, modified and then implemented. Indeed, the Swatch product has unique characteristics. Even if it was designed on the basis of the new quartz techniques, it introduced itself on the market as the heir to the Swiss-made label, to its tradition of quality and its quest for distinction. The target was no longer the elite and the 'happy few', as it was before for the classic brands, but young people and the growing middle class consumers. The Swatch watch, over and above its utilitarian functions, was immediately accepted as a fashion, sport or leisure object and even as jewellery.

Therefore, like the Japanese, the Swiss decided to mass produce quality watches but with the added dimension that followed the principle of constantly renewed variety, reflecting the rhythms of season and fashion. As early as 1980, two new collections were created each year and each collection consisted of 30 distinct models. The watch was not only an instrument for measuring time but also a fashion object which, like all fashion, determined its own obsolescence. With success lending a helping hand, it almost became a collector's item.

The success of Swatch was startling. Between 1983 and 1988, Swatch produced 50 million items, and by the beginning of the 1990s (ten years after its launching), the market was absorbing 100 million. The Japanese and even more so the Hong Kong producers were sent back to the defence lines. They took refuge in the very low-end LCD quartz watch market, which was to decline rapidly òver the second half of the 1980s.

From Roskopf to Swatch: Tradition and Renewal of the 'Cheap' Watch

Many anecdotes can be told of the story of the design of Swatch and, in the great tradition of 'success stories', the story of the destiny of individuals and improbable encounters is combined with those of major entrepreneurial initiatives. In the written and oral tradition of SMH, the custom is to start the story of Swatch in 1978. At that time the ETA firm had developed an ultra-flat watch called 'Delerium' whose main feature was an exceptional miniaturisation of watch mechanics: all the savoir-faire of the Swiss watch-making industry was concentrated into a two-millimetre thickness. This watch was positioned 'up-market' but it did not meet with much success. Thereafter from 1980, the possibility of transferring the savoir-faire to a more modest and 'really cheap' product which would impose itself on a very wide market was envisaged. Research began by trying to develop a so-called 'Delerium Vulgaris'.

This eventually give birth to Swatch, but only after numerous detours and with certain individuals playing a particularly important role (Box 4.4). The Swatch concept as we know it today was the fruit of the ideas and the will of a small number of people who had the capacity to renew the watch in various aspects (technique, marketing, image and price) and to invest in the sector during a period of crisis. The Swatch experience should also be placed in a broader context by viewing it within the framework of a watch-making tradition which provided important signposts of the best direction to take.

In fact, the story of the cheap Swiss watch is marked by at least three inventions and really outstanding experiences.

Box 4. 4
The Swatch Designers

Towards the middle of the 1970s (the time of crisis), the engineer, Jacques Muller, who had been made redundant by a watch making firm, joined ETA at Grenchen and met another engineer, Almar Monk and the chief executive of ETA, Dr. Thomke. Muller was a great admirer of the 2CV Citrôen car, and dreamt of a watch that was as simple as the 2CV. His idea was that less pieces meant less breakdowns and assembly problems' [*Carrera 1991*].

However, there was an essential difference between a watch and a car in that, even if they both possess a motor, a watch must tick night and day for years at a speed corresponding to a car speed of 90 km/h. And what is more, in order to get the *Swiss Made* label and benefit from the approval of legal technical control, it could only lose one second per day.

Muller developed a simplified watch assembly design (never a complete success in the sector) whilst Mock was responsible for the design of a plastic injection unit for micro techniques. These two men worked separately and on 27 March 1980 they presented the first Swatch project on paper to Tomke who enthusiastically accepted the two engineers' idea. The initial small group grew larger on a family basis when Jacques' brother and wife joined the team. They were responsible for the design of the watch.

A work unit to develop the Swatch project was only set up at the end of 1981, with the arrival of Franz Sprecher, a marketing specialist from the United States who confirmed the concept of 'a cheap but prestigious product' [*Carrera, 1981*]). The implicit hypothesis of the market study was that the trend towards a demand for fashion accessories was developing rapidly.

---

1. The first dates back to 1867 when the arrival of the Roskopf watch introduced a series of innovations which were unequalled by any innovation up to the arrival of the quartz watch[3].
2. The second important innovation came only 15 years before the arrival of the Swatch with Astrolon by TISSOT. For the first time, this company introduced synthetic materials into the making of a watch[4]. However, this watch, which was sold at a price of SF80, had little success as the quartz watch had already arrived and was beginning to dominate the market.
3. The third revolution belongs to Swatch itself as it partly incorporates the advances made by its two elder sisters, while capitalising on certain innovations acquired with the design of the 'Delerium'. Eventually,

Swatch introduced a very cheap watch based on high-performance plastic materials (designed in the laboratories of Swiss chemical firms, including Ciba-Ceiby).

Compared to Astrolon, Swatch distinguishes itself less by the quartz technology it was using than by a new, innovative idea of design, which itself was the basis of a complete overhaul of commercial strategy. The merger of these two experiences represents the dynamism of Swatch, which knew how to bring an idea back (only 15 years after the Astrolon failure), by proposing the same technical basis (plastic parts), but by using a new market strategy at a particularly difficult time for the Swiss watch sector.

Simplification, New Materials and 'Vertical Assembly': An Integrated Process-Product Innovation

As has already been argued, the key to the success of the Swatch strategy was that it was not a passive response to the Japanese offensive. Swatch did not submit to the competition in 'down-market' products, and did not try to replicate the quartz technology strategy imposed by the Japanese. Instead, it developed a strategy which allowed it to change the rules and conditions of its competitors. Apart from the design and marketing dimension, to which we will return below, this meant that the product itself had to be completely renovated. Swatch only found the solution by completely modifying the classical connection between the design of the product and its manufacturing conditions, or, in other words, between the technologies of process and product. From this perspective, the Swatch watch was a completely innovative product.

The Swatch innovations, to make things simple, had three related dimensions. First, the Swatch watch was designed to reduce the number of components as much as possible. Secondly, these components were themselves designed so that the assembly would be perfectly original (and very cheap) following a technique called 'vertical assembly'. Finally, an essential part of this assembly was undertaken on a heavily automised production line.

Each of these important innovations was only possible by confronting and solving a large number of technical difficulties. However, the choice of certain basic extras structured and weighed heavily on the overall design. Thus, the most profound innovation was brought about by the choice of adopting a plastic case, which was a solution inspired by the Tissot Astrolon watch. Once this choice had been made, ultrasound soldering techniques had to be designed to fix the glass of the watch to the plastic case, or again the difficult problem of fixing the bracelet to the watch had to be resolved.

Reducing the number of parts that make up a watch by more than 50 per cent (Table 4.2) was a technological achievement in itself. This made possible and conditioned the innovations in assembly which differed greatly from traditional assembly methods. The traditional process of production was carried out in three stages: manufacture of the case, manufacture of the parts and assembly of the mechanism, and putting the mechanism in the case. Swatch, combined these three stages into one. The simplification was such that it was possible to reduce the Swatch assembly phase to eight basic operations (instead of several tens or hundreds of operations applied in traditional assembly) [*Blanc, 1988, p.234*][5].

TABLE 4.2
REDUCTION OF THE NUMBER OF PARTS THAT GO INTO THE
MAKING OF A WATCH

Traditional mechanical watch	130 parts
Electronic watch	90 parts
Swatch	52 parts

A last word should be said about the process of assembly for Swatch. It is a quite common practise for other manufacturers (even within the SMH group) to use robots - but no robot is used in the manufacture of the Swatch. The reason for this, according to the engineers who designed the assembly process, was that for mass production it is unnecessary to use sophisticated and polyvalent machines to carry out what an ordinary machine could do Therefore, automatisation was based on relatively simple and efficient equipment and there was no need to worry about the difficult problems of maintenance and adjustment that a robotised assembly line would bring.

These changes brought considerable benefits. The innovations in most of the design/manufacture assembly line, together with those in automation, permitted Switzerland, where labour costs are high, to produce an analogous quartz display watch for a sale price of SF50 and a production cost of about SF10.

IV. THE CONDITIONS FOR SUCCESS: MARKETING, DIFFERENTIATION AND FLEXIBLE PRODUCTION

However important they may have been, these innovations in the design of this watch would not have been successful if the Swatch had not simultaneously revolutionised marketing techniques through a particularly innovative commercial policy. This marketing policy could only function if it was founded on a policy of product differentiation, which itself demanded a high

70

level of flexibility in the productive structure of the Swatch. These were the ultimate conditions for success.

A Remarkable Set of Innovations in Marketing Strategy

As far as marketing is concerned, the Swatch distinguished itself by a series of practises which were highly innovative for a watch-maker. They can be summarised as follows:

The major innovation (especially for a Swiss made product) was that the product was sold in the super and hypermarket which meant that it could attract a wide public and presented no competition for traditional outlets. To make sure that it was noticed, the launching of the products (and the renewal of the collections) was backed by a strong advertising campaign which focused attention on the fact that a watch 'was bought to show who one is, or more often to show how we consider the person to whom the watch would be offered' [*Crevoiser, 1990: 37*]. One of the Swatch advertisements simply said 'Just Imagine'. If it was necessary, marketing became very aggressive. This is how a 165 metre Swatch came to be hung from buildings in the centre of Frankfurt, Barcelona and Tokyo.

An essential point is that at the time when the product was entering the big distribution networks, the Swatch image was built around the idea of guaranteeing its owners with 'the exclusivity of a mass produced product'. In order to do this, the collections were renewed twice a year which, as we shall see, created a problem where flexible production was concerned. This permanent renewal made people forget the banality of a 'down-market' product, creating the illusion of custom made products. It instigated an unprecedented race to buy up the new models which, thus, became collectors' items: the most prestigious items such as the watches designed by Kiki Picasso or Mimmo Pladino, for example, reached a value of SF50,000 at the beginning of the 1990s

Particular care was taken in the outward design of the watches. Colour was used for the cases as well as for the straps. There were multiple facets in the design of the figures or the hands. In addition, famous painters or decorators designed special series (the case of Kiki Picasso and Mimmo Paladino), and these thematic series were not renewed, but were valid for only one collection. This dimension became so important that in order to strictly follow the tastes of the consumers and the trends of the market, SMH installed a specialised design centre in Milan, one of the world's large fashion capitals.

This was possible because the strategy followed was not only that of the Swatch product range. It benefited from the vertical structure that had been integrated into the SMH group. It must be remembered that other important brands, apart from Swatch, belong to this group such as Tissot, Longines or

Omega. If the marketing policy of each brand was decentralised so that each brand could develop its own image, strong synergies were available in the distribution networks, in advertising, in the policy for national or international commercial agents, etc. Each particular brand benefited from the international alliances which bound the group together.

Lastly, one must not forget that this marketing strategy, whose policy was to present the Swatch watch as an object of distinction, art and collection was dealing with a product sold at a very low price - around SF40 for the cheaper models.

Differentiation, Modules and Productive Flexibility

We have emphasised that the variety offered in the products, and the capacity Swatch had to renew these was a major feature of the Swatch strategy. The question was, how could this level of variety be reached without compromising the cost which could not go beyond certain limits?

A part of the answer was given in the preceding paragraphs. The process/product innovations of the Swatch were indeed at the origin of the lowering of important production costs. The reduction in the number of the components and the consequent reduction in the number of mounting/assembly operations constituted a key factor in Swatch competiviness. Other essential elements must be added that explain how long series and variety , mass production and differentiation could be reconciled.

It should be said that in spite of appearances, the Swatch essentially remains a standardised product in the sense that at least the technologies that have made it what it is, such as its shape (round face), are identical for all the models of each collection. The distinctive characteristic of each design change was only introduced through colour and graphic details, in the bracelet and the face, and in the size of the face. So, the viability of the long term product strategy of SMH was built on what could be termed almost traditional principles of mass production and the economies of scale that are associated with it.

Another key element in Swatch strategy, which conditioned its policy of differentiation is linked to the setting up of a modular strategy of product conception. The strategy of design is to follow standardised sub-groups following different specifications, according to the model. The use of flexible equipment enabled the manufacturing of the different formats needed for the different modules. Thus, the changes required by a policy of differentiation could be rapidly adopted.

This productive flexibility built into the core of its organisation and which conditions the efficiency and the variety of its product, allowed Swatch to move in this direction by multiplying product innovation on 'down' and 'middle' market products. Early on Swatch emerged with a feminine watch.

72

Although it did not seem to be anything spectacular as far as revolutions go, this type of product gave rise to numerous technical problems caused by the size of the watch which necessitated the components being redefined and reformatted.

In the same way, and applying a policy of vertical differentiation, in 1990, Swatch offered the first cheap stop-watch (sold at SF100). Thereby, Swatch broke with a tradition that in Switzerland itself - a country which almost had a monopoly in this niche - constitutes an up-market product (sold between SF2,000 and SF15,000). Note that Swatch chose to call its product a 'chronograph', even if it only really was a stop-watch with the official Swiss label for stop-watches. Within a few hours of its launch, a delivery of 200 items was sold out within an hour in a large department store in Geneva.

The most important event concerning diversification within the sector was, however, set up by the launching on the market, at the beginning of the 1990s, of a mechanical watch, still designed according to Swatch philosophy. By returning to the great tradition of the automatic watch, Swatch reaffirmed its links with the past, yet still took a place on the market of tomorrow: that of the 'ecological' watch, the mechanical watch that did not produce the waste linked to quartz[6].

The Changes in the Jurassian Industrial District

Undoubtedly, the success of Swatch has spread over the entire Swiss watch industry, including the up-market watch segment even if it was only to impose the 'Swiss made' label as a sign of quality and innovation in world watch making production. More directly even, Swatch stimulated innovation in other middle market firms. This was the case, for example, for Tissot where its the Rock Watch model took its inspiration from a technical and marketing design similar to those of Swatch. Thus, the Rock Watch was introduced with a stone case which, because of the shading and the veins in the stone, guaranteed its owner originality and exclusivity. It cost between SF200 and SF300, which targeted it on a potentially large market.

More generally, the impact of Swatch on the watch industrial area in the Jurassian district (the birthplace of the Swiss watch industry) was very important. Conversely, it is likely that the Swatch phenomena would not have been possible without the changes this industrial district had to undergo to adapt to the new order it had imposed on itself since the 1970s.

Having come from a traditional structure marked by a 'corporatism' which heavily penalised its efficiency, the watch industry had undergone essential changes. These cannot be neglected when considering the reasons for the return to competiviness of the Swiss watch makers. Indeed, until the 1970s, the Swiss watch sector was characterised both by the massive presence of small firms (each specialised in making just one of the components in the movement or in the outside casing) and by very large manufactures that often held the monopolistic positions in the market. The industry was thus organised on the base of a typical 'horizontal' structure [*Piotet, 1986*]. This situation had been inherited from a long tradition of corporatism and in particular from precise and restricting regulations set up during the crisis in the 1930s. The result was that in the majority of cases, these firms (small or large) had no competence in the other phases of the production cycle. They either benefited from their situation of partial monopoly over a component or sub-ensemble, and tried to control the industry without modifying it, or they subcontracted with only a minimal amount of capital and a non-skilled workforce[7].

The paradoxical consequence of this situation was that the structure of the market was also characterised by the existence of a very small number of 'super-holdings' ruling over some de facto cartels. Two 'giants' dominated the watch making activity. The first was the Société Générale de l'Horlogerie Suisse SA (ASSUAG), founded in 1931 and consisting of the Longines, Rado watches and clock mechanisms. The group Ebauches SA is part of the holding and it produces nearly all of the mechanisms used by the SA ASSUAG, while still supplying other firms. The other giant is the Société Suisse pour l'Industrie Horlogère SA (SSIH), founded in 1930 and includes firms like Omega and Tissot. This group has a strong position in the production of clock mechanisms.

This structure was gradually modified over time and through necessity - in particular when it was necessary to stand up to the threat from the east and from the quartz technology. Restructuring was first financial and industrial, with the setting up of the SMH (see above Section). However, progressively and subtly the place and the role of the actors were modified to accommodate the new know how in design.

After the heady days of the 1950s and the 1960s, when the markets were demanding and when the Swiss watch making industry dominated the world, a first change came about in understanding better the nature of the markets and consumer demands. The move towards quality products but with a positioning on a more modest price range came about at the same time as the rationalisation of the distribution channels. It is remarkable to note here that the attempts to adapt 'from bottom up' by delocalising production towards countries with cheap labour costs and by using inferior quality components, ended in failure. It was by using its own tradition and in giving it dynamism, that the watch-making industry adapted successfully.

Also, numerous initiatives were taken as the new technologies of the quartz channel were mastered: creation of research centres, alliances with new partners in the micro electronic sector, long-term supply commitments and partnership with specialised firms in the production of components whose know how was not available in the Jurassian district.

It was in this spirit that the Regional Industrial Fairs were developed, the rendez-vous of trades and know how, as well as being the shop window for innovation of the products of tomorrow. These fairs played an ever more important role in ensuring a greater visibility of the market, the trends that animate the market, and in facilitating actors who occupy complementary positions in the industry to meet.

Finally, the major change concerned a progressive re-arrangement in the relationships between creator, designers and manufacturers. The former division of work was based on a strict separation by the setting up of formal networks and the multiples exchanges organised along the whole manufacturing chain, between the different suppliers and manufacturers. As all observers remark, from then on the industry functioned according to a real, 'industrial district' logic.

V. CONCLUSION

The case of Swatch presented here and of the Swiss watch-making industry provides many lessons. First of all, the case illustrates the way in which the challenge posed by the Japanese and by the developing countries of Asia can be met by countries where production costs, notably labour costs, are considerably higher. Swatch has shown how it is possible, by using tradition and know how and by renovating them by means of a resolute commitment to a policy of innovation, to confront this new competition even through 'down market' products. The search for distinction and reputation finally compensated for the late start in mastering the new techniques.

A second lesson concerns the importance of the marketing and distribution strategies. In the age of globalisation, the mastering of this dimension is decisive. The capacity Swatch had to break with the traditional circuits in order to promote its production in a 'global' way, whilst not losing track of the 'Swiss made' label image, is worth consideration by other European firms, which could also put value on their national 'Made in' labels.

Finally, the case of the Swiss watch industry and the changes it brought about, remind us of the importance of the link between the technical, social and organisational dimensions of innovation and competitiveness. Swatch was only made possible through coupling the benefits of product innovation and the marketing. The management of these different dimensions of innovation meant mastering profound changes in the division of work between the actors of the industry. The setting up of new types of relationships of cooperation between firms, to give dynamism and to renew the Jurassian industrial district, is one of the major lessons that can be drawn from the Swiss watch-making industry.

NOTES

1. A presentation of the characteristics of the watch industry is given in Section IV of this paper. (See Courvoisier [*1993*] for a more detailed analysis of its history).
2. The inventor of this technology offered it to a number of Swiss firms which refused it. He then went on to offer it to the Japanese.
3. In many aspects, the Roskopf was welcomed very much like the Swatch was. Carera writes as early as 1867: 'Orders came in from all parts of the world even if they were only to satisfy curiosity. And what was extraordinary was that the proletarian watch had been adopted by people such as Escher de la Linth, from Zurich, the famous professor of geology, by royal countesses as well as by the warrant officer of the heir to the Prussian throne, the future emperor of Germany and by a number of lords who had used the Roskopf as a political lever by offering it to their farmers, or to their electorate if they were members of parliament - and they did not disdain to keep one for themselves. The phenomenon was to reproduce itself a hundred and fifteen year later with the Swatch' [*Carrera, 1991: 108*].
4. These innovations permitted the making of a watch 'for the proletariat' at a very attractive price. And like Swatch, success was immediate; it was used by ordinary people as well as by the European elite.
5. The process in the making of the Swatch is described in eight operations: (a) manufacture of the case in synthetic materials which is also used as a support; (b) implanting and riveting of the electronic module; (c) mounting of the unit that regulates the electronic module; (d) mounting of the bobbin and the motor module; (e) mounting of the gearing and the support plaque; (f) date; (g) calendar; and (h) face and hands, soldering of the glass to the case.
6. Parallel to this strategy of differentiation, Swatch was also involved in a policy of diversification outside the watch sector. With a series of objects of Swatch typical technology design such as telephones, the watch that receives calls (the number of the person calling could be read), glasses and other objects that were linked to fashion. In addition, plans are underway for the production of an innovative car (the 'Swatchmobile'), probably electric and developed in collaboration with German manufacturers.
7. The proportion of skilled workers in the watch making industry is below the national average. In 1980, there were 32.3 per cent skilled workers in the whole of Switzerland for only 22.9 per cent in the watch industry. This results from a long process of mechanisation and de-qualification of labour since at the beginning (in 1950) skilled workers made up 42.3 per cent of all the occupied workforce.

REFERENCES

Benko, G. and A. Lipiets (éds) (1992), *Les régions qui gagnent*. Paris : PUF.

Blanc, J.F. (1988), *Suissse Hong-Kong, Le défi horloger*, Lausanne: Collection Nord-Sud.

Brusco, S. (1982), 'The Emilian Model: Productive Decentralisation and Social Integration', *Cambridge Journal of Economics,* Vol. 6., pp. 167-84.

Carrera , R. (1991), *Histoire de la Swatch*, Geneva: Antiquorum Editions.

Chevalier, J.-M. and V. Gremont (1988), *Le Cas Swatch*, Paris: Economie Industrielle, MEI, Université Paris 13, ronéoté.

Chandler, A.D. (1962), *Strategy and Structure,* Cambridge, MA: Harvard University Press.

Chandler, A.D. (1977), *The Visible Hand*, Cambridge, MA: Harvard University Press.

Crevoisier, O., *La transformation de l'industrie horlogère dans l'arc Jurassien Suisse de 1960 à 1990*, Neuchâtel: IRER

Federation de L'Industrie Horlogère Suisse (1990), *Industrie horlogère et concurrence internationale en chiffres*, Bienne: Fédération de L'industrie horlogère.

Federation horlogere Suisse (1967), *L'horlogerie demain étude prospective de l'industrie horlogère Suisse,* Bienne: Service de l'information de la Fédération horlogère Suisse.

Glasmeier, A. and Pendall, R. (1989), *The History of the World Watch Industry*, Austin, TX: Document ronéotypé.

Institut de Microtechnique de l'Ecole Polytechnique de Lausanne (ed.), *Conception de produits en vue d'un montage automatique*, Lausanne: EDFL.

Maillat, D., Nemeti, F., Pfister, M. and A. Siviero, *L'industrie microtechnique en Suisses*, Neuchâtel: IRER/ EDES.

Piottet, G. (1988), *Restructuration industrielle et corporatisme: Le cas de l'horlogerie 1924-1949*.

Société de Microelectronique et d'Horlogèrie S.A. (1990), *Rapport de gestion 1989.*

5

ORGANISATIONAL ROUTINES AND COMPETITIVENESS IN THE AUTO INDUSTRY: THE CASE OF PEUGEOT SA

Benjamin Coriat

I. CONCLUSIONS

The car industry has been subject to a process of continual change over the past two decades. Globalisation, the opening of markets, new concepts in the field of products as well as that of processes, (where Japanese producers have been especially influential) have overturned the industry's competitive structure.

The purpose of this chapter, based on a study of the French automobile group PSA, is to stress some of the key orientations to which all car makers now have to submit. The organisational changes and adjustments to new routines required by the new market conditions have played a critical role. The main idea that is explored in this chapter is that following the pattern set by Japanese producers, who have introduced innovated a remarkable set of innovations in the sphere of production, the car industry has to transform the traditional methods of the Taylorist and Fordist inheritance, and centred around mass production techniques. As I intend to show, one of the import-ant dimensions of change arises in the division of labour in the whole of industry.

The chapter comprises of three parts. The first part identifies the new constraints that makers have to cope with, and discusses the new orientations imposed upon the relationships between manufacturers, distributors and subcontractors. The development which is highlighted is that the classical order of mass production is being substituted by a different order based on what is called the regime of variety. The second section deals with the new protocols that the PSA Group is developing to cope with these new con-straints and to secure its competitiveness. As will be seen, organisational transformation is the keystone of the adaptations on hand. The third section presents one important dimension of the new structure that increasingly characterises the car industry, namely the development of networks of firms which provide the basis for the competitiveness of the sector as a whole.

II. CHANGES IN THE EXTERNAL ENVIRONMENT, AND THE DEVELOPMENT OF NEW CONSTRAINTS: THE EMERGENCE OF THE REGIME OF VARIETY.

The essential changes that force automotive firms to revise their methods and forms of organisation can be summarised as follows. First they have to face an increase in the variety constraints: for each basic design the firms must be able to produce and deliver in a very short time thousands of variants (see below where this point is developed in more detail). This occurs in the context of a significant shortening of the product life-cycle, arising from the influence of Japanese producers; thus automobile product life has fallen from an average of about ten to only four years. These changes have themselves triggered off a deep reform of trading methods, closer proximity to the market and customer demands have become necessary. In these conditions the search for enhanced productivity together with flexibility through substantial organisational modifications (whether these be internal or in the relationships between other actors of the automotive 'filière'), has become imperative. At the operational level all these points are well accepted today and do not require any further development. However if we try to estimate the significance of these changes at a conceptual level, it is clear that the conditions of mass production - in its traditional pattern - are irrevocably altered. These are progressively giving way to a new regime of production, the connections and implicit logic of which must be clearly understood if we want to interpret correctly the new orientations adopted by the firms in terms of management of their cycles of production and the role to be played by organisational innovations.

From Mass Production to Bariety: Towards a New Production Regime

For reasons that will become clear later in this chapter, it is evident that all the changes in the firms environment listed above, can be linked to the emergence of a general constraint of 'variety', which is the central factor driving reorganisation in the industry. It affects both internal methods of production management and the relationships that exist between the firms in the industry.

To characterise briefly the changes that have taken place it can be said that the present moment is that of the passing from a regime of production centred and organised around the principles of specialisation to that of a new one, in which the organising logic is dictated by the demands of variety.

Confronted by stagnant or decreasing markets in which, beyond the strategies of differentiation, the capacity to operate in a universe organised around multiplicity has become both a condition of survival and an essential source of relative advantages. Automobile makers have progressively had to deal with variety in a new frame - no longer as a simple 'constraint', but as the central axis of their production and supply strategies.

The central thesis put forward here, therefore, is that the entire productive order has swung towards new forces and bases as reflected in the movement towards variety. We need, however, to look more closely at the characterisation of this new regime, since it is decisive for understanding the changes that currently affect the traditional structure of the mass production system.

Approaches to Variety

From a strictly empirical viewpoint, the passing to a regime of variety may be expressed in a few simple figures. The combined result of the multiplication of the products required by the market, which are increasingly diversified and specific, is seen in the fact that the number of variants (or 'titles', as in Peugeot internal language) has increased from a few dozen in 1960 to a few hundred thousand in the 1980s (Table 5.1).

TABLE 5.1
THE EMERGING REGIME OF VARIETY

Item	Number of variants as of April 1966	Number of variants as of April 1978
Body type	2	4
Engine	2	4
Carburettor	2	2
Type of fuel	2	3
Transmission	3	7
Grade of luxury	4	8
Seat shape	2	5
Option	1	20
Colour	14	13
Final specification of vehicle	322	101,088

Note: The number of orderable different final specifications of the vehicle is not equal to the number of possible combinations of selectable items calculated by simple multiplication. This is because some combinations are not offered by the company as a whole.

Source: Adapted from Asanuma [*1989*].

Nowadays, it has become commonplace for an automobile maker to be able to produce a hundred thousand or so variants for each basic model offered (the Peugeot 205 or the Toyota Corolla, for example). Of course, a relatively limited number of titles comprise the bulk of sales, which means that most of the advantages of mass production and repetition can be realised [Coriat, 1993a]. But we can see that this production regime is itself clearly different from the previous one where 'customers could chose the colour of the car they wanted so long as it was black' - to repeat the well-known words of Henry Ford.

From a conceptual point of view, the production regime that is required by this general change in the market must be distinguished from the previous regime of mass production based on the principle of specialisation and distanced relationships with suppliers. One could say, that while product differentiation remains compatible with the principle of specialisation - by keeping uncertainty within limits that make it predictable and programmable - the regime of variety as it emerges brings its entire operations into a realm of 'virtuality'. Rather than trying to manage uncertainty by limiting its scope and trying to make it predictable with the new constraints of variety, the principle of non-predictability is accepted in order to be able to manage it efficiently. Under these conditions, apart from the core car-maker itself who remains in charge of variety, it is the entire automobile activity through the 'demonstration effect' that has been affected by a series of major transformations. A number of uncommon features can they be associated with variety and what this demands influences the relationship between the various actors of this sector.

Some Features of the Regime of Variety

As soon as variety is accepted as the central regime, it strongly contradicts several principles of classical mass production. They can be identified as follows:

(1) Variety is a regime of 'virtual' production, based on the property of reactivity: First, it is clear that variety in its larger sense which is our concern here, demands, apart from the flexibility and adaptability of production structure, a de-multiplied operating speed which can be designated also as a property of reactivity. Flexibility is useless unless its effective time-span lets it satisfy variety and its own order. Market time-span is not production time-span. In order to obtain variety, the second needs to be brought closer to the first. So, to continue to typify the order of variety by differentiating and contrasting it with the preceding order, one could say that, apart from flexibility (required by differentiation), reactivity that characterises the regime of variety must be considered as the possibility of a rapid response to a large range of virtual demands.

Two important new lines of rationalisation which are also springs of productivity inherited from specialisation economy organisation will themselves be opened up by the new economy of time that comes from variety. The first concerns stock and work in process inventories. The second concerns quality.

(2) Variety implies a regime of low-stock and just-in-time production: The passing over to a permanent regime of variety can only be accomplished at the expense of drastically reducing work-in-process and other types of inventory. It is out of the question to stock work-in-process necessary for the manufacturing of hundreds of thousands of 'titles' that may only satisfy a limited market. Models only get their true existence, and only have an object of manufacture, if they can be sold. In this sense, and we are now going one step ahead, the regime of variety can only be, in principle, that of just-in-time production. To exist in variety, that is in permanent virtuality, means reacting over a very short time period. To exist in variety is to exist without stock, but to be able to produce the item demanded 'just-in-time'. Thus, as we shall see, this property of variety will, of course, bring about an upheaval in the relationships between the car-makers and their suppliers and subcontractors (see below).

(3) Variety requires a regime of original and better quality: In its turn, production 'without stock' means a leap forward in the quality of the finished product as an intermediary asset. If market time schedules have to be respected without stock, the manufactured products must be faultless. As soon as the security net of stock disappears, production must leap forward with respect to quality. Thus, a regime of variety necessarily means a regime of better quality. This property, like the preceding one, will become a central element in the relationship between car-makers and their subcontractors. In practice, the passing-over to a regime of variety goes alongside the assembler's decision to set up new and more stringent procedures of selection for subcontractors in which quality criteria are decisive. These procedures, ending in a process of certification, are carried out by following a finely and precisely codified protocol termed Supplier Quality Assurance (SQA). As we will see further on, this is also the basis of new 'organisational routines' in the relationships between contractors and subcontractors, which profoundly affect the manufacturing methods themselves of both the contractor and the subcontractor.

To conclude on this point, the regime of variety is both a regime that is still highly virtual and a regime that is already in process, in the remaking of the automobile assembly line as more generally in the whole 'filière' of the industry. At the moment, the most visible change brought about by the passing over to the regime of variety is that of a series of changes in places and roles allocated to the key actors in the industry, who have begun materialising the order of variety. At this level, three essential changes need to be highlighted. They describe certain key elements of how the regime of variety has penetrated into the core of the industry.

Places and Roles: Three Key Changes Brought About by the Transition to the New Regime

The Place of the Market and the New Role of Distributors and Dealers

The first change is the one that concerns the place of the market-place in the global production cycle of the industry. Where in a specialised economy the market constitutes an arriving point and the ultimate moment in the cycle of operations, at present it tends rather to be more the departure point and 'impulsion centre' as it sparks off the whole of the manufacturing cycle. The exchange of information between the dealers - who have a direct relationship with the market - and the car manufacturer thus plays a decisive role in the parenting, planning and pace of exchange of products at the core of the industry.

The Place of the Final Assembly Plant

The second change is that the final assembly plant no longer resembles the Fordist picture of a 'long river with its converging tributaries'. As final assembly has a very direct relationship to the market (in the form of information on dealers daily sales that become a central element in the choice of the models put into production) it has become the 'nerve centre' of production operations. A large part of the orders to manufacture come from the departments of the factory to other factories in the group and to the subcontractors. Final assembly receives and distributes essential information. It has become a sort of 'revolving point', as much for information flows as for real merchandise flows. Telecommunication networks that receive and redirect the orders to manufacture play are frequently an essential component in ensuring the effective working of the regime of variety.

The New Role of Subcontracting

It is clear that it is this category of actor that is most profoundly affected by the passing over to the regime of variety; three different implications are evident.

At the most visible level, the first consequence is that the subcontractor is put in a situation where it must operate 'reactively' with respect to the demands of the order-giver, and deliver 'just-in-time' the components that have been asked of him. Even if the 'time' considered is in itself variable (hourly, daily, and perhaps weekly) and even if the reserve stocks put aside can help in certain cases to limit the excesses of variety, the new order demands a refocusing of routines that have been broadly renewed.

A second consequence is how the quality of the supplies is envisaged. If the car-maker produces without or with very little stock, all supplies from the subcontractor must be usable in the finished product that was made and delivered in the just-in-time mode. Thus the new situation means that the subcontractor feels the pressure of an upswing in the demand for quality. As we will see, the rising strength of the regime of variety is on a par with the setting up of complex and harsh protocols, concerning quality which affect the relationships between contractors and subcontractors.

The third consequence of variety is a gradual but steady transformation of a part of the subcontractors to pass from the status of ordinary suppliers who manufacture components to that of component-makers who design or co-design integrated units, and who are directly involved in the manufacturing of the automobile.

Having recounted the wider characteristics of the change to variety, it now remains to explore the way in which protocol and production routines have been modified in practice. Using empirical data gathered mainly from PSA innovative practices, this is the object of the following two sections.

III. PSA: THE STRATEGY OF ORGANISATIONAL CHANGE

Under the weight of constraints and new requirements that have occurred in its external environment, the PSA Group became deeply involved in a set of innovative devices, designed to secure the mastery of the new world in which they were to live. . One of the essential features of the Group is that very early they became aware of the fact that essential dimensions of the transformation to be carried out were to be applied to a general revision of internal protocols of organisation and routines to fit with their partners, dealers and subcontractors. In this section, we will underline two dimensions connected to the changes that have occurred.

The first one is linked to the relationships with subcontractors. As will be seen below, the change in roles and places that have taken place requires much closer relationships between makers and subcontractors, implying complex processes of selection and quality certification, corresponding to the new division of labour that is progressively taking place in industry. The second one is related to the passing to different techniques and modes of 'just-in-time' production, involving not only subcontractors but also dealers in a wholly modified design/production/trading cycle.

New Division of labour and the Building of New Routines Inside the Industry

Three directions of the changes pursued are essential, for they introduce a series of crucial mutations in the relationships between suppliers who were at the origins of new routines.

This has meant that the manufacturer

- sought systematically to reduce the number of suppliers, by forcing them - directly or indirectly - to merger;
- revised drastically his criteria concerning schedules and abo e all the quality of delivered products;
- favoured a development in subcontracting which tended towards sub-contracting integrated subunits from design point, which implies for the subcontractor, a technical capacity on R&D issues.

Reduction in the Number of Suppliers and Encouragement to their Concentration and Multinationalisation

Begun in the early 1980s, this process reached its peak at the end of the decade and continues today. Thus, for example, PSA had in 1980 some 2,000 direct suppliers for mass produced parts. In 1988, this figure was halved and the process was speeded up even more over recent years. In July 1990, there were no more than 770 official suppliers (a fall of 21.8 per cent in two years). The aim is to reach a figure of about 650 suppliers in 1994. For the other manufacturers operating in France (Renault and Ford) the same tendency is to be found. The most remarkable aspect of this movement is the decisive part played by the manufacturers. Even if the more important groups of component-makers follow their own strategies, manufacturers are particularly active and take action in several ways.

First, the weight of their intervention is most visible in a series of assessment procedures called 'Quality Assurance', which allows them to give (or withhold) the approval that has led to the taking of orders. By this means, and sometimes by more direct financial intervention, they have favoured regrouping on criteria that are specific to them and that are aimed at a double objective:

- to keep at least two suppliers by product type to maintain the principle of competition between suppliers, and not to risk being subjected to the effects of abusive monopolisation;
- to ensure that their suppliers take on an international, dimension as they are globalised. Hence regrouped suppliers must aspire to at least a European dimension. One criterion put forward is the capacity of suppliers to become European leaders in their respective areas of

competence. At the same time, they must be established on a national and international basis near the manufacturers' assembly plants. This last condition is linked to the new 'synchronous' production techniques of just-in-time delivery and in certain cases, demands proximity (see below). Thus suppliers who survived the selection process may now have 25 per cent of their productive sites situated abroad close to the manufacturers' foreign sites.

Quality Selection

A second trend in manufacturer-supplier relationships is connected with a general redevelopment in quality criteria. If the rise in the preoccupation for quality is long standing in industry - and in particular in the automobile industry - 1987 was, in France, a turning point, for it was the year that the French groups set up a common reference system - Supplier Quality Assurance - which was elaborated according to a precise five stage protocol (see Box 5.1).

Box 5.1
The Five Stages in Supplier Quality Assurance

1. The first stage consists of a procedure of 'assessment of quality aptitude' that permits an appreciation of the potential quality, after a minute's inspection of the subcontractors production units.

2. After this, a stage centred around suppliers improvement of the handling of the production process. Help is eventually offered by the manufacturer through know-how transfer.

3. In the third stage, suppliers first samples are accepted by the manufacturer.

4. The fourth stage, which to many is a decisive one, is the stage that admits the supplier to enter the Product Quality Assurance circle (PQA). If it manages to reach this stage, the supplier retains entire responsibility for the quality of the products. Thus, following the 'quality charter' that governs relationships between firms in the automobile industry, 'the PQA gives concrete expression to the suppression of systematic reception control and marks the beginning of an approach toward a permanent improvement of quality'.

5. The fifth stage is characterised by a continual assessment of the quality performance of the supplied products, where 'demerit' marks are utilised if delivery does not conform to agreement (notably concerning criteria of quality and schedule).

Firms are assessed right from the first stage and they are given marks (from A to D). In practice, the selection process means retaining only those suppliers that have grade A. Adaptation time spans are set up to allow B-graders to become A-graders. In practice, B firms have two years to achieve A standards. This rigorous process of selection was established with severe selection effects[1].

Again, it is important to appreciate these developments in their wider sense as it takes in criteria of time span and reactivity, this being understood as a rapid response capacity to unforseeable demand from the contractors. The idea of rapidity also has to be strictly understood. In certain cases, it means a response capacity on the hour[2].

Finally, it is important to note that an essential criteria of the A grade is 'to be capable of product development and to develop the (AQP) approach alone'. As we will see, over and above quality the suppliers organisational and technical capacity in matters of design are essential criteria for selection.

Reactivity and Technical Capacity in Product Development

Once selected by these procedures of quality auditing, it is the assembly line plants that choose their suppliers who from then on become particularly loyal to them. The outcome is a series of requirements and complementary constraints for the supplier who must possess very strong reactivity in respect to the requirements of the assembly plants. In practice this assumes, other than networks of information that are capable of working in real time, *the setting up of an adequate organisational capacity* that itself requires the command of techniques such as the 'rapid change of tools' that are required by tight flow production techniques and the multi-purpose nature of pre-assembly islands when the supplier delivers integrated sub-units.

Finally, and parallel to organisational capacity, an essential criterion is the real technical capacity of participating in the design of products, at least at the development level on the basis of the specifications given by the manufacturers and, notably, when new models are launched. To reduce the time span of product design, one of the procedures that the Peugeot group set up was to separate (as far as possible) the finalising of innovations from the launching of the vehicle. The objective was to make sure that any delay in the design of certain elements or sub-units did not interfere with the launching of new products.

This method implies the setting up of a permanent innovation group that regroups manufacturers and suppliers and that functions as a real innovation bank, feeding design and new product development groups. In the same way, the vocation of the project groups that have been set up is to follow the project from the onset of the design right through to the launching of production.

Also, the assessment of the suppliers R&D capacity is a decisive element in their insertion into the new manufacturer-supplier networks.

Production in 'Real Time': The New Protocol for Mass Production

As we indicated, the growth of the regime of variety brings about a rise in the diverse forms of production in real time because of the acceptance that customer demand is primordial. It is particularly the methods and principles of manufacture programming that have encountered these essential changes. They are now carried out centrally from sales made by the dealers. This gives birth to a series of protocols and routines that reshape the whole relationship between agents at the core of the automobile industry. Having briefly introduced the principles at the origin of these new protocols, the main techniques used by PSA will be:

A First Presentation of the New Techniques of Just-In-Time Programming

Once the principle of manufacturing and delivering some 100,000 variants per model has been accepted, the revolution is under way. As far as possible only variants that have really been ordered and sold beforehand should be made and the manufacturing process should be organised on this basis. The universe of just-in-time production, under the authority of the manufacturer and final assembler, necessarily becomes the reference universe for all the actors in the industry.

However, in practice, 'tight flows' function under different tensions which each requires the setting up of specific procedures. These procedures may differ in the information exchange systems as in the methods of preparing and launching manufacture and delivery techniques[3]. Induced by the entry into a just-in-time universe, the essential change is a new pacing of programming. In the information that comes from the manufacturers and that is destined for the subcontractors, everything is built on the principle of three series of temporality, that correspond to yet shorter time spans. Each series of temporality corresponds with information and manufacture set-ups or delivery instructions that are more and more precise. In certain cases, the last instructions may then consist of delivery orders in strict just-in-time - with a time limit of less than one hour separating the delivery order from delivery itself. Thus everything happens in three phases.

Phase 1: The contractor analyses real and estimated load plans on the basis of customer order, and communicates these to its subcontractors. At this stage these load plans are still highly provisional[4], but they allow the subcontractor to organise its own provisional load plans (in workers and machines) and in certain cases to launch a pre-manufacture series.

Phase 2: Clearly defined programmes are sent out on a weekly basis (the virtual dimension fading out as the confirmation of titles from dealer orders progresses) and correspond this time to almost definite production orders. The subcontractors commit themselves to production.

Phase 3: Finally come demands for daily delivery(ies) following a schedule that varies from D+1 (delivery order of one day for the next) to a few hours.

On the basis of such a general principle, several just-in-time protocols are applied that correspond to a more or less strong subcontractor integration into the rhythms of manufacturers programming and production[5]. This concerns the looped or synchronous production methods, from RECOR or SPARTE, of which the essential principles will be laid out now.

Synchronous Production, (SPARTE, RECOR): Some Practical Devices used for Just-In-Time Production

Synchronous Production: This is the most demanding and rigorous method for the subcontractor and the one that, corresponding to strict just-in-time, fulfils the highest possible level of virtual integration of the subcontractor to the manufacturer. At this point, the protocols of information exchange and effective delivery are highly formalised and codified. Nothing is left to improvisation. It is also the technique in which telecommunication networks are the most systematically used. They must be particularly speedy and reliable and the information contained on them must be perfectly readable.

The conditions of application of this method are themselves also very strict, and its setting up is only justified in limited cases: only large volume parts are concerned (seats, exhaust pipes, tanks) or parts of a great diversity (several dozen varieties of the same part). The risk factor of variety is thus carried by the supplier whose final and daily load plan is highly uncertain both for quality and sometimes quantity[6].

In all cases, in a strict just-in-time configuration, the subcontractor has to deliver the different parts in the exact order in which they will be assembled and to deliver them to the assembly line itself at the exact moment when these parts are needed. Because of this, geographical proximity is a prerequisite as the manufacturer has no stock. The parts are delivered directly to the assembly line. For this reason, this method of production is also called 'looped', as the subcontractor is perfectly integrated into the manufacturers production cycle. This type of looped production at present at PSA and comprises about 15 to 20 per cent of the total volume of subcontracted supplies which is already a remarkably high percentage considering the very demanding nature of these techniques[7].

Box 5.2
Synchronous Production:
An Illustration of the New Protocols Required by Just-In-Time

The protocol applied can be described as follows. As soon as the automobile is in a phase of its production where the next required part can be forecast, a requisition order is sent to the supplier who can then begin its production. It then knows exactly when it will intervene and the order in which it can introduce the variety of its own sub-assembly parts into the more global assembly of the manufacture.

In practice, and in a very short interval, two distinct messages are sent to the supplier. The first is sparked off by a camera that is linked to an electronic system of information transmission. As soon as a given section in the manufacture of the automobile is picked up by the camera, often in the workshop, a first message for going into production is automatically sent to the supplier. The second message which deals with the effective delivery order is sent out moments after, once respect to the theoretical cycle has been checked: if any unknown factors have occurred then the message integrates them and the instruction given to the supplier is 'delivery delayed'.

In such a regime of synchronous flow production the supplier must startup and function according to a definite delivery plan that has contractual value[8]. In this procedure, direct telephone links are provided for, that complement tele-information links, as well as emergency delivery services on light, highly mobile vehicles and by using reliable pre-established itineraries.

The SPARTE Method: The SPARTE method or 'system of rationalised supply programming through economic techniques is also a very strict variant of just-in-time based, as the preceding one, on a principle of coordinated, quick selling automobile production. Citroen has used this method for a number of years, particularly at Rennes, which was a pilot site for the different types of protocols analysed in this section[9].

The principle applied is that of 'consumer anticipation'. In practice, everything functions in the following way. Definite manufacturing orders for six days (from D+5) are sent out to the suppliers on a daily basis on tele-information networks. These orders are brought up to date and clarified every day, and are then transformed into delivery orders which must be carried out at least on a daily basis and in the majority of cases several times per day.

The advantage of this method is that it allows the final assembler to function in 'near synchrony'; it also allows the supplier time for its programming (production can be set up from D-5). Furthermore, in this particular case, the proximity of the supplier is not an absolute prerequisite. This method, which offers almost the same advantages as synchrony, but which

91

is less restricting, is being increasingly used. It is thus that the addition of the SPARTE and Synchronous methods at the Citroen Rennes site already makes up some 45 per cent of the plants supplies.

RECOR or 'kanban' Delivery: The RECOR method (or work-in-process replacement on real delivery) need not be considered in detail. The reason is, as its name states, that it is just a classic application of the initial Japanese 'kanban' method, often quoted and now very well known[10].

The manufacturing principle is as follows. The suppliers work with reduced stock and production start-up replenishes these stocks as they become the object of delivery to the automobile makers to fill their orders. The procedure follows the classic method of using tags and kanban boxes. When an empty box arrives, this means an order to set up production to replenish the stock that has just been delivered[11].

IV. 'VIRTUAL INTEGRATION' AND ITS COMPETITIVE ADVANTAGES

In this final part we will concentrate on three series of questions which permit a general conceptualisation, notably concerning the social forms mobilised for the new type of production regime now required. I will focus on the characteristics that set it apart from other forms of production organisation that developed after the breaking up of the traditional Fordist forms of production organisation. The following points are relevant.

Some Basic Characteristics of the New Production Regime

Virtual Integration Implies a Changing Division of Labour Inside the Industry Considered a Whole

First of all, it is to be noted that the changes affect the entire industry. They are not intelligible if they are considered at the individual firm level. As I have pointed out, variety and the virtual regime that this implies assumes a new division of tasks and functions at the core of the industry. This new allocation of tasks takes on three new characteristics:

1. The tasks of interfacing production and marketing are passed over to the agents with the pacing coming largely from the orders they collect and give to the car manufacturer and that complete the swing from the 'pushed flow' Fordist principle of production organisation towards a new principle of 'pulled flow'. It is the agents orders that transform virtuality into reality.

2. The role that the final assembly plants play is modified and gains in importance. They are more than terminal 'pouring out' points and take

on fine-tuning tasks of subcontractor management and more generally of production flow management at the core of the industry.

3. Finally, apart from the constraints that the tightening up in just-in-time delivery have brought on them in particular, the subcontractors take on the task of the design of entire sub-units.

Thus, the industry as a whole is built around the principle of a virtual network that makes firms, *de facto*, stand by each other, much more than they could have done in the preceding production regimes[12]. It is thus that the new regime paradoxically means a greater integration of relationships between firms, although it would seem that tasks and functions that were beforehand dealt with inside the firm have been thinned out and decentralised. We have chosen to qualify this paradox as the one that is closest to what we call 'virtual integration'.

The Crucial Role of Organised Networks

More precisely, if we go further into analysing the structure of the network that includes virtual integration, it would be appropriate to note here that these networks are fundamentally built upon the basis of hierarchical principles under the influence of the car manufacturer.

This influence shows up in all the essential practices that characterise the new regime. Indeed, on the one hand the agents are subjected to quota/price negotiation processes that leave them little initiative and small to very small profit margins on the sale of new models. What they gain is more help and assistance from the car manufacturer. On the other hand and above all, the suppliers are subjected to a very harsh process of selection that uses stringent criteria such as quality, reactivity and design, that operate through an industrial restructuring process and that strive towards a concentration and regrouping of the component makers as it does towards their multinationalisation. The reason is that during the selection process headway is made on several fronts: economies of scale and price competition, the transferring of activity and a diminution of stock, delivery time schedules, quality and economy of variety of the products manufactured.

Co-operation and Long Term Contractual Relationships

In practice, however, the setting up of new protocols that go alongside the setting up of a network of actors within the industry also has its counterpart that essentially consists in tacit (and sometimes explicit) contracts for long term orders. Thus, the result of the setting up of these new firms is a sort of partnership that operates by externalising its functions while multiplying the bonds of dependency. Specific procedures are necessary at which point I will now clarify the essence and bring us to the core of the *social forms* in the building of the regime of variety.

Variety and Its Social Forms of Production Organisation: 'Partnership' and the Building of 'Relational Rents' Through New Routines

In practice, two series of new routines are set up with the break through and strengthening of the regime of variety. (For a first characterisation of the notion of firms routines see Nelson and Winter [*1992*]).

New Inter-firm Routines

These routines first concern inter-firm relationships. What is to be noted here particularly is the nature of the relationships established at the core of the network built up by the car manufacturers, their subcontractors and component-makers. The core is built from *certification procedures* which have been made from the codifications that are part of SQA procedures. What is remarkable about these procedures is that at all stages one feels the presence of a highly visible hand that substitutes itself for the market. This can be verified at the inter-firm network formation stage, the stage of subcontractor selection and during the functioning of the ordinary regime once the network has been set up.

The procedures used to set up the network are those of subcontractor selection and do not follow at all market procedures of 'auctioning' the products to be made. The potential supplier network is made up of these procedures of inspection, assessment and certification. Still following non-commercial methods at this phase of the setting up of the network, practices of a co-operative nature come into being to allow those who do not satisfy the required criteria to progress and to be eventually admitted into the network. Following on from this, in a stable functioning regime the procedure of attribution of demerit points that accompanies and completes the process of selection is close to administrative practice that cannot itself be analysed according to traditional categories of market coordination[13].

Let us add again that in return for these procedures of inspection-"assessment"-selection and for the effort the subcontractor puts into it, once the subcontractors have been selected they do benefit from a relative guarantee of continuity concerning the orders that are sent to them. The reason is that the setting up of just-in-time production modes corresponds to the establishment of minute, complex routines. In this area investment and learning are heavy and costly. So, as far as possible, due weight must be given to this to obtain the better part of mutual learning effects that result from the repetition of co-operation in the setting up of these procedures. Thus, even if market procedures based on auction mechanisms have not been completely eliminated - the car manufacturer trying to maintain certain competition between the suppliers - one must note that in these new routines (both in the selection procedure and the functioning modes of a stable regime network) the universe of coordination between firms both at contract signing and at implementation level is not that of the market.

In fact, the partnership that has been set up is very special in that it is made up of a very special mix of selection and co-operation. From a theoretical point of view this is an 'administrative' procedure even if, at the core of the network, a principle of competition is maintained between the suppliers[14].

Intra-Firm: Sequential Versus 'Dialogue' Model

If one looks at intra-firm relationships, remarks of a similar nature can be made. The new routines that have been set up do not consist of contracts signed between agents but of new modes of distribution, access to and sharing of information. One enters into the area defined by Ken Arrow as 'nano-economics' [*Arrow, 1976*], which characterises the new institutional micro-economy.

The important point here is that the setting up of these new routines relative to information management happened at the same time as a change in organisational forms - the traditional functional division of the Fordist firm faded away to allow less hierarchical forms to emerge. Thus the final assembly plant manages the subcontractor network in just-in-time. In the former division of work mode this activity was under the exclusive monopoly of the Groups purchasing department. In the same way the firm has progressively swung away from a sequential model to a dialogue model (to use Clark and Fujimotos expression [*1989*])[15] through the setting up of innovation banks and other such structures in the area of project development policy.

Partnership and the Building and Sharing of a 'Relational Rent'

Following a conceptualisation proposed by Asanuma [*1988 and 1989*] (see also Aoki [*1988 and 1990*]), one can say that this new growing partnership built upon these new routines is really a social procedure of building and sharing of a relational rent[16]. Things happen here as if the passing over to a regime of variety and the constraints that go with it, were too serious an issue to be left in the hands of market trade-offs. Through the procedures of selection-certification and their counter-effects on the guaranteeing of orders, through the multiple forms of co-operation between car makers and subcontractors that have developed at the core of production, the market is mainly rebuilt and reinserted in minute protocols and routines that affect inter-firms relationships as much as intra-firm relationships.

Thus the coming closer together of the market and customer demand makes itself increasingly felt as essential and necessary, even though it is a paradox, as it assumes the setting up of routines and multiple procedures that have been built up using a social pattern, and has bonded agents together with forms of coordination and arbitration that are essentially non-commercial. Thus, a growing pressure of the markets needs and constraints can only be obtained through the building of more and more complex social networks.

V.   CONCLUSION

As we can see the changes that have been described are broad and have thoroughly modified all the organisational practices used in industry. Yet it would be a mistake to consider that it is an exceptional display of innovations. Practically speaking, they have become common place for all the major car-makers, even if, according to national particularities or firm uses, these innovations are carried out differently. Common points can be identified everywhere, whatever local specificities can be found. Car-makers are now compelled to take better account of the market that has now become crucial in terms of techniques for programming manufacturing, to have new relationships with subcontractors who are now better chosen, according to quality and technical competences criteria, and to apply 'just-in-time' production techniques (according to modes of applications that can vary themselves). Thus, and this is the reason why this example has been chosen, in the case of the car industry, organisational change is not a more option among others: for car-makers it is the price to pay if they wish to continue in the present conditions of competition and competitivity. Organisational innovation has become a decisive condition as regards the life and reproduction of a firm. Beyond that, mastering it to a better or lesser degree may be the source of particular relative assets. Thus the quick and determined commitment to such changes, allowing a firm to associate the benefits of experience with those of apprenticeship so as to be able to innovate in its turn, seems to be unavoidable.

NOTES

1. For example, at PSA, only 330 of the assessed firms were ranked A. This is less than one in three of the total assessed and offered an adaptation time.
2. The case of one contractor interviewed. This point will be developed further in the description of the different just-in-time methods set up with the selected partners.
3. Note that in certain cases temporal constraints can become spatial ones: the tighter the flow, the more the distance must be short, or at least mastered. The result is that certain just-in-time procedures imply paradoxically a multiplica-

tion of stocking points and new sites. The result is new 'mobile' logistics, built on mobile lorry-loads in a proximity compatible with the given supplier time.

4. As was indicated, at this stage, the virtual load plan only takes effect after real orders have been put through which is in itself a basis for forecasting new orders that will be made during the month.

5. Even if most of them only concern suppliers that have reached at least level 4 (AQP level).

6. In most cases, two or several subcontractors supply the same part or sub-unit, each being specialised in a part of the varieties required for each model. Definite orders that privilege certain varieties over others contribute to the risk factor that is part of each subcontractor's load plan. Thus, for a particular gear box, the orders that are put through to a supplier can fluctuate greatly every day.

7. If one takes the more general case of French firms, the percentage of just in time delivery is already more than noteworthy. At Renault, for daily delivery, it reaches 60 per cent of the added value of which 10 to 20 per cent is in strict synchrony. At Citroèn in Rennes where three models are produced - the XM (since 1989), the re-designed AX (since 1991) and the BX (since 1982) - practically the entire three month forecasting system has been replaced by a just in time form which is 80 per cent of purchase value. It is true that the Rennes site is a pilot site for just-in-time techniques.

8. The suppliers plan must include the means to anticipate and absorb the solution to all types of unknown factors that could arise as final assembly cannot be subjected to an interruption of this sort. If this happens, and according to AQF conventions, the suppliers are attributed demerit points.

9. The Citroen marque is also owned by the PSA Group.

10. See, for example, my paper [*1991b*] that introduces synthetically the main lessons of the Japanese masters. On this theme see Monden [*1983*], and of course T. Ohno himself [*1989*].

11. This method suits certain types of parts (e.g. door panels and certain mass produced small parts), but it is also seldom used. It has proved to be too restricting, only allowing limited economic profit. In particular, in the case of high variety in the products, the stocked quantities (if one wants to have all the variants available beforehand) are a heavy burden on cost.

12. It must be noted that the market does not generate in any way the spontaneous necessary solidarity that is needed for virtual integration. On the contrary, as we will shall show in a moment, this solidarity comes from a social construction that sets up complex protocols and routines that assume a high level of apprenticeship on behalf of each of the partners.

13. These demerit points sanction the subcontractor if flaws have been found in one of the key criteria of quality, reactivity or scheduling.

14. Substituting administrative selection and cooperation principles for market ways of functioning according to 'auction logic' is neither accidental nor contingent. Indeed, if the regime of variety is a just-in-time and quality regime, a unity of codification and minute routine must substitute itself for market procedure.

15. Let us finally note that substituting administrative selection and cooperation principles for market ways of functioning according to 'auction logic' is neither

accidental nor contingent. Indeed, if the regime of variety is a just-in-time and quality regime, a unity of codification and minute routine must substitute itself for market procedure.

16. I have emphasised in this chapter the conditions and ways in which a relational rent at the core of the manufacturer/subcontractor network has been set up. It does not seem possible to bring out a general rule concerning the *sharing* of this rent as this seems to depend on the state of the balance of power between agents. As we suggested previously, it would seem that *manufacturers should try essentially to reserve for themselves most of the monetary gain*: for example, most of PSA's suppliers find themselves obliged to maintain a steady price. If yearly inflation is taken into account, this means a significant lowering in prices in real terms. The advantages to be gained by the subcontractors can mainly be found in the guaranteeing of orders which allows them to set up strategies by which they lengthen series and more generally rationalise production.

REFERENCES.

Aoki, M. (1988) *Information, Incentives, and Bargaining Structure in the Japanese Economy*, Cambridge: Cambridge University Press.

Aoki, M. (1990), 'Towards an Economic Theory of the Japanese Firm', *Journal of Economic Literature*, March, Vol. XXVI, No. 1.

Arrow, K.J. (1967), 'Vertical Integration and Communication', *Bell Journal of Economics*, Spring, pp. 173-83

Asanuma, B. (1988), 'Transactional Structure of Parts Supply in the Japanese Automobile and Electric Machinery Industries: A Comparative Analysis', *Working Paper*, Kyoto: Faculty of Economics, Kyoto University.

Asanuma, B. (1989), 'Manufacturer- Supplier Relationships in Japan and the Concept of Relation Specific Skill', *Journal of the Japanese and International Economies*, March, Vol. 3 (1), pp. 1-30.

Bar, F., Borrus, M. and B. Coriat (1989), 'Information Networks and Competitive Advantage. Issues for Government Policies. *OCDE/BRIE Telecom Users. International Synthesis, Final Report*. Brussels: The Commission of the European Community.

Clark, K.G. and T. Fujimoto (1989), 'Product Development and Competitiveness', Paper Presented to the International Seminar on Science, Technology and Growth, April, Paris: OECD.

Commissariat General du Plan (1992), *'L'Automobile, les défis et les hommes' - Rapport du GSI 'Automobile' - La Documentation Française*.

Coriat, B. (1990), 'L'Atelier et le Robot - Essai sur le Fordisme et la production de masse à l'age de l'Electronique', in C. Bourgois (ed), Paris.

Coriat, B. (1991a), 'Penser à l'Envers -Travail et Organisation dans l'Entreprise Japonaise', in C. Bourgois (ed.), Paris.

Coriat, B. (1991b), 'Technical Flexibility and Mass Production: Flexible Specialisation versus Dynamic Flexibility', in G. Benko and M. Dumford (eds.), *Industrial Change and Regional Development: The Transformation of the New Industrial Spaces*, London and New York: Belhaven Pinter Press Publishers.

Coriat, B. (1992), 'The Revitalisation of Mass Production in the Computer Age' in M. Storper and A. Scott (eds.) *Pathways to Industrialization and Regional Development*, Routledge.

Coriat, B. (1993a), 'Variété, Informations et Réseaux dans la Production de Masse -Le cas de l'Industrie Automobile', *Rapport Final de Recherche AMES/MRT*.

Gorgeu, A. and R. Mathieu (1990), 'Partenaire ou sous-traitant ?' *Dossier de Recherche*, No. 31, Paris: Centre d' Etudes de l'Emploi.

Gorgeu, A. and R. Mathieu (1991), 'Les pratiques de livraison en juste a temps en France entre fournisseurs et constructeurs automobiles'. *Dossier*, Paris: Centre d'Etudes de l'Emploi.

Landau, R. and N. Rosenberg (eds.) (1986), *The Positive Sum Strategy: Harnessing Technology for Economic Growth*, Washington DC.: National Academy Press.

Midler, C. (1991), 'L'Apprentissage de la gestion par projet dans l'industrie automobile', in *Réalités Industrielles, Revue des Annales des Mines*, October, Paris.

Monden (1983), *Toyota Production System*, Institute of Industrial Engineers, Atlanta.

Nelson, R. and S. Winter (eds.) (1982), *An Evolutionary Theory of Economic Change*, Boston, MA: Harvard University Press.

Ohno, T. (ed.) (1989), *L'Esprit Toyota*, Paris: Masson.

Priore, M. and C. Sable (1984), *The Second Industrial Divide*, New York: Basic Books.

Taddei, D. and B. Coriat (eds.) (1993), *Made in France: L'Industrie Francaise dans Competition Mondiale*, Paris: Livre de Poche, Hachette.

Volle, M. and D. Henriet (1987), 'Services de telecommunication: integration technique et differenciation economique', in *La Revue Economique: L'Economie des Télécommunications*, March.

Williamson, O.E. (1975), *Markets and Hierarchies*, New York: New York Free Press.

Womack, J.P., D.T. Jones and D. Roos (1990), *The Machine that Changed the World*, London: Macmillan.

6

SMALL FIRM, MAJOR CHANGE: ZILVERSTAD SILVERSMITHING

Hanno Roberts, Friso den Hertog and Mieke van den Oetelaar

Zilverstad Silversmithing is a small Dutch company which has to cope with fierce international competition. This chapter gives a detailed report[*] of the organisational journey undertaken by the firm in order to safeguard its future. The report shows that even small firms can be trapped in their development by too much complexity in and too little of control over their production processes. Zilverstad simplified its organisation by the introduction of a model of flow-oriented production. This opened the way for pushing the control capacity to the lowest possible level in the organisation: the self-managing task group. The firm made use of the principles and instruments of a Dutch design approach: Socio-Technical Organisation Design (STOD). This approach enables the members of the organisation to redesign their own working environment.

SITUATIONAL BACKGROUND

Zilverstad is a small-sized company which was founded in 1875 as one of the many silversmithing shops in Schoonhoven, a city dedicated to this one industry since medieval times. After the Second World War and, more specifically, during the 1970s, severe competition from firms in the Far and Middle East resulted in a dramatic reduction in the local silver industrial activity. During the 1980s, however, this trend was stopped by emphasising quality over low-cost production. And, as Zilverstad is the name-bearer of

---

* For a more detailed report see: Roberts [*1993*]. Management and workers of Zilverstad, particularly the Pluut brothers, are gratefully acknowledged for their willingness to participate in this study.

Schoonhoven's silversmithing tradition, this was reflected in the economic prosperity of Zilverstad.

Zilverstad is a family-owned and run company. The present two family members, brothers Arne J.P. Pluut (commercial executive) and Arie Pluut (production executive and engineer), have taken over the company from their father. Collectively, they constitute the Board of Management. The family ownership was reflected by the internal culture. People work their whole life for the firm, which therefore has little personnel turnover. Also, people are relatively well paid and receive a share of the profits. Labour conditions are good, mediated by the small community Schoonhoven, resulting in few labour and payment differences in the various local silver companies. Managerial control and decision-making is of an enlightened autocratic type. The two brothers frequently consulted and discussed with key personnel on important decisions, but they were clearly the ones who actually made the decisions. The vision of the two brothers on labour affairs and human resources has always been based on a strong perception of social responsibility and 'taking care of your people'. The organisation is largely structured according to the product market (combination) with two functional departments, that is, Procurement and Administration.

The craftsmanship tradition of Zilverstad can still be found in the three main product market combinations: premiums and corporate gifts, jewellery and souvenirs. The jewellery and souvenir lines are also exported; approximately 25 per cent of sales are designated for export to 26 countries. The premium and corporate gifts markets are the fastest growing and most dynamic market, characterised by a large variety of design-to-order and customised products and a constant pressure for product rejuvenation and line development. Product quality, delivery time and technical capabilities are the main competitive parameters in this market. The jewellery and souvenir markets are in a more difficult position. The constantly decreasing number of jewellers, competition from alternative luxury articles (for example, audio equipment and exotic holidays) and the hard monetary position of the Dutch guilder put a constant squeeze on sales. Again, quality and delivery time are important here, supplemented by the factors of a large product range and high-service level. The common denominator of all the markets served is that they are characterised by high-quality, customised and small-batch production with short delivery times. The product mix consists of a large variety of different products, ranging from relatively inexpensive, easy to manufacture souvenir spoons to full silver, traditionally crafted candlesticks.

Two-thirds of the annual sales are from in-house production with the last one-third coming from wholesale activities. For the manufactured products, Zilverstad has all the required production facilities available. They range from tool shops and product development to the final finishing stage. The technology-in-use is dependent on the various craftsmanship domain, that is, forging, casting, stamping, enamelling, engraving and electrogalvanizing, with the latter requiring the most technically advanced and complicated machinery. Most of the other crafts are inherently low-tech and high-skill manufacturing functions. Further manufacturing relationships exist with a fully owned enamelling job shop (since 1986), sub-contractors in India and the Far East for low-cost, semi-finished products, and independent manufacturers in England, Germany and Italy for additional product specialities. Zilverstad employs 70 people, has a Return On Investment (ROI) and an inventory turnover of about 18 per cent and 5.5 respectively. Its balance sheet amounts to a total of 5.7 million Dutch guilders (all figures from 1990).

Initially, Zilverstad was specialised in just one manufacturing operation, that is, stamping. In the 1970s, a limited number of standard products were made in large batches, mostly souvenir spoons, cheap nickel-plated ashtrays and cigar boxes.

> But our products were being copied in the Far East. Which meant it was over and out for us. We couldn't compete against this. We had to find a way to survive, it was as simple as that. We had to find alternative products and markets. We more and more started to manufacture products according to customer specification: high-quality products which allowed us not to compete on price alone. There is now, except for a basic assortment, almost no product left from our assortment of fifteen years ago (Commercial executive).

From the 1980s onward, Zilverstad experienced an explosive growth. The number of employees doubled while the sales figures almost tripled. Also, various production techniques were acquired and used in manufacturing, for example, casting and forging. The success of the company necessitated a change as the company went from a pioneer phase to an organisation phase, increasing product diversity and production capabilities at the same time.

> Orders came into the factory and, at some time, came out again but what happened in between we didn't know. In the factory everything was milling about, and there were bottlenecks in manufacturing. This was mainly caused by our own occupation with special customer orders, and therefore, with new and unknown products with all the quality and planning problems that went with it (Production executive).

> We got delivery time problems in the years 1985-87, also due to the fact that sales increased very fast. Our continuous need for a sufficient number of adequately trained personnel couldn't be kept up. The organisation didn't fit the fast growth. Furthermore, the market was changing rapidly

and increasingly kept asking for shorter delivery times and higher product quality. It really became necessary to control quality in all phases of production. This is how, at the end of the eighties, the need arose to improve the structure of the company (Commercial executive).

Rapid growth and a clear inability to deal with rising complexity urged the firm to develop policies for fields which were previously viewed as being self-evident: the organisation design and personnel management. The appearance of personnel shortage forced the firm to reconsider personnel policy for the very first time. This bottleneck was approached in two ways: first, by starting internal training for tool and stampmakers and, second, by acquiring a computer system that could engrave stamps from an engravings database thus taking some routine work away. Unfortunately, the large product variety with its subsequent large number of machine changeovers make automation and even mechanisation of production a troublesome affair. In order for automation, and technological innovations in general, to succeed, it was felt that the organisation first had to be made fit for such changes. Only then could technological interventions be successful.

To the extent that the organisation was felt to be in need of direction, a business plan was made in 1986 by the commercial executive. Typically, the business plan focused mainly on the commercial aspects. However, the business plan also clearly indicated the need for intensified quality control in all production stages. It did not give any information yet as to how this could be achieved. The business plan did not prove to be satisfactory because of its limited focus, and the shopping for additional help was continued. This help was found through the Dutch employers association for the Metal Industry (CWM). By October 1988, the CWM introduced Zilverstad to the executive course on SocioTechnical Organisation Design (STOD, see box 1) for small and medium-sized companies. This course was taught collaboratively by the CWM and the Dutch Foundation for Quality of Work and Organisation (NKWO); they later also involved a consultancy company, practising what they preached, called KOERS. The brothers Pluut and the head of administration returned with the impression that this could be what they were looking for and asked their key people to go and see what they thought of it.

The STOD approach had been developed during the past 15 years by a group of Dutch organisation researchers and consultants directed by Professor Ulbo de Sitter [*de Sitter, 1994, de Sitter, Dankbaar and den Hertog, 1994, Dankbaar and den Hertog, 1991, Roberts, 1993*]. The essence of the approach is *selfdesign*. The members of the organisation make use of a set of well-elaborated redesign rules, principles, instruments, and follow a clear design sequence. In this respect, the approach is also an expert approach, that is, the members of the organisation are trained to fulfil the expert role themselves. They are the ones that make the choices between the design options.

Central to STOD is the differentiation between production and control structure. The production structure stands for the actual primary process by which orders (products or services) are processed. The control structure consists of all activities by which the primary process is managed and monitored. The objective of STOD is a simplification of the production structure in such a way that the need for control is drastically reduced. This is done by the changeover from functional structures into parallel product flows and by re-integrating tasks into meaningful segments. This can only be done by changing simple, monotonous tasks into more complex and challenging tasks. The redesign of the production structure goes top-down, from the rough organisational-structures to detailed work structures. The design of the control structure goes bottom-up. Here, the general rule is applied that anything that can be controlled at the lowest organisational level *should* be controlled at that level. STOD has been practised in more than 25 Dutch firms. The redesign results in the formation of whole, self-containing and interlinked groups at different levels of the organisation: the whole-task group on the shopfloor, the operational group on the plant level and the business unit at the business level.

Box 1: STOD

In February 1989, the production manager and two other production staff members completed a middle management course on STOD, and everyone came out very enthusiastically about the integral redesign ideas presented. The educational trajectory thus started with the two board members and the head of administration, followed by key people. The courses explained what system design was, how it was done and what was the best way to depict and describe organisational processes. At this moment in time (June 1989), a consultant of KOERS was introduced. Her main role was that of process facilitator, not of an expert, as she served to keep the project within the tracks set out.

A group of six people was again trained by this consultant, repeating the main design principles. This group consisted of the initial course partici-pants: head of administration, production manager, two production staff members (the galvanising foreman and the foreman in charge of jewellery articles) plus the job scheduler, and the board secretary, also being export and import manager; that is, four from the production department and two from non-production. The job of the design group was to do the general redesign. All design groups reported to a steering group which monitored the process and made the final decisions.

Two different types of work groups followed up the general design of the design work group: A sales work group and various detailed design work groups. The sales work group, consisting of the commercial executive, market groups' sales managers and, to maintain the link with production, the job scheduler and the production executive, started in mid-1990. Their job was to asses the commercial position of the firm by means of a SWOT analysis and propose measures to bridge the gap between desired and expected performance. Almost naturally, this flowed over into a strategic orientation round (SOR) as prescribed by STOD (September-December 1990), the preliminary work of the SOR already being done by the business plan made earlier.

The SOR brought forward that a decision had to be made on what Zilverstad would look like in the 1990s. Strategy was discussed in terms of market capacity, production and sales capabilities, and product range. Two strategic directions were considered: continue the present flexible organisation with its large and varied product range, or change towards an organisation with a clear image, having a relatively limited product range and market coverage. To date, while the strategic discussion is still continuing, the firm is becoming aware of the necessity of bringing more focus into its market orientation.

The second type of project group following up the design work group is the various production work groups. They zoomed in on the general design of their production segment and made a detailed design, paying special attention to interfaces (that is, work flow boundaries). Typically, it involved all the members working in that specific production segment. These detailed design work groups were headed by the design work group participant under whose responsibility the specific part of the organisation fell. Meanwhile, the design work group was maintained for feedback and cohesion in the various detailed designs.

Therefore, the project structure unfolded simultaneously with the various redesign activities, their sequence and responsibilities coinciding: The redesign work group came up with the general design, then the upstream part (coupling job scheduling and production) was designed in detail, followed by the downstream part (coupling finished product and shipping). The end of the detailed design was marked by the completion of the control structure and information structure in December 1990.

THE CHANGE TRAJECTORY

In July 1989, the two board members, supported by the consultant, made a company-wide presentation. It was outlined to all organisation members gathered, what the reasons for the change were, what was going to happen, and what generally would be their future role in the upcoming change process, explicitly stating their participation and involvement. In this one big event, which was unequalled in the firm's history as well as in the fact that the board directed itself to all personnel, the upcoming change was openly laid out and discussed by the two brothers Pluut, showing their own commitment to the changeover.

The change trajectory started formally with the installation of the design work group and the concise rehearsal of the STOD design principles by the consultant (August 1989). As an immediate result, a phased approach to the change process was prepared, linking up with the project structure. For example, phase 3 is where the above-mentioned detailed design work groups came in. Remarkably, the phased approach and the project structure related only to Production. Sales started up its own track later on.

TABLE 6.1
FULL TASKS PER REDESIGN PHASE

Phase 1	Formulating design specification Bottleneck listing	
Phase 2	Look for parallel flows in the production Link flows to the pre-production and past-production trajectories as much as possible Determine in outlines all operational and control activities Match production and control structure with design specifications, plus make a choice (the Board enters the trajectory) Present new organisation structure to the entire company	Executed by: design work group
Phase 3	Determine in detail operational and control activities of groups/units Determine (possible) layout changes Determine (possible) changes in technical equipment List changes in information supply & demand List the need for training Make an implementation plan	
Phase 4	Formulate group goals Systematic problem solving Situational leadership Introduce work counselling Training Conflict management & team building Performance appraisal	Executed by: work groups under the design work group

The four-step approach consisted of the following main phases (Table 6.1):

* formulating design specifications and categorising organisational bottlenecks (phase 1);
* actual design (phase 2);
* elaborating the organisation model (phase 3);
* implementing it, using an implementation plan (phase 4).

The design work group started off with listing bottlenecks or what was felt to be a bottleneck ('points of attention' and 'points of annoyance'; September 1989) and with formulating the design requirements (October 1989). In other words, it was stating the framework and boundary conditions for the upcoming design (see Table 6.2). 'That listing showed the way for the detailed final proposals. Those proposals have, to a certain extent, brought about a culture shock: Many things which were taken for granted, were suddenly discussed or abandoned' (Head of Administration).

The functional requirements are preceded by a short statement of General Company Goals, a sort of mission statement, which was unprecedented because it was the first time goals were explicitly stated and ratified. The functional requirements focus on structure, structure allowing for product quality, quality of work and functional integration. Furthermore, the explicit attention for the cost structure of each product market group is important: It states cost-structural targets simultaneously with the targets for delivery time and reliability and product quality, that is, cost structure and performance are considered to be two sides of the same coin. Cost structure targets are thus norms for the overall accounting system to be designed, that is, norms to be attained *by means of* rather than *within* the accounting system.

Bottlenecks were listed according to their system level and to whether or not they had a structural cause (September 1989). System level refers to the six sub-systems making up the primary process at organisation system level; sales, preparation, production, storage, shipping and procurement. These six sub-systems return in phase 2, where a process model of the existing organisation is made in order to establish interfaces and information flows between subsystems. The analysis of these sub-systems forms the basis for the latter control and information structure design. Non-structural bottlenecks are then prioritised and serve as inputs for quick improvement actions. Structural bottlenecks are inputs for the subsequent redesign of the production structure.

Bottleneck listing was most visibly used for starting up improvement projects, such as improving specific working conditions that have been annoying people for a long time, for example, bad ventilation in the foundry as a result of plants growing on the roof of the shop. It involved considerable

TABLE 6.2
FUNCTIONAL REQUIREMENTS FOR ORGANISATIONAL REDESIGN

General Company Goals

- Sales spread across the various market segments   Market opportunities
  (approx);
  gift articles (export)   30% growth, mainly export own products
  souvenirs   10% stable, on approx. 1 min.
  retail trade   15% growth possible
  premium/business gifts market   45% growth possible
- In order to operate successfully on the various markets, a wholly owned production of sufficient size per technology (foundry, presses) is needed. This means a size which can sustain a good market position per technology.
- Priority in choosing to make or   • Profit maximisation is more important than sales growth.
  buy is determined by: • In building up the order position targets are:
  - higher added value;   a) a well-utilized production capacity;
  - own product as image;   b) high-running wholesale articles;
  - short delivery time possibilities   c) supplementing sales with premium/business gift
     articles.

Functional requirements for the executing and control structure

- A structure that allows for the implementation of Total Quality Management.
- A structure in which a high quality of work is realised.
- A structure in which the qualities of all personnel are optimally realised, allowing people to develop involvement and/or motivation.
- A structure that allows for the integration of wholesale and production activities.
- A structure in which the sales activities have to be integrated with the strategically set production capabilities and are not autonomously directed at wholesale.
- A structure in which the procurement activities can have a clearly delineated position.
- A structure that, supported by the administrative department and computerisation, is controllable for the Board.
- A structure that allows for a clear and effective consultation structure.
- A structure that allows for good planning.
- A structure that improves communication between departments.
- A structure that prevents pigeon-holing.
- A structure that develops team spirit instead of creating 'little bosses' everywhere.
- A structure that allows for standards/norms in general.

		Retail	Souvenirs	Business/premium	Gifts/export
Delivery time:	Factory	0	6 weeks	6 weeks	2 weeks
	Customer	48 hours	7 weeks	6 weeks	3 weeks
Delivery reliability:		± 24 hours	± 1 week	± 1 week	± 1 week
Quality A/B/C/:		A	B/C	A/B	A
Cost structure:					
Acquisition		10	4	11	4
Wholesale/materials		67	25	44	44
Processing costs		14	48	30	30
Margin		0	23	15	22
		====	====	====	====
		100%	100%	100%	100%

outlays on equipment such as hoods with extractor fans and flexible clench-ing arms. The production employees were invited to go to the trade fair and buy the equipment themselves. Apart from showing involvement and broadening the support base for the changeover, a beneficial effect was the improvement of communication. The various departments came into much closer contact than before, because they had to work together outside the daily routine.

Figure 6.1.: Timepath, main events and project structure of organisational change

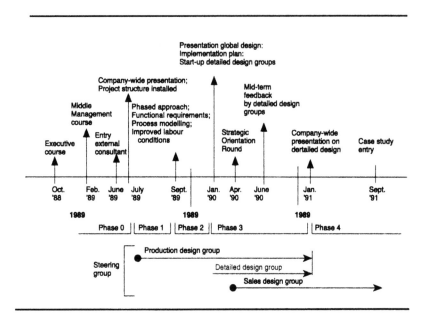

By the end of 1990, a project structure was installed, the primary process was charted, analysed in terms of bottlenecks, and provided with functional requirements for the upcoming redesign, and the Board could be offered a general design. Meanwhile, some alternatives were considered on how to redesign production, for instance, a structure according to batch size or according to manufacturing complexity, but none of these was found to be satisfactory. The main difficulty in choosing the best alternative was the delineation of tasks, because one of the goals was to improve interaction between the sales department, which knows the signals from the market-place best, and the Production department. In the final design offered to the Board, this point resulted in placing the warehouse under the responsibility of the Sales department.

In January 1990, the general design was presented to the Board and approved. It marked the start of the detailed design work groups and extensive participation of all personnel. The design immediately resulted in an actual reform consisting of a primitive task group structure and flow-oriented production. The rest of the year 1990 was used to further refine this general design. Mid-term feedback implied the various work groups commenting on the assumptions and starting points employed by the overall design work group, thus providing a larger framework and a 'warming-up' on the design task. The linking-pin project structure was turned into reality as work groups were headed by the representative of that particular production part, who was also a member of the overall design work group. In fact, task groups turned out to become design work groups, thus bringing the change process 'into the line'. Design focus at this stage was on the upstream and downstream parts of the production process and on how linkages between parts could be established. This also included the first adaptations to the available control systems of, for example, inventory, order processing and registration. In this process, the external consultant from KOERS acted as a sounding board. Nevertheless, most problems were solved by the Zilverstad staff itself. Personnel acquired skills and knowledge at a high speed, doing things they had never done before: providing feedback, making presentations, having meetings, and informing and relating to each other on how their design developed.

At the end of 1990, a detailed production design was ready and an implementation plan formulated. At the traditional New Year's reception in January 1991, the full design was festively introduced to all company personnel. Reactions of personnel were reserved, not negative nor resistant. Especially some of the jobs that had to be done in the task group were felt to be unpleasant, as they involved loss of status. For example, quality control is now done by the group itself, and it was something of a culture shock the first time a product was refused and returned to the responsible worker for additional treatment. In addition, nobody wanted to do the packaging as it was considered an inferior type of work. In other words, it took some time to get used to the full implications of self managing teams.

THE ORGANISATIONAL REDESIGN

Production Structure

By January 1991, the final production structure was selected and ready for implementation. Based on the systems analysis, four self-managing teams were formed. Three of them occupied themselves with manufacturing (blue, white and yellow), and one with the warehousing activities (green). The systems diagrams resulted in a general design which was handed over to the various work groups for detail and linkage (see Figure 6.2).

Figure 6.2.: Global Production Structure

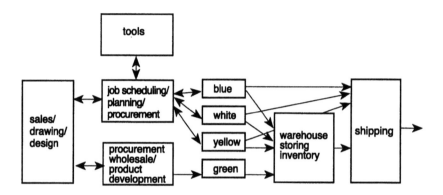

In fact, the warehouse group can be considered an 'inventory management group', since its task is to balance the wholesale and Zilverstad standard product inventories with demand. Its tasks include sorting, repackaging and order processing for wholesale products. The main reason for creating this group was, as it was experienced over time, that the wholesale and own standard products were overrun by the specialised customer orders. For example, the habit developed to manufacture standard products only when production slackened and there was time left, that is, standard products filled the gaps in the production schedule. As a consequence, Zilverstad's own standard products were not available and often had an order backlog. In other words, Zilverstad was undercutting its own sales performance.

> We deliver both on order and from stock. Then, it showed that customer orders always got priority over inventory orders. Because one order was for ourselves and the other just for inventory, it was never urgent. And you know, if things are not urgent, they don't get done. So if they have few customer orders, sales performance could drop. But if, in contrast, they produce on inventory when times are slow, that part of sales will be added to their performance since inventory and sales are the same thing. To them, it doesn't matter whether they deliver to the warehouse or to the customer: the internal transfer price values their sales turnover. So thats also a reason why you could say that they *can* influence sales; not directly, but indirectly all right (Head of Administration).

The warehouse group is separated from the factory and is placed directly under the Sales department. Presently, the warehouse group is treated in the production schedule as another customer, equalling both inventory and customer orders. The equal role of wholesale versus own products can also be derived from Figure 6.3. There are two inputs to the inventory function (the triangle in the picture) and the Sales responsibility domain embeds that of production. The detailed design of the production structure maintained the larger framework of the general design.

Figure 6.3: Production Structure Redesign

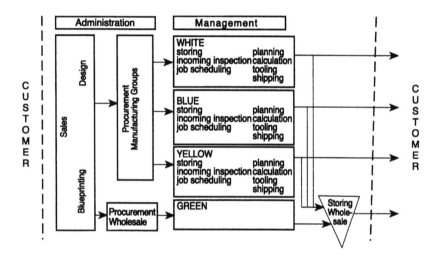

The '*White*' group is made up of 14 people and manufactures so-called single products, that is, products made out of one piece, and batch products, for example, spoons and commemorative medals and coins. The '*Blue*' group consists of 26 people and generally manufactures composite products in small batches, for example, teacup holders and rattles for babies. The '*Yellow*' group consists of eight people and also manufactures composite products in precious metal, in even smaller batches, for example, silver miniatures, brooches and hallmark-quality decorative ware. This is the group where the fully experienced silversmiths are predominantly situated.

Several production typologies at the same time are available. From top to bottom, the order is of decreasing batch size: the *White* group manufactures the largest batches, mainly spoons, while the *Yellow* group manufactures the smallest batches, mainly jewellery. Next, the *Blue* groups has also input of semi-finished products purchased in the Far East. The *Yellow* group is a full

113

product manufacturing group and therefore has a somewhat different expertise build-up as well as a different way of working, including the craftman-
ships culture that accompanies it. Nevertheless, each production group is
autonomous in terms of jobs: planning, quality control and tooling are
performed by the group.

Each group is headed by a group leader. Although circulating group
leadership is intended, it is not as yet effectuated because there is not enough
know-how available in each group. Other than high quality and maximum
employment of individual qualities, no explicit rotation target was mentioned in the preceding functional requirements. This was done deliberately,
because its limitations were clear in advance. Some people do not want to
rotate and view such demands as being threatening, while others simply do
not have the capacity or qualifications. Changes in the work included shared
responsibility for tasks and the availability for various tasks. Group responsibility was the main argument used in the inferior packaging job example
above - have all group members do packaging jobs. Availability, of course,
is restricted to tasks requiring a short learning period on the job, learned from
colleagues.

> Of course it is true that some difficult operations can only be performed by
> a few people who really know their business. It's hard to get other people
> to do this. You need time to enable all the people in a group to perform all
> sorts of operations. That's a next step in the process on which we're
> working right now. We're starting with training, job classification and all
> that sort of thing. Again, it's an example of taking up things we're able to
> handle. The process will never stop, you have to be inventive constantly
> (Production executive).

Consequently, the task group structure resulted in a different responsibility structure in Production, replacing the functional foreman by flow-
based units (see Figures 6.4 and 6.5).

The drawing function is renamed 'design' and is coupled to Sales and
brought upstream. Basically, because Sales generates the sample requests,
Design has to draw and Production has to manufacture. Samples are important to convince the customer of the quality and appearance of the product
and get him to confirm the order. The designer is located next to the job
scheduler (which is a production staff function) in order to enforce preliminary planning and communication by proximity.

The task of higher management is to keep all groups together and have
them act as one. For example, it is set up in such a way that a group which
is low on orders assists another group. The 'assistance hours' are being
registered and 'sold' to the demanding group using an internal transfer tariff.

Figure 6.4.: Former Production Organisation Chart

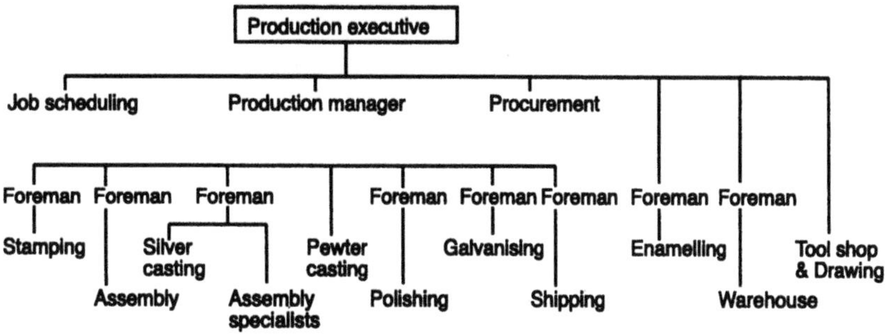

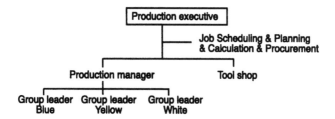

And the present chart of the responsibility structure:

Figure 6.5.: Present Production Organisation Chart. The 'Production manager' function is considered temporary and will eventually disappear

Changing the organisation brought numerous other changes with it. The first one was the grouping of people. It meant a significant change for people. Previously, they worked on a manufacturing operation and now, they're working on a product. Work was something they did on their own in the past, and now they have to work together and in mutual agreement. This has to grow over time. For example, at the start there was clearly visible resistance to having meetings. People were saying to one another: 'Do we have to go and sit around the table again; it'll cost me ages, all this blabbering.' But by now, it has become clear to everyone what the use is of having regular meetings; one is able to say one's piece, people listen to you and problems get solved. Employees have far more responsibility in this group structure and it seems that they can handle it very well. A second important thing is that planning and job scheduling are made much easier and more precise. It improves your insight into the organisation and into the throughput of orders. You *dare* to look ahead, so to speak. Which was far more difficult in the earlier situation. A third point is that it is easier to deliberate on problematic matters. It improves with groups getting smaller.

Solutions do come up quicker from a group. And because people are directly involved, they come up with workable solutions (Production executive).

The overall organisation structure underwent a subsequent redesign. The former product market structure was replaced by a structure according to business function (see Figure 6.6), framing a combination of product market and task group typology.

Figure 6.6.: Present Organisation Chart

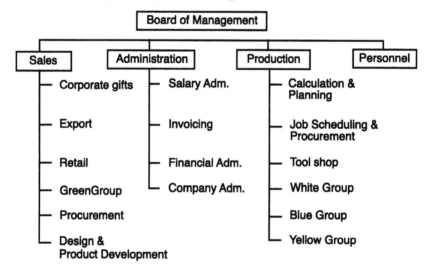

Control Structure

The control structure design can be seen as resting on two mutually supporting tracks, that is, meetings and agendas. Both meetings and agendas form parallel links between the elements in the production structure (see Table 6.3). The primary process is supplemented with a combination of agenda-setting reporting forms and concurrent meetings in which this information is discussed. Three meetings annex forms support the business process:

- the sales meeting with the sales order ticket;
- the procurement meeting accompanied by the purchase order form, and
- the post-calculation meeting using the calculation ticket for agenda setting.

TABLE 6.3
CONTROL STRUCTURE DESIGN

	Function	Goal	Input	Output	Agenda	Frequency	Participants
Sales Meeting	Balance customer demand with manufacturing supply	To accept sales proposals	Sales proposals	Realisable (R) & nonrealisable (non-R) proposals	Select prioritize and decide on R, non-R and R?	Weekly	Sales reps & all group leaders
Procurement Meeting	Coordinate purchasing orders	To purchase effectively and efficiently	Purchase proposals	Purchase orders	Select combine and delivery time coordination	Weekly	Group member & member Procurement department
Post-Calculation Meeting	Enlarge insight into manufacturing process	Minimal costs & 'pure' manufacturing data	Calculation tickets	Tested & corrected norms	To evaluate decisions, correct yes/no and how much	Monthly	Management & group reps
Product Development Meeting	Product mix management		Product development proposal	Mix extension or pruning	To evaluate proposals: prune, take in or don't	Quarterly	Group reps, Management, people from Sales and Design

Two other combinations of meetings and reports which are less related to the primary process are the product development meeting with its subsequent product development proposals, and the after-sales meeting which has filled orders as input.

Originally, it was meant to conduct the after-sales meeting as a separate meeting, but it turned out to be more effective to have it coincide with the sales meeting, which is more related to the primary process. The main reason was that improvement proposals go across functional boundaries. Since people from both Sales and from Production groups are present in the sales meeting, it could be coupled and simplified. The goal of the after-sales meeting is to obtain insight into the customer's experience with the product so as to optimise and continue customer relationship. Management is also present at this meeting. The problems and improvement proposals that result from this meeting have somewhat the same function as the post-calculation meeting, which, however, is oriented more towards the business process, towards continuously improving organisational performance by solving incidental and structural market-oriented problems.

A longer-term-oriented meeting, which requests the presence of board members, is the one concerned with product development and post-calculation. Aptly referred to as the product development meeting and post-calculation meeting, they can be considered as a sort of control mechanism of both product mix composition and manufacturing costs. The product development meeting is held quarterly and discusses the various development proposals which are put forward on the product development ticket. If the product is technically and commercially feasible, it is supplied with a product specification and taken into the assortment.

The post-calculation meeting has the objective to enlarge insights into the manufacturing process. Management and group representatives discuss on a bimonthly basis the actual consumption of resources and the standards against which they are set. Calculation tickets are explicitly used to match standards with actuals and to come up with variances which are then used as input for discussion in the meetings. Discussing standards often implies discussing their own knowledge on how products are manufactured, that is, results are improvement proposals based on cost efficiency. An alternative benefit which is targeted is the supply of up-to-date financial data for order bidding. Monthly discussion *within* the production groups of these calculation tickets is considered ideal but is at the moment of study not yet realised.

> In the production groups, discussion takes place at management level. Which has to do with this being just a test year (= 1991); it is the first year we started with all this. We used the first couple of months to clean up the figures and to correct things which were not all right so that we can now work with the numbers. The next step is to have the figures discussed with the group leaders. And the step following that is indeed to discuss them within the group, but there are still some differences between people. Production people are even less used to dealing with figures than sales people. And that is not without significance. It has also something to do with education. The people in Production usually have vocational training only, or didn't even finish it. So you have to introduce things very slowly, otherwise people get jumpy or frightened (Head of Administration).

After six months it was evaluated how the various new forms were experienced in daily practice. It turned out, according to the task groups, that no significant changes were needed. The layout of certain forms was changed, an additional form for warehousing was added and the job ticket used for scheduling and production operations was considered for integrating both commercial and technical product information. The specific comments and critiques received indicated, however, that the forms were used and understood in a production system by people not used to administration and documentation: It was something for the bosses to handle and they would know. Now, people speak up in detail.

RESULTS OF THE REDESIGN

As Sociotechnical redesign inherently links improving efficiency to the framework of a (more) effective and reshaped organisation, results are first and most clearly noticed at the efficiency level. 'There have been many results up until now. Of course, one cannot express a number of things in hard figures, for example the involvement of people, their attitudes. Still, I think that is the most important change, which results afterwards in figures' (Production executive).

Cost control and cost traceability have increased considerably. There is increased insight into product cost build-up and the causal factors driving costs, as the MAS design matches the organisational processes more closely. The relative simplicity of the design and the full participation of group members in designing it are mutually dependent factors. Responsibility in designing it seems to make it easier to have the responsibility accounted for.

In terms of hard numbers, Zilverstad improved its sales by 15 per cent in 1989, while at the same time experiencing a reduction in personnel of five per cent (natural turnover). Inventory turnover in 1989 was 4.7 and 5.5 in 1990, with a norm of 4.0 for the industry. Absenteeism (sick leave) dropped to six per cent which is below the Dutch average of 9.1 per cent (1989). Furthermore, the number of complaints on product quality dropped considerably. Another indicator of quality is the number of orders delivered on time. In 1988, operating in the former organisation mode, delivery reliability was 40 per cent (three out of five orders went wrong somewhere somehow). In 1989 it increased to 60 per cent while in 1990, it increased even more and is now reaching 85 per cent. This percentage relates to the busiest time of the year, that is, the fourth quarter, which is the gifts season. A by-product of the improved delivery reliability was a reduction in orders that were delivered in different batch sizes; most orders are now being delivered in one single batch, thus saving extra shipping costs.

> It results in customers staying customers more easily. We get many repeat orders. So all the energy you put into customer acquisition you direct at getting new customers instead of replacing them. Price adaptations are hardly necessary since the organisation has improved and we are able to supply much better quality, service and delivery times for the same price. Our competitive position has markedly improved, also internationally. All segments have done well. The sales department has less internal problems to solve and, thus, can concentrate far more on its commercial activities. Of course, we've just been operating this way for nearly a year so the effects are still young (Commercial executive).

> Of course not everything can be accounted for by the organisational change. There are many other factors, for example the dollar exchange rate, the economic climate. Or one Saddam Hussein spoiling everything. You can be perfectly organised but if you don't get any orders. On the other hand, it is also true that you can't get any orders if you don't have a

well-organised company. It's a bit a question of which came first, the chicken or the egg (Production executive).

No additional investments in assets were involved, apart from a one-time-only outlay for equipment to improve working conditions.

Yes, and for the rest: working conditions - we've spent a bit more on the costs for working conditions than we had the last couple of years. But those costs don't get any lower because for people to perform well they need a good PC, a good terminal, chair, etcetera. And that's of course a very natural thing because these are really legitimate demands and they speak up far more easily when they take the initiative to purchase or replace something. But again, that's all right in itself but nevertheless it does lead to higher organisation costs (Head of Administration).

A more structural increase in cost level is initiated, however, regarding personnel and human resources. The accentuation of group initiatives and the decentralisation of problem solving has made people aware of both their abilities and capacities and, consequently, of the value they represent for the organisation.

Well, I think personnel costs tend to increase. Putting more demands on people or on groups is coupled to an overall performance target. By the end of the year, they know whether they've attained their group performance or not. And you try to steer it in that manner, which has consequences for your personnel policy. If you ask a bit more effort from your people, and if they perform accordingly, they'll demand more regarding salary conditions and payment. Also, people become more important for the organisation because if people drop out, if you end up with fewer people, and certain key personnel in a group drop out, it can be quite harmful. So people, if they perform well, do become aware that they have gained importance for the company. But that has to do with the subject of personnel policy in the organisation. That's what we have picked up lately, putting up a job classification system and keeping appraisal interviews (Head of Administration).

1994

Organisation renewal is an ongoing process. In fact, the redesign process enables the firm to set the process of continuous improvement into motion. That certainly holds true of Zilverstad. After completion of this case study in 1993, a number of important changes were implemented. Some of these changes can be regarded as direct consequence of the redesign process: the implementation of a job classification system, a sales information system and a training programme.

Other changes were of more fundamental nature. In 1993, Zilverstad merged with two other Schoonhoven silverware companies. This merger was induced by the need to build up a stronger position in the fierce international competition. It opened the way to a more effective organisation of the firm's sales and distribution function. During this process, the principles that provided the basis for the redesign were never abandoned. The merger and the deteriorating market conditions temporarily took a lot of attention away from the internal development process. In 1994, Arne Pluut presented his experience during a management conference. At the end, he was asked to summarise the costs and benefits of the redesign. His short and direct answer is perhaps the best indication for the present status of the project: 'That's simple: I would not have been here today. Our firm would not have been there tomorrow' (Arie Pluut).

REFERENCES

Dankbaar, B. and J.F. den Hertog, 1990, 'Labour Process Analysis and Socio-Technical Change: Living Apart Together?' *New Technology, Work and Employment*. Vol.5, No.2, pp.122-35.

Roberts, H.J.E., 1993, *Accounting and Responsibility. The Influence of Organisation Design on Management Accounting*, Maastricht: Datawyse/University Press Maastricht.

Sitter, L.U. de, 1994, *Synergetisch Produceren*. Assen: Van Gorcum.

Sitter, L.U. de, Dankbaar, B. and J.F. den Hertog, 1994, 'Simple Organisations, Complex Jobs.' Maastricht: MERIT.

7

THE BROAD SCOPE OF ORGANISATIONAL INNOVATIONS

Christian Berggren

The three contributions to this section highlight the breadth of issues and efforts addressed by the theme of organisational innovations. The Swatch case is about a fundamental, three-pronged innovation strategy in the Jurassian watch industry: the Peugeot case illustrates the new regime of variety in inter-firm relationships within the auto industry: and the Zilverstad case is noteworthy for the way it demonstrates the complexity and richness of change within a small company.

For a future European research programme within this field, however, it would be desirable to broaden the scope further. I would like to see action and research in at least three other sectors, by themselves very different. One is the telecommunications industry, the telecom corporations, like Alcatel, Ericson and Nokia as well as the new private operators, and the transformed state-controlled agencies. If it is true that Europeans have a certain knack for managing and innovating complex technological systems, this is the prime case, where Europe has advanced far ahead of Japan. What can weaker sectors learn from this high-growth industry? Another field where Europe demonstrates skills in complex management is the new breed of cross-border mergers, like Swiss-Swedish ABB and Anglo-French GEC-Alsthom. If we were to write a European 'In Search of Excellence', which might be a most worthwhile venture in order to harness European will and skill, we should certainly include these corporations, and the organisational lessons in cross-border learning they teach us.

Discussions of innovations and competition often tend to get on a conventional track, first analysing production, then moving on to research and development and finally saying something about public policy. What about the users? Is it nobler to produce than to use? Certainly that is the case in Japan. which causes the Japanese many problems, not only permanent trade friction but also a relatively underdeveloped information society. In Europe there are several countries with a very high penetration of information technology, cellular phones, personal computers, software-sharing networks, and so on. This advanced state of the users is a valuable competitive asset, the problem is that so much of the equipment used is supplied by non-European firms. Japan has the reverse problem. A comprehensive enquiry into organisational innovation should look at the potential links between advanced users and new strategies of developing manufacturing and marketing products and services for these sophisticated markets.

Finally, there is the whole area of environmental initiatives, recycling being one prominent case in point. In analysing and adopting public policies to cope with these problems several European countries are at the very forefront, certainly far ahead of the Asian countries, where most of these concerns are simply externalised. Recycling of cars, design-for-recycle, etc., has progressed much further in Europe than in Japan. Still there remains to transform these measures to international competitive advantage in what is to become one of the world's premier growth industry. Here there is certainly a need for organisational innovations, concerning both intra-firm structures, inter-firm relationships, business-governments relations as well as the relations between users and producers. In this sector, too, Europe could build on its important segments of advanced consumers. From this overview of emerging issues in the area of organisational innovation, let me look somewhat closer at the three cases presented in the following chapters.

SWATCH - CONSERVATIVE SWISS ENGINEERS TURNED RADICAL INNOVATORS

The story of the Swatch is probably the most innovative and successful European response to Asian competition in any industry, and Benjamin Coriat presents its principal features succinctly. In the midst of a dual crises, caused by rapid technological change and potentially deadly low cost competition, the Jurassian watch industry did not pursue a segment retreat, it did not withdraw from the mass markets to concentrate on luxurious up-market products. Instead it attacked the competition head on in the low cost segment - but with a strategy of surprise. This strategy combined a radically new product design, a greatly simplified and automated production process as well as a most novel set of marketing principles, which fused high-tech and fashion. Upon reading this fascinating story, however, one is left with one crucial question: why did all this happen? The Swiss, the bankers as well as the manufacturers, have a solid reputation for competence and sophistication, but also for conservatism, and for a strong tendency of going up-market in competitive industries, be it photographic equipment, machine tools or garments.

So, why did they not choose the 'natural strategy' of segment retreat in this case? For being a small nation, Switzerland has a uniquely broad array of internationally competitive industries: pharmaceuticals, chemicals, food, machine tools, banking and financial services, just to mention the most well known. Were they able to mobilise particular resources and skills from other sectors in order to resurrect the Jurassian watch industry? What role did national pride, tradition and history of corporatist arrangements play in this effort? How could the conservative inertia of the banks be overcome?

Most important, what are the broader lessons learned, or perhaps so far, not learned? Hitherto there are precious few Swatch cases in Europe. Why is this so? The answer has something to tell us about the obstacles inhibiting so many industries from reinventing their tradition, combining innovative marketing with new forms of production and innovative product concepts.

THE CASE OF PEUGEOT - NEW SUPPLIER PROTOCOLS, OLD FACTORY REGIME?

Benjamin Coriat's study of 'the new protocols of mass production' in the auto industry is a forceful argument for the important inter-organisational consequences of a new 'regime of variety'. The chapter mainly focuses on changes in buyer-supplier relations and their new processes of assessment, selection and inter-organisational learning. Very importantly, he points out that these practices cannot be analysed according to traditional categories of market coordination, since these do not account for the crucial mutual learning effects. In fact, the pressure of market needs, the intensified international competition, is paradoxically creating much more complex social networks and inter-organisational integration. In this process, there is a highly visible hand (the auto makers) re-configuring the production chains.

The Peugeot case is different from the Swatch study. Whereas the latter signified a genuine strategy of European innovation. Coriat's auto study raises the dual question: Compared to the Japanese, what is new in Peugeot's strategy of variety? What is European? Certainly, all industries cannot be innovative at the same time. Much change is driven by learning from others (by itself often a creative undertaking) or sometimes just by copying successful 'best practices'. In the case of Peugeot, it would be interesting to know if there is any genuine innovation, or it is a straightforward case of adopting Japanese practices. This might be necessary in order to catch up, but is seldom enough to establish a competitive advantage.

Coriat emphasises the all-pervasiveness and unpredictability of the new variety in modern car production. However, key to profitability in markets demanding a large variety at the user end is the ability to produce modular systems with flexibility. This makes it possible to maintain economy of scale at the point of production. That is the secret of Scania trucks, for example, the most successful heavy truck producer in the world. And this necessity is certainly felt by the Japanese car-makers. As early as in the late 1980s Toyota's profitability was declining, in spite of brisk sales and increasing volumes. The major reasons was that the strive for engineering uniqueness - combined with a 'Lexus syndrome' - went out of control. Currently, all Japanese producers are reducing options, introducing common components across models, and enforcing strict discipline in their design and engineering departments. All this means less, not more variety. The dream of market segments 'the size of one' is over. From a longer time-perspective, variety has increased dramatically, but it is important not to be carried away with the new concepts, 'regime of variety', 'principle of non-predictability', and in the process lose touch with the economic reality of cost-effective production and sourcing.

The case study of Peugeot conveys the image of all-inclusive change, that the entire organisational set-up has been transformed. Certainly there has been a lot of novelty in purchasing and quality control, but what about work under the new regime? A few months ago I had the privilege of visiting Peugeot Poissy outside Paris. My main impression of this plant was not the novelty of a flexible post-Fordist regime. On the contrary, I was struck by its very traditional organisational mode of operation. The age-old French organisational hierarchy was very much in place. In the assembly shop, for example, it comprised Agent Fabrication (operator), Chef d'equippe, Regleur, Contremaitre (supervisor), Chef d'Atelier and Chef Secteur. The physical working conditions on the assembly line seemed to be very Fordist too. Perhaps the plant was operating very efficiently, so why change? The interesting thing, however, was that the plant did not operate well in relation to the labour market. After many years of downsizing, Poissy had to start recruiting workers in the early 1990s. The high unemployment could not stop an enormous turnover among young workers recruited by Poissy. In order to expand the workforce by 2,500 persons, management had to hire 12,000 people! Japanese manufacturers, the role models for the new 'regime of variety', are experiencing similar problems. That is one of the reasons why Toyota started a new and very different plant in Kyushu in 1993, and why it is reforming the Motomachi plant along the same lines.

There is a long European tradition of analysing industrial work and suggesting new principles for improving the quality of life. We should not forget and forego this heritage in the present time of intensified competitive pressures. Otherwise the Japanese will take the lead in this area too.

ZILVERSTAD SILVERSMITHING - THE FAST FEEDBACK LOOP IN A SMALL FIRM

In this study of a small-scale Dutch silver firm, Friso den Hertog makes a strong case for the virtue of studying small firms as a method of accelerating learning. Small is not simple, this firm of only 70 employees displaying an amazingly rich history of change. Moreover, the relationship between cause and effect, in this case between product line expansion and production bottlenecks, is much more obvious in small firms, and so are the learning loops. However, the case would profit from a more elaborated contextual setting. If we are discussing Europeans answers to global competition, it would be interesting to know what other Dutch firms in this industry are doing. Den Hertog only mentions Asian competition. To my knowledge, Italy is the world's premier jewellery exporter, however. In an expanded study, it would therefore be most interesting to compare the Zilverstad case with strategies adopted by Italian firms.

The major reform strategy to cope with increased product variety at Zilverstad has been the STOD-approach, understood as Socio-Technical Organisation Design. Could this be conceived as a European or Dutch alternative to Business Re-engineering? What are the similarities and differences? The problem of the one-firm-study is that it is so difficult to evaluate one approach. Was STOD the only alternative, or are there similar firms in similar circumstances, adopting quite different strategies? Studies of matching cases, be it pairs of large multinationals or small-scale artisanal firms, are often most rewarding in the discussion of options and constraints.

The three cases discussed in this introduction are empirically rich and very different. They illustrate the broad scope of current organisational innovation in Europe, and the need for comprehensive research and action in order to improve the effectiveness of these changes. There is a strong need for learning from non-European competitors, but also for reinventing some important European traditions in this process.

PART III:
ORGANISATION AND INNOVATION IN RESEARCH AND DEVELOPMENT

The three case studies in Part II were focused on the introduction of new organisational techniques in the sphere of production. The two following chapters reflect the introduction of new organisational procedures in the sphere of R&D, by reflecting on the recent experience of Renault and SGS Thomson.

Renault has shown itself capably of shrinking its product development cycle very significantly. At the same time it was able to launch a small car, potentially threatening to the market share of its existing small car (the Clio), into a new market niche. Consequently both sales and profitability were expanded. The key to this successful process of product development was to be found in the development of effective product development teams. Cutting away the traditional division of labour both within its internal operations and with its suppliers, Renault has proven itself adept at the use of new techniques of concurrent engineering.

SGS-Thomson achieved similar results in the design of integrated circuits. This is an extremely competitive - but rapidly growing - segment of global industrial production, in which the technological barriers to entry are substantial. Time is of the essence in semiconductor development and here SGS-Thomson's introduction of the 'lab manufacture' (integrating prototype design and testing with manufacture) was both innovative and effective. Further organisational reforms involving the construction of R&D alliances with other firms have also helped the firm to move up the global pecking order in terms of sales and technological leadership.

In both cases, significant investments were also required. But without these innovative approaches to the organisation of R&D, the returns to this heavy capital expenditure would have been limited.

8

ORGANISATIONAL INNOVATION IN PROJECT MANAGEMENT: THE RENAULT TWINGO CASE

Christophe Midler

INTRODUCTION

Many companies in the Western world are currently implementing far-reaching reforms of their project management systems for new products. This trend is affecting many different sectors [*Giard and Midler, 1993a*] and in it can be seen the effects of a shift from the competitive modes of a mass-market economy to those of an economy typified by variety or reactive adaptability. In this context the competitive edge of any company depends, firstly, on its capacity to market genuinely innovative products rapidly and at satisfactory levels of quality and pricing, and secondly, on targeting them at specific market niches, with the aim of outclassing more ordinary products [*Dertouzos et al., 1990; Stalk and Hout, 1990; Cohendet and Lléréna, 1992; Coriat and Taddéi, 1993*]. The combination of these strategies multiplies the number of projects needing to be managed.

The automobile sector, which typified mass-market industry up to the 1960s, is a particularly good example of the trend [*Womack et al., 1990 ; Clark and Fujimoto, 1991, Midler 1993*]. This chapter aims to provide an illustration using a European corporation in the forefront of these developments - Renault SA. In the first part we analyse the transition process in the project management field through which this company has progressed over the last thirty years. From the 1960s to the 1990s, a four-phase transition process can be seen as a growing influence of project roles versus functional roles [*Galbraith, 1971*]. The second part analyses the Twingo project, which has tried out the new project organisation modes and techniques set up in Renault. I characterise these organisations and management practices within the transitory project team and evaluate their results on the project performances. In the last part, I analyse the current, fourth phase of organisational evolution. Empowerment and the growth of project structures lead to classical but important questions: what is the future for skill-based functional departments of the firm? Are they going to disappear, scattered into different project teams? How is it possible to keep the long-term technical learning process, when organisational structures focus energies on more short-term and product-oriented objectives? I will show that Renault's present dynamic leads to an balanced and cooperative model between project teams and skilled-based structures. Skilled-based departments are not bound to disappear but to implement deep internal reengineering to meet the demands of concurrent engineering.

The paper is based on longitudinal research which combines different methodologies: historical analysis, ex-post project diagnostics in the 1980's and real-time analysis of Renault organisational experiments from 1989 to 1993 during the Twingo project [*Midler, 1993a*].

II. RENAULT'S PROJECT MANAGEMENT ORGANISATION FROM THE 1960S TO THE 1990s

The changing process which Renault went through in the project management field can be broken down into four phases:

(1) First Phase: Functional Organisation and Informal Project Coordination in the 1960s

In the 1960s, Renault was typical of functional structures. It was divided, as showed in Figure 8.1, into powerful, compartmentalised skill-based departments: engineering design, methods, production and so on. No direct link existed between these operational divisions.

Therefore, the 1960s were a time of informal project coordination (*artisanat projet* in French as used by Pierre Dreyfus, Renault CEO [*Dreyfus, 1977*]). Each project was managed on a case-by-case basis. The only person who linked and arbitrated between them was the CEO himself. This approach was suited to the manufacture of few non-diversified products, but by the 1970s was no longer capable of dealing with the growth in the number and complexity of products.

(2) Second Phase: Lightweight Project Managers and Centralised Project Regulation from 1970 to 1988

The beginning of 1970 was time for a first important evolution in new product development management. Project management and marketing experts were recruited, especially from American firms which had already experimented these techniques. Organisational structures cutting horizontally across the corporation were set-up as shown in Figure 8.2, involving

Figure 8.1. : The Functional Structure
[adapted from Clark, Hayes and Wheelwright, 1988]

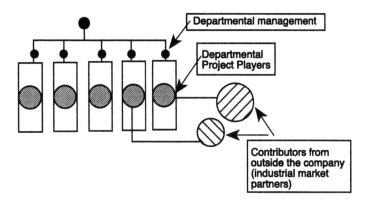

Figure 8.2. : The Lightweight Project Manager Structure
[adapted from Clark, Hayes and Wheelwright, 1988]

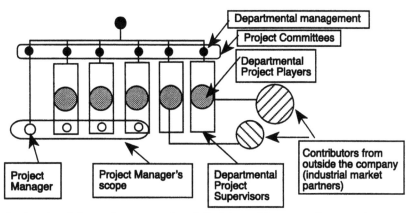

the heads of the various operational divisions. These met in committees to look at the project-related problems. Project coordinators were appointed: these were people whose corporate status was fairly low and whose competence was not yet fully confirmed (in other words - lightweight project managers). Their task was to gather information for the committees of departmental managers and they obviously possessed no decision-making powers.

Project control techniques were implemented at that time. A general standard of product development planning was set to coordinate the different contributions. A common economic language based on the project Return On Investment (*Taux de Rendement Interne*) concept was defined, to arbitrate trade-offs between the various corporate departments.

133

This second project organisational form was successful in overcoming Renault variety strategies of the 1970s. But it had weak efficiency on controlling financial slippage in a project [*Midler, 1993a*]. Matching the skilled-based department strategies and contributions without a powerful coordinator was a particularly difficult and ineffective process. At the same time, international comparison revealed more generally occidental project management practices to be far less competitive than Japanese automobile product development processes [*Clark and Fujimoto, 1991*].

(3)   Third Phase: Empowerment and Autonomy of Project Management Structure in 1989

These results were already known by 1986-87. But Renault was then in an important crisis and all concerns and energies were focused on short term programs in order to improve the firm's financial situation. Developing project management performance was not a priority in that context. As soon as short term profitability objectives were met, the new CEO, Raymond H. Lévy, introduced a reform creating Project Directors in December 1988.

This change was both a small one and a major one: as we have already seen, the real innovation was not in the project management structure (it had existed since the early 1970s) but in the importance given to this role. Project managers now have a powerful formal position in the firm, giving the project enough status to carry on an equally-matched dialogue with top departmental echelons. The project management role was entrusted to experienced and successful executive personnel, with considerable influence due to their prestige and know-how. The project structure surrounding the Project Director was also developed to a complete team of departmental project supervisors (products, engineering, industrial production, purchasing, sales, quality, planning controller, economic controller, personnel relations) with one foot in each hierarchy and operating within a matrix-type model [*Galbraith, 1971*]. Figure 8.3 illustrates this 'heavy-weight Project Manager' organisational structure.

In January 1989 the Twingo project was the first to experiment with this project management structure. This application, as we will see in Section III, was to be a decisive factor in the success of the project. It has been since adopted in all the following projects.

(4)   The Fourth Phase: Toward 'Integrated Design': The Impact of Project Management on Permanent Corporate Departments

The implementation of the heavy-weight project management model is not the end of Renault's development processes transition. A number of problems still remain, in spite of the progress which has been made. Professionals trained for years in a compartmentalised corporate environment have not been prepared for inter-department, or even inter-company, dialogue. Long term technical research and learning within the skilled-based departments must be reorganised to cope with the new situation of concurrent engineering. What therefore is the future route of the improvement process in project performances? There seem today to be two likely candidates.

Figure 8.3. : The Heavyweight Project Manager Structure
[adapted from Clark, Hayes and Wheelwright, 1988]

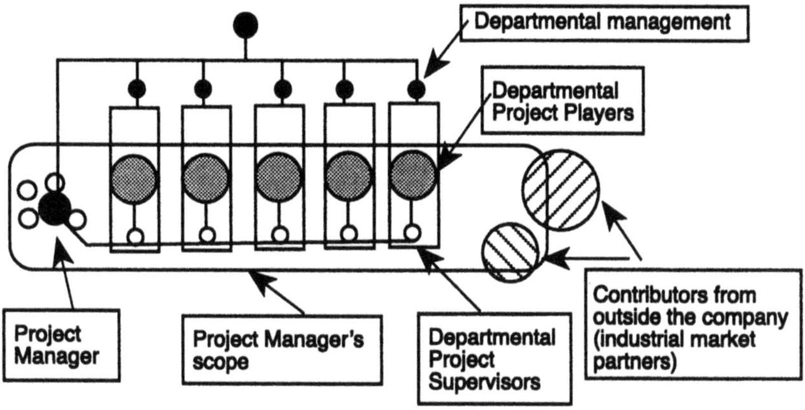

The first is to continue to reinforce the importance of project structures. If this happened, there would be increasing development in size and responsibility of project teams, skilled-based departments becoming simply labour pools on which project managers could draw. Some corporations do operate in this way in other sectors. It can be said that it was on exactly this issue that the debate centred at the beginning, expressed in the concept of the 'zero-sum game' in which project players would win exactly what department players lost.

Instead, the route down which Renault has gone is not this one and their choice seems to be better suited to the auto industry. In fact, Renault has chosen to balance out strong project identities and strong departmental identities, setting up a complementary relationship between the two.

In fact the effectiveness of a project management structure lies not in doing things directly but in enabling them to be done by others - both inside and outside the corporation. In addition, the logic specific to technical skill departments, cannot be ignored in the context of the automobile industry: maintaining and developing a sales network, increasing the productivity of a multi-product fabrication system and the level of the technical skills of engineering design personnel are objectives which are just as crucial as the success of any project. The raw material of future projects depends on the development of departmental expertise. It therefore seems to be a more efficient solution to strengthen the two complementary identities and to enhance the co-operation between them.

Against this background, the developments now to be expected are no longer so much in relation to project team management or even at the project/department interface. Rather, new developments will occur in internal reengineering of corporate departments or supplier companies. We will analyse such changes in part III.

II.   THE PROJECT MANAGEMENT PRACTICES IN THE TWINGO PROJECT

We saw that in the last 30 years, Renault achieved a succession of important changes in its formal organisational patterns and decision processes, concerning new product development. These structural changes are only the most visible part of the changing process, the part that was much studied after Chandler famous theory of adjustment of structure to strategy [*Chandler, 1962*]. Organisational change analysis needs also to focus on practices, behaviours and know-how within these formal patterns. The development of a new car involves more than a thousand professionals and hundreds of different firms. These complex co-operative processes cannot be changed in an instant by the creation of a new project structure. The Twingo project, as the first one to experiment with the heavyweight project manager model, was an important attempt to create and test more efficient know-how and practices in project management. I shall now describe the project, its management and its results.

(1)   The Question of Strategy and Repeated Failures

At the World Automobile Show in October 1992, Renault announced the launch of a small car, the Twingo, in spite of the fact that the company was already in this market with a leading product, the Clio. The new model, with its highly innovative concept, design and monobody architecture, was immediately an enormous media success. In fact, the idea of being present at the entry-range end of the market with two different, but complementary, models is an old one for this manufacturer. The notion can be seen as early as 1973, just after the launch of one of Renaults all-time star products, the Renault 5. The company then made five separate attempts from 1973 to 1985 to give this idea concrete expression. But all these projects were abandoned in the end because they could not unite the three key conditions for success in a programme of this type:

- The automobile must be sufficiently attractive to gain a significant market share (that is to say, it should not appear to a 'cut-down' model);
- The programme must be profitable in spite of the strong pressure on sale price typical of this range level;
- The automobile must differ enough from the other Renault not to be direct competition for it.

The possibility of initiating just such a project began to be discussed again in 1986. The pre-project exploratory phase was problematic: given past experiences, there were many skeptics and the financial computations did not yield satisfactory answers. Aiming to break through this bottleneck, Renault's CEO Raymond H. Lévy appointed a manager for what was now called "Project X06", in the just born heavy-weight project organisation.

(2)   Management Design in the Twingo Project

The Twingo project was a spectacular experiment to demonstrate how empowered project teams could create an organisational context which could drive all energies and concerns to the very problems of a specific project.

The Design-to-Cost Programme

In the traditional development process, the early phase is driven by market experts who give the new product specifications and technical engineers who develop technical solutions to fit them. Then, economic analysis and purchase are made from this product and process proposals (the cost-to-design process) from extrapolations from existing data. As the end of 1988 approached, this logic did not seem to be able to obtain significant reduction in cost and investment of the pre-project scenarios that was an absolute constraint for the project. Therefore, the just-appointed project manager decided to reverse the process. He initiated the development process on the base of voluntary economic targets for each sub-system of the car and piece of the manufacturing system, targets which were consistent with the global objective of the programme. Then, the development went on to find technical solutions to fit these initial economic constraints.

Such a process proved to be particularly efficient [*Midler, 1993a:26-33*]. It led to significant changes in the manufacturing process (the first technology scenarios included a high degree of sophisticated and expensive automation, the design-to-cost operation leading to a 30 per cent cut in the body shop investment for example); these were also evident in basic components

137

such as the engine (the investment cost of the engine finally chosen for the Twingo was less than the half of the investment needed with the first engine proposed by the motor engineers of the firm). On the sales side, the work done by project management led to innovations in distribution modes and in communications; these led in turn to major savings in programme costs.

All these cuts were not obtain by weakening the product competitiveness on the market but by focusing the development specifically required for the Twingo product. The changes revealed that the first technical proposals integrated the broad lines of the strategy defined by corporate technical departments, but those lines were not always consistent nor suited to the specific problems to be resolved. The design-to-cost operation showed how heavyweight project structures could now negotiate development methodologies and solutions with due regard for the project's particular constraints and opportunities.

Partnership Development

The application of this design-to-cost philosophy did not remain only within the company. Materials and component purchases account for approximately 70 per cent of the cost of the car. The introduction of concurrent engineering principles into relationships with suppliers took the form of co-development processes. Early selection of suppliers was carried out using contract specifications which were sufficiently open to enable suppliers to help in the search for solutions. The Project Manager polled equipment suppliers as early as the beginning of 1989 using component price targets as a basis. The technical solutions they submitted in response were then negotiated with engineering design personnel following a route which is exactly the opposite of what is normally done; that is, purchasing personnel normally use detailed and unchangeable technical specifications to call for competitive bids from suppliers, the goal being to arrive at the best possible price [*Womack et al., 1990*].

Following this, the chosen equipment suppliers were closely integrated into the project development teams working inside the company in order to make quality cost and time savings in dealing with the many questions related to the interfacing of the areas for which suppliers were responsible with closely connected or interdependent project areas. The implementation of these new procedures was to have a dramatic effect on the Twingo project: it enabled a reduction in costs of 18 per cent to be made on the components in the design-to-cost programme (compared with initial estimates made by project costing personnel). Reductions on certain components even reached 30 per cent without affecting either quality or profit margins, simply by better targeting of specifications following a complete functional analysis of the product.

The project management teams made major contributions to this evolution since their responsibilities cut across boundary between the corporation and the outside world: they spoke, for instance, in terms of 'internal' and 'external' suppliers, placing Renault plants and the facilities of Renault suppliers in a novel peer-to-peer relationship. They helped promote competition between engineering design personnel within Renault and like departments in outside equipment supply firms with the objective of widening the search for technical solutions, and so on. Purchasing personnel were naturally right at the heart of this revolution in the relationship between the corporation and its partners, a fact which implied an updating of both its supplier relations and its contacts with internal technical personnel, providing new meanings and new tools for traditional notions such as supplier quotation requests, selection and monitoring.

Implementation of Concurrent Engineering

From that starting point, project managers set out to implement organisational structures and working methods aimed at more effectively mobilising the many contributors to the project, at enhancing communications between the various expert workers in order to anticipate possible problems, at improving the trade-offs between the various logical systems involved, and so on. All these principles can be summed up under one generic heading: 'concurrent engineering'.

These principles first took concrete form in the project scheduling [*Wheelwright and Clark, 1992*]. Formerly, the work of the various experts was performed sequentially, starting with marketing and design, going on to engineering, production methods, materials purchasing and serial production and ending up with sales. On the Twingo project, contributors traditionally playing 'downstream' roles (plant personnel, outside suppliers, sales personnel) were involved right from the beginning. The aim of this was, firstly, to enrich input into the search for solutions while some freedom of manoeuvre still existed, and secondly, to contract for solutions with those who would later be responsible for their implementation. The symmetrical opposite was also true: 'upstream' players (engineering and production methods design) were increasingly called on to implement downstream what they had designed.

These same principles were also concretised by physically gathering together all expert personnel, to the maximum extent possible, in the same location - known as the 'project platform' (*plateau du projet* in French) - with the physical media and tools for development near at hand: drawings and models at the beginning, prototypes later and, finally, the production machinery. Formerly, workers on a project stayed where their departments were physically located, which often meant that they were far apart. Physical proximity therefore enabled time measured in weeks to be saved in solving interface problems, in particular the management of modifications dictated by industrial feasibility.

Finally, a new project guidance structure was set up with the goal of decentralising the monitoring of costs, schedules and quality risks out to those contributing directly to project development. To achieve this, the project was broken down into some two dozen sub-projects based on physical sub-assemblies or specific client services (automobile noise and behaviour studies for instance). In each of these sub-projects, a group was formed to represent each of the skills involved: engineering, methods, purchasing, outside suppliers, industrial production etc. This decentralisation made it possible to mobilise extremely effectively the project players involved at ground level to achieve project objectives and make major improvements in the quality of the decisions reached. Members of the project team ensured the overall coherence of the work done by the various sub-groups.

From Sequential Organisation to Management of 'Focus-Down' Convergence

One of the major changes implied by the development processes introduced by project teams was to bind the corporation to a specific temporal progression, a progression defined by the project itself. In traditional development processes, each department contributes to the overall project at a given point in the sequence, working toward a limited horizon. Now, all contributors work within a common time frame [*Sayles and Chandler, 1971*], which we have modelled in a theoretical diagram represented in Figure 8.4 [*Midler, 1993a:98*].

In this model, a project is represented by two connected processes: a learning process (dotted line) in which uncertainty about product features, industrial feasibility and market reception is gradually reduced, and a work process (solid line) in which the freedom to change the project is gradually reduced as the degree of irreversibility of project decisions rises. Project management is the search to optimise these coupled processes between the moment, in the upstream initiation phase, where virtually anything is possible - but where nothing is actually known for sure - and the downstream phase when everything is known, but virtually no free choices remain.

This theoretical model shows that in order to optimise project convergence there is no point in hurrying the process at the outset since the level of actual project knowledge is too low. Conversely, there is no longer any point at the end of the project in raising the degree of sophistication of analysis because the freedom to act on the results is virtually nil. Projects are therefore more effectively expedited by starting to take decisions later and then locking the project into them as completely as possible. It is at the end of a project that a sense of urgency should dominate. The diagram in Figure 8.5 shows these three separate phases in graphic form.

Figure 8.4. : Project Convergence

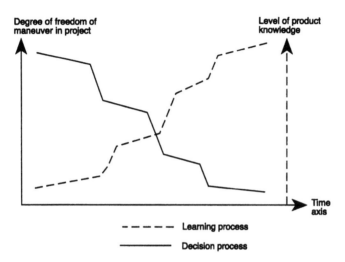

The Twingo project implemented a similar process to this. When the project team was formed, no decision had been taken to go ahead with the project. At that time it still seemed impossibly risky in economic terms. Project managers then capitalised on the risk of abandonment of the project to look at each and any route which had not really been explored up to that time. Studies went on for more than a year before the decision to build the automobile was finally taken. When the point of no return had been reached, and the project had been able to demonstrate that it could in fact be profitable, it went into a second 'control' phase in which maximum stabilisation was sought for all development parameters. Finally, at the end of the project speed and rapid reaction were given maximum priority in order to expedite the finding of solutions to the remaining technical obstacles.

Therefore, the classical variable of development time must be precisely defined. If development time goes from the project manager's nomination to the first day of production ('job one' day), Twingo development time is 48 months, which is a good but not excellent performance, as compared to best development practices [*Clark and Fujimoto, 1991*]. If development time begins with the no-return point of the project to job one (the time from product decision from product on the market), development time is 33 months, which is certainly a very good performance.

Figure 8.5. : Accelerating the project cycle

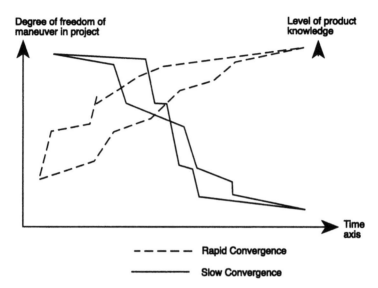

Project Convergence, Career Management Evolving Management Style

This theoretical model shows that convergence improvement needs continuity in the involvement on a project. Learning needs memory process in the project team. If those involved at the end of the process were not there at the beginning, there is a strong likelihood that they would have no understanding of the compromises and trade-offs negotiated by others, that they would not accurately assess the risks taken by others in full awareness of the context, and there would even be a risk that they would not feel personally bound by commitments entered into by others.

The effectiveness with which a project may be managed therefore depends on the capacity of the corporation to manage with foresight the careers of those involved, to plan ahead for transfers, organising them around project programmes and carefully setting up 'hand-over arrangements' whenever they cannot be avoided. All Twingo project team members, with only one exception, followed the project right through from the beginning to the end. Ideally, all players in functional project groups would follow through to the conclusion of the process. This was not possible for all since such continuity implies a fundamental change in personnel management in a type of organisation where this has until now been based on an ahistorical view of personnel activity.

Finally, the focus-down convergence logic leads to join continuity *and* rapid adaptation in management styles on the project [*Midler, 1993b*]. The emerging phase needs strategic insights, creativity and charisma, and a capacity to sustain high uncertainty contexts; the control phase requires precision, realism and negotiation talents; the last phase is a permanent race against time, where remaining 'details' can stop the process if they are not taken care of rapidly and where the project team has to undergo a very conflictual context.

(3)   The Bottom Line of the Twingo Project

The Twingo Project went on the market at the beginning of 1993 at what was a very difficult time for European auto manufacturers. Recalling the five previous attempts that had led nowhere, the fact that the project reached its natural conclusion can itself be seen as an significant indication of the effectiveness of this new approach to project management. Compared with previous failures, the difference was due less to a more favourable context than to management procedures capable of adapting to and taking advantage of the overall economic situation. To be more precise, the project had three objectives:

- *to gain a market share*: it is obviously too early to reach any certain conclusion on how this product has been received, but the results at the beginning of 1994 can be said to be satisfactory given the general slump in the market. The Twingo programme was of significant help in sustaining the Renault brand during a black 1993 (the total market in France regressed by 25 per cent).
- *to achieve profitability*: the effect of these management practices on reductions of cost and investment was determinant. The global results, as one can estimated it in 1994, met the forecasts made at the point of no return on the programme.
- *to market a product to complement the other small Renault model, the Clio*: once again the results are good and are even better than target (a gain of more than 60 per cent).

The Twingo project can be said, then, to be a success story. This result was a important reason confirming and developing the new development practices in the following projects of the firm.

III. THE MOVE TOWARD 'INTEGRATED DESIGN': THE IMPACT OF PROJECT MANAGEMENT ON PERMANENT CORPORATE DEPARTMENTS

As we saw, further improvement in project performances require deep evolutions in the functional departments, in order to reconcile concurrent engineering requirements with technical learning orientation.

(1) Changes in the Technical Skills of Corporate Departments

The Taylorist work division has had the effect of making some personnel specialise upstream and others downstream in a linear process. The 'upstream culture' thus became habituated to abstraction, developing the capability for strategic reasoning (in other words, defining scenarios and constraints in situations with high levels of freedom of manoeuvre). 'Downstream culture' became reactive in outlook (capable of reacting in situations in which freedom is restricted but uncertainty comparatively low), aware of the importance of detail, of the approximate character of both forecasts and theoretical presentations, and habituated to pragmatic reasoning.

Putting these two corporate cultures, as different as they are complementary, together in a context of concurrent engineering without any preparation cannot be immediately effective. The dialogue between very different departmental skill areas requires that each must show a higher capability for rationalisation than in communicating with players of their own team. This requires suitable communication tools to be developed. How can it be possible, for example, to have meaningful discussions on the industrial feasibility of a component with only drawings for reference? New modes of individual knowledge and team action, in addition to new media for communication between skill-based departments, therefore need to be invented.

A further major change is the integration of technical skills and value-control expertise: in other words - controlling costs, scheduling and quality. The process whereby work was divided up led previously to a sharp separation of these two types of competence, a fact which was harmful to projects. What a project manager wants a technician to do, for instance, is to fit his technical decisions to quality and cost targets, to work not towards technical sophistication for its own sake, but towards the final success of the project as a whole.

The final project debriefings operated as revealing the degree of expertise and relevance of skilled-based departments and pointed to the need for developing new areas of knowledge. One spectacular evolution within Renault was the recent decision to merge the product engineering department and the process engineering department under the same location and responsibility, in order to develop technical knowledge combining product and process expertise. Another area for deep professional reorientation is the purchase departments. New co-development strategies with suppliers need new ways to evaluate, select and coordinate the suppliers, compared to classical buying practices. The re-engineering of buying departments is currently one of the main fields of transformation, and it is not by chance that the new Director just appointed this year for conducting this transition is an outgoing Project Director.

(2)   Changes in the Relationship between Departmental Management Echelons

If horizontally-based project groups, bringing together personnel from workshops, engineering offices, purchasing departments and so on, are to function properly, those who take part in them need sufficient levels of competence and decision-making power, in particular the need to be able to undertake negotiations that will commit their departments (and therefore the managers of these departments). This is incompatible with the Taylorist type of organisation in which delegation is unheard of and in which competence is strictly shared between high-echelon experts and those who carry out the orders. Such organisational principles are still encountered frequently, and not just in industrial plants.

(3)   Changes in the Tools for Assessment of Departmental Performance

The standards by which the performance of project contributors is assessed also need to be reinvented; it is an illusion to think that project players will seek to optimise global project criteria if they are themselves assessed in isolation on criteria only partly related to their work. The upstream involvement of plants in the project is a typical example of this: the evaluation of the performance of individual plants is arrived at essentially on the basis of the ratio of the number of plant personnel to numbers of automobiles produced. The involvement of workshop foremen or technicians prior to the launch of a new model, hiring and training the manufacturing team six months to a year before serial production - none of this is reflected immediately in any productivity indicator. This explains why it is so difficult to mobilise high levels of energy just at the moment when it would be most effective for the final design of facilities and the preparation of the teams involved.

(4) Changes in the Relative Social Status between the Different Functions

In western technically advanced corporations such as automobile firms, upstream technical and strategic departments used to be in a dominating position (a push forward hierarchy). Concurrent engineering and project managers concerned with global compromise on the project tends to change this relationship between the different functions of the firm (towards a more pull hierarchy). It offers downstream people new opportunities to express and enforce their constraints and value-adding rationality.

(5) Changes in Career Management within Permanent Structures

Projects are historic and temporary activities. One difficult problem is to match the continuous but temporary involvement in the project teams with the career management constraints in the permanent structures. We have already seen how people rotation had dysfunctional effects on project convergence. However, this rotation is generally the direct consequence of rational allocating of scarce expertise among different projects. Team dismantling at the end of a development is also a difficult problem: permanent structures or new projects rarely open satisfactory job opportunities at the right moment.

(6) Changes in the System of Industrial Equipment Supply and the Professionalism of Corporate Buyers

The traditional attitude of the corporate buyer is to seek out the cheapest sub-contractor to make a component carefully defined by drawings and specifications. The result of this is a fragmentation of sub-contracting work: taking stamping as an example, there are sub-contractors supplying serial production tooling, others for the first wave of prototypes, and yet others for the second wave. The cheapest suppliers are often those who have made the greatest reductions in their overheads and, by the same token, in their design costs. Modern project managers challenge the worth of this kind of narrow specialisation. They are looking for partners capable of undertaking an entire development process from the first prototypes right through to serial production, with the objective of anticipating as early as possible the constraints which will exist for industrial-scale manufacture to ensure the lessons learned upstream will be remembered downstream. It will be readily understood that this implies fundamental changes in the way in which equipment suppliers are organised [*Banville and Chanaron, 1991*].

CONCLUSIONS: MANAGING THE TRANSITION FROM PRODUCTIVE TO CREATIVE ORGANISATIONS; LESSONS FROM RENAULT'S COLLECTIVE LEARNING PROCESS

The importance of organisation as a factor in production (the term *re*production might be more appropriate) has long been recognised. However, creation has been seen until recently only as an essentially individual activity, as a quality of lone inspired artists or, at best, small groups of innovators. One of the major challenges of the 1990s has probably been to unite all the factors that have made mass market industrial manufacture such a success, while accenting the need for innovation and creativity.

The media success of the Twingo project was unprecedented. We see in that welcome, in addition to the recognition of the qualities specific to this small automobile, an intuitive insight that the Twingo embodies a new reality in our society, a particularly sharply focused symbol of an industrial revolution in the very process of occurring: the shift from productive to creative organisation. What lessons may we draw in the end from Renault's experience? In our opinion, there are two of major importance.

The first, which is evident if one analyses the route taken by this corporation, is the difficulty and time involved in the kind of move towards project management. This is attributable to several causes:

- The fact that the capability for project development depends on collective skills. The whole set of behaviour patterns must be taken along in the organisation if significant results are to be achieved. A project is as effective as its weakest link. The effect of introducing efficient project managers is sure but limited: their role is basically that of providing leadership for the process of change throughout the whole range of corporate practices.

- The development of project management raises difficult questions which are a source of conflict within the corporation. These questions concern the relationship between the top and the bottom of the corporate pyramid, between the inside and the outside of the corporation and they highlight the importance of the interface between the different logic systems which exist.

- Development is a long process, compared, for example, with production. The learning curve for a new procedure is therefore longer.

- Building on shared experience between different projects does not occur spontaneously because it is part of the very nature of this type of activity to want to cultivate originality.

Analysis of the route taken by Renault in this area also enables identification of a whole set of conditions favouring a radical corporate shift towards more creative organisational modes:

- The existence of outside forces pushing the organisation into the change: the project management development in auto context is typical of Lawrence and Lorch's [*1967*] adaptive process. If European automobile manufacturers are changing today, it is because they have been forced to do so, notably by competition from Japan.

- The looking for external managerial innovations, both from corporate practices and the academic field. Learning from other firms and researchers was a permament strategy from the first move in the late 1960s to the actual experimentations. In the late 1960s, Renault hired managers with American project and marketing experience who took an essential role in the changes. In the 1980s, the Centre de Recherche en Gestion was asked to analyse the project practices that had been implemented the decade before. In the 1990s, Renault created for the first project directors a club (named 'Montreal Club') which gathered managers of major projects in various other sectors (construction and civil engineering, acronautics, information technology and so on) and two researchers.

- The close involvement of professionals in pooling and building on past experiences in the field of project management. Looking outside is not sufficient. Many companies feel today that buying new project management software or applying standardised procedures are enough to change the situation. I have tried in this chapter to show that the problem is much more deep-rooted and that what is in fact needed is a complete restructuring of corporate know-how - a new corporate culture. This cannot be done without full-scale trials and processes aimed at assessing and sharing what these trials have to teach us. The changing process following 1988's reform is typical: the creation of project management functions initially focused on spaces of responsibility and enlarged autonomy, it being the task of project players to regulate their own activity and to define broad guidelines. This open situation was the determinant reason for our research, the project manager needing an external view of the assessment, evaluation, formalisation and diffusion of emerging managerial knowledge in the organisation [*Nonaka, 1994*]. After some time, groups of managers formalised 'project meta-rules' [*Jolivet and Navarre, 1993*] that reconciled the necessary project autonomy (to adjust management to particularities of each project) with a minimum of coherence in the management practices.

- The strong and durable commitment on the part of the highest level of corporate management to the pursuit of these reforms [*Chandler, 1962*]. It is striking that as soon as top corporate management ceases even for a moment to put itself explicitly behind the process and directs its attention to other priorities, the logic of technical specialisation returns in force.

- The step-by-step changing strategy: it is not possible to jump directly from the functional organisation of the 1960s to the autonomous 'heavy-weight project managers' of the 1990s. We see a progressive pattern as described for example in Galbraith [*1971*].

- The ability to develop project management without destroying depart-mental identity. Approaches such as career management which alter-nates project responsibilities with roles erquiring technical expertise seem to be attractive solutions to the problem of combining professional identities which, while very different, remain necessary because they are complementary.

Finally, we have shown that this fundamental change cannot be separated from the essential, classic problems of all organisations: relations between management levels, performance assessment, inter-company co-operation and so on. The speed with which project management can develop will therefore also be dependent on the solutions found from all these points of view within the organisations concerned.

REFERENCES

Banville, E. de and J.J. Chanaron, 1991, *Vers un système automobile euro-péen*, Paris: CPE-Economica.

Chandler A.D., 1962, *Strategy and Structure*, Cambridge, MA: MIT Press.

Clark, K.B., Hayes, R.H. and S.C. Wheelwright, 1988, *Dynamic manufac-turing: Creating the Learning Organization*, New York: The Free Press.

Clark, K.B. and T. Fujimoto, 1991, *Product Development Performance: Strategy, Organization and Management in the Auto Industry*, Boston: Harvard Business Press.

Clark, K.B. and S.C. Wheelwright, 1992, *Revolutionizing Product Develop-ment: Quantum Leaps in Speed, Efficiency and Quality*, New York: The Free Press.

Cohendet, P. and P. Lléréna, 1992, 'Flexibilité et mise en cohérence des données de production', in *Les nouvelles rationalisations de la production,* Dubois et Terssac Edts, Cepadues, Toulouse, pp.25-41.

Coriat, B. and D. Taddéi, 1993, *Made in France, L'industrie française dans la concurrence internationale,* Paris: Hachette (Le livre de poche).

Dertouzos, M.L., Lester, R.K. and R.M. Solow, 1989, *Made in America,* Cambridge, MA: MIT Press.

Dreyfus, P., 1977, *La liberté de réussir,* Paris: Simoèn.

Galbraith, J.R., 1971, 'Matrix Organization Design. How to Combine Functional and Project Forms', *Business Horizon.*

Giard, V. and C. Midler (eds.), 1973, *Pilotages des projets et entreprises; diversités et convergences,* Paris: Economica.

Jolivet, F. and C. Navarre, 1993, 'Grands projets, auto-organisation, méta-règles : vers de nouvelles formes de management des grands projets', *Gestion 2000: Management et prospective,* No.2, April.

Lawrence P. and J. Lorch, 1967, *Organization and Environment: Differentiation and Integration* Cambridge, MA: Harvard University Press.

Midler, C., 1993a, *L'auto qui n'existait pas, Management des projets et transformation de l'entreprise,* Paris: InterEditions.

Midler, C., 1993b, 'Le responsable de projet, portrait d'un rôle d'influence' *Gestion 2000: Management et prospective,* No.2, April.

Nonaka, I., 1994, 'Dynamic Theory of Organizational Knowledge Creation', *Organization Science,* Vol.5, No.1, February.

Sayles L. and M. Chandler, 1971, 'The project Manager: Organizational Metronome', *Managing Large Systems,* pp.204-26.

Stalk G. (Jr.). and T.M. Hout, 1990, *Competing against Time,* New York: The Free Press.

Womack, J.P., D.T. Jones and D. Roos, 1990, *The Machine that Changed the World,* Cambridge, MA: The MIT Press.

9

INTEGRATING R&D WITH MANUFACTURING TO BUILD WORLD-WIDE COMPETITIVENESS: SGS- THOMSON INTEGRATED CIRCUITS

Benjamin Coriat and Nathalie LucchinI

Most European suppliers of semiconductors are facing a declining relative competitive position in a sector of critical strategic importance. SGS-Thomson (a Franco-Italian consortium), a firm which is one hundred per cent European-owned, provides an exception to this trend. As will be seen below, the reasons for this success are multiple. Broadly speaking, they can be summarised as follows: in recent years, the firm has learnt how to combine and add a systematic search of usual advantages linked to this field (concentration, specialisation, economies of scale) with an audacious policy built around organisational changes, aiming at taking advantage from the most up-to-date experiments about present sources and criteria of innovation and competitivity.

The strategy followed by the company provides us with a clear illustration of the resources and potentialities offered by a policy of organisational change, leading to the recovery of competitiveness. The example is all the more persuasive since it is in a sector which is highly exposed to international competition; moreover, SGS-Thomson is a firm of relatively modest dimension whose resources are considerably smaller than those of its big American and Japanese challengers.

In order to estimate the nature and quality of the company's capacities, we begin by outlining the characteristics of the Group, and recounting the difficulties met by individual operating firms. The second section will then address the critical conditions for the Group's recovery. The third part will identify the importance and significance of the organisational transformation which has taken place and which provide the route to a revival of competitiveness.

I. THE SEMICONDUCTOR INDUSTRY: A REFLECTION OF EUROPEAN DIFFICULTIES WITH COMPETITIVENESS

The semiconductor industry is a core component of the current technological revolution; it is also emblematic of the difficulties being met by Europe within the field of information technology. These weak European capacities are all the more so since the industry is one of the high-growth sectors in which, as we saw in Chapter 1, Europe has performed poorly.

High-Growth Industry, yet Cyclical and Marked by Permanent Technological Jumps

Since its birth at the beginning of the 1950s, the global semiconductor industry has registered one of the most explosive rate of growths among all industrial branches: an average of about 15 per cent a year. It developed three times as quickly as the whole of industrial production, 2.5 times as quickly as the chemical industry and 1.4 times the pace of the aeronautics industry. In the 12 years between 1980 and 1992, the turnover of the world semiconductor market jumped from $14bn to almost $60bn, which is remarkable even for a new industry. As Jean-Philippe Dauvin Responsible for Economic Studies for SGS-Thomson put it, 'everything enables us to believe that this trend which has been registered over about 30 years is bound to last in a future that is far from darkening for the semiconductor industry'. Specialists foresee that this industry will not reach maturity before 2020 and, furthermore, from then on, the market will keep increasing about five per cent a year.

This growth, tumultuous because of its cyclical aspect, has involved structural transformations in its user industries. Beyond the applications that have now become traditional - final consumer goods such as TV, video recorder, cameras, data processing, telecommunication and military sector - semiconductors are penetrating the automotive and transport industries, households, machine-tools, and thus comprise the raw material for an increasing part of the manufacturing industries (see Figures 9.1 and 9.2). In fact, semiconductor uses have diversified since the 1960s when their applications were mainly limited to the military and data-processing sectors. In addition, the industry generates an intense rhythm of renewal of its products, the different generations of chips quickly following one after the other, and each new generation bringing about substantial modifications in their production conditions for equipment as well as for processes. This has turned the industry into a highly risky one, both because of its strong requirement for investment and because of the continuous transformations that are involved. Thus, today all systems are being invaded more and more by microelectronics: as Dauvin put it, we are witnessing a growing phenomenon of 'the pervasiveness of silicon' within the whole range of electronic products and systems. In addition, different studies foresee the development of new applications that are strongly demanding in terms of semiconductors such as cellular telecommunications, digital video and wireless digital telecommunications. Semiconductors have become therefore as essential as steel or petroleum used to be in the past. A sentence by Pasquale Pistorio, Director-General of SGS-Thomson pinpoints this aspect: 'No advanced industrial society can exist without controlled access to an advanced electronics industry, which in turn cannot exist without controlled access to an advanced semiconductor industry' (extract from internal activity report). Similarly, Dauvin emphasises the strategic nature of this industry: 'controlling the semiconductor industry almost means controlling economy at large'.

Figure 9.1.: Semiconductors Market Distribution According to Applications in 1992

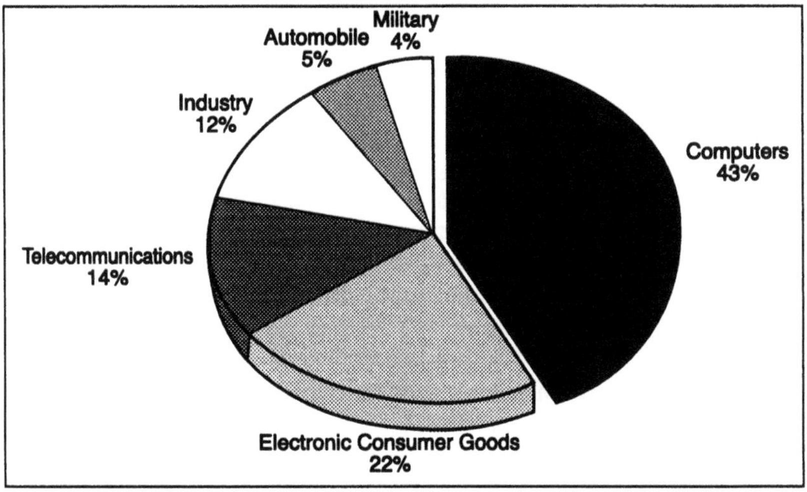

Source : SGS-Thomson

If semiconductors are so crucial in industrial priorities and if mastery of them represents a strategic challenge, Europe then finds itself in a vulnerable position. An analysis of the global landscape of production and consumption of semiconductors clearly underlines this vulnerability. It accounts for one-fifth of global consumption, but at only ten per cent of world production, represents a marginal source of supply. Worse, the deficit in the balance of the semiconductor trade has worsened consistently since the 1970s, amounting to $2.365bn ECUs in 1991. This persistently worsening shift between the internal market of the Union, and its capacity to supply and produce what it consumes, is obviously of serious policy concern[1].

Figure 9.2.: Semiconductors Relative Weight in the Cost of Electronic Equipments.

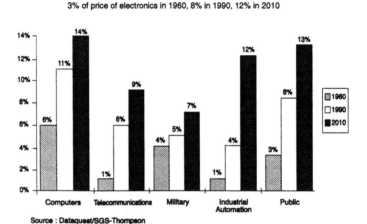

3% of price of electronics in 1960, 8% in 1990, 12% in 2010

Source : Dataquest/SGS-Thompson

If we pass on from these aggregate data to the analysis of the evolution of the competitive positions taken by European firms, the landscape gets even darker. If Europe satisfies only about half of its home consumption, producers of European origin cover only 38 per cent of the domestic market; this rate is declining as the leading European firms are compelled to give up more positions year after year.

Thus in 1991, Philips, Siemens and SGS-Thomson still held the first, second and third positions in the European market, together accounting for 27 per cent of the European internal market, followed by three main American firms producing in Europe, Motorola, Intel and Texas Instruments. However, as early as 1992, Siemens and SGS-Thomson started losing their market share and by 1993 the two largest suppliers were American (Intel and Motorola) (Table 9.1).

The weakness of the European semiconductor firms can also be seen in their world ranking. In 1991 and 1992, Philips was the only European firm in the top ten world firms. It lost this position in 1993, falling to fifteenth in rank, some distance behind Samsung of Korea. Within this general context of decline, SGS-Thomson today is the only European firm capable of maintaining and improving its global position. As the only European firm within the first fifteen world suppliers (see Table 9.2), it is beginning to reap the rewards of the efforts made over the previous years.

154

TABLE 9.1
TEN LARGEST SEMICONDUCTOR SUPPLIERS IN EUROPE (1992-93)

RANK		FIRMS	Sales 1993 ($m)
1993	*1992*		
1	2	Intel	2.070
2	3	Motorola	1.190
3	1	Philips	1.100
4	4	Siemens	1.030
5	5	SGS-Thomson	990
6	8	Texas Instrument	920
7	7	NEC	610
8	8	Toshiba	580
9	12	Samsung	510
10	9	National Semiconductor	450
		Total Europe	15.100

Source: Dataquest (December 1993 estimation).

TABLE 9.2
SEMICONDUCTORS SUPPLIERS OVER THE WORLD IN 1993
(MILLION DOLLARS)

Rank 92	Rank 93	Firms	1992 Sales ($bn)	1993 Sales ($bn)	%	Market shares %
1	1	Intel	5.091	7.950	56	9.6
2	2	NEC	4.869	6.173	27	7.4
3	3	Motorola	4.834	5.973	29	7.2
4	4	Toshiba	4.676	5.754	23	6.9
5	5	Hitachi	3.851	5.038	31	6.1
6	6	Tex.Inst.	3.087	4.003	30	4.8
11	7	Samsung	1.900	3.047	60	3.7
7	8	Fujitsu	2.553	2.931	15	3.5
8	9	Mitsubishi	2.213	2.804	27	3.4
*	10	IBM	-	2.610	-	-
14	13	SGS.T	1.483	2.060	28	2.5
		Others	32.398	39.398	22	47.4
		Total T.O.	65.271	83.071	27	100

Source: DATAQUEST (December 1993 estimation).

II.   SGS-THOMSON: FROM DIFFICULTY TO SUCCESS

In this context of declining market shares, the early years of the Franco-Italian group were not very easy, indeed, the very life of the Group was at stake.

A Slow but Spectacular Recovery

It was in 1987 that SGS-Thomson and SGS Microelettronica, two European companies with a 30-year presence in the semiconductor industry decided to merge their resources. Being of similar size, the partners gave birth to a new company called SGS Microelectronics. The rationale of the merger was to take advantage of economies of scale and the potential effects of complementarity in terms of products, customers and markets, specifically outside Europe.

At first the new company remained small; in 1987, sales amounted to $850m only and its competitive position was fragile. The company started by experiencing heavy losses that were only reduced with much difficulty ($203m losses in 1987, $68m in 1988, $97m in 1989, a weak balance in 1990, and another setback with a heavy losses of $102m in 1991). Clearly the joint venture's very survival was then at stake, particularly as it required heavy subsidies to maintain operations.

However, recent performances prove that SGS-Thomson is now heading towards a remarkable recovery. In 1992 the firm earned almost $4m post tax profit (on a turnover that has almost doubled since 1987 to reach $1.6bn). In 1993 post tax profits grew to $100m on a turnover that was a little over $2bn (see Box 1).

The huge growth of the semiconductor market certainly contributed to its success but this conjunctural element is not the only explanation. Did not other European firms' relative positions decrease at the same time? In fact, SGS-Thomson led its recovery in a very dynamic manner, working out a multiple dimensions strategy.

Five years ago, SGS-Thomson had 22 manufacturing sites but Pistorio implemented a programme of industrial rationalisation and the number of sites has been lowered to 15.

Reliance on a Multidimensional Strategy

One of the key orientations comprised an important financial and industrial restructuring elaborated by the General Headquarters with Pasquale Pistorio at the head. The financial restructuring was implemented in two stages; the first was decided on in 1992 by the French and Italian governments (each owning 45 per cent of the equity) involving a recapitalisation of SGS-Thomson by injecting $500m in the spring of 1993; the second stage would involve a similar capital injection in 1995. This partial increase of capital was necessary to reduce the firm's debt which fell from $900m in 1992 to $350 millions in 1993.

Box 1
SGS-Thomson: A few key figures

Basic shareholder: CEA Industrie (France)

Main shareholders:

- France Telecom and Thomson CSF (France): 45%
- IRI and Comitalo SIR (Italy): 45%
- Thorn EMI (U.K.): 10%

The group employs almost 18,000 people globally, owns nine advanced R&D centres, 15 production-facilities, and 25 design centres located in Europe, the USA and Asia.

In 1992 SGS-Thomson sales organisation comprised 44 offices located in 21 countries plus 600 agents and distributors.

Turnover: 1992: about
                  $1.6bn
                  1993: $2.06bn

	1983	1993
Europe	65.1%	49.1%
USA	23.2%	23.6%
Japan	1.3%	4.2
Asia-Pacific	10.4	22.9%

Source: SGS-Thomson.

Five years ago, SGS-Thomson had 22 manufacturing sites but Pistorio implemented a programme of industrial rationalisation and the number of sites has been lowered to 15.

Meanwhile, at the industrial level, a major restructuring has been implemented. This involved a reduction in the number of facilities (from 22 to 15), an investment in new production facilities and the modernisation of existing ones, the opening of trade delegations all over the world (notably in South-east Asia and Northern America), a commitment to an intensive R&D programme (at 20 per cent of sales, an unusually high figure even by the semiconductor industry's standards), progressive specialisation in new products and high added value products, and partnerships with a few large firms (section III below).

The result was that in seven years, SGS-Thomson has managed to win leading positions in a range of products which are emblematic in the industry and in areas of anticipated growth:

- largest global supplier for IC power, bipolar analog and digital circuits, telecommunication circuits and circuits for automobiles;
- largest global supplier of EPROM memories in 1992 (leapfrogging the previous leaders AMD and Texas Instrument);[2]
- second largest global supplier of EEPROM memories (14.9 per cent of the market) and of special SRAM memories (13 per cent of the market) in 1992;[3]
- third largest global supplier of transputers, and microprocessors used in RISC systems in 1992.

In fact these positions were achieved only as a result of key strategic choices and a consequent focus of the firm on its strong points such as reprogrammable memories. At the same time, however, and to cope with increasingly diversified customers' demand, SGS-Thomson's range or products was widened and now covers all the sectors of application of electronics: most of the product portfolio has grown faster than the market did in 1993 and the firm's yearly increase between 1987 and 1993 was about 16 per cent compared to an overall market growth of 14 per cent. So, after difficult beginnings, it seems that the decisions that were made were the appropriate ones, and it is generally accepted by specialists that the merger of SGS and Thomson semiconductors in 1987 has been one of the most successful in the history of industry. Such an achievement is even more remarkable if we bear in mind that one out of two mergers in Europe failed during the last two decades.

Given the progress that has already been achieved, future progress is likely to be enhanced by SGS-Thomson's commitment to investments in equipment and R&D (Table 9.3). However, these investments in equity, equipment and R&D only constitute a part of the explanation for the recovery and success of the Group. One of the very particular features of SGS-Thomson is that they supported their policy of industrial and financial restructuring and their commitment to R&D through an innovative policy of organisation, co-operation and partnership.

TABLE 9.3
SGS-THOMSON BETS UPON THE FUTURE

Investments in 1993	R&D in 1993
$480m	$300m
85% more than in 1992	20% more than in 1992
23% of sales	15% of sales
8% greater than the industry average	2% greater than the industry average
Ranked ninth globally	Ranked tenth globally
	327 applied patents

Source: SGS-Thomson.

III. THE KEY ROLE PLAYED BY ORGANISATIONAL INNOVATIONS

SGS-Thomson is an excellent example of a firm that rapidly realised its survival was dependent upon innovation in organisation. More specifically, an effort was made to integrate R&D activities with manufacturing. Meanwhile, and because they constitute two connected dimensions promoted by the Group, the search for this integration between R&D and manufacturing has been supported by a systematic policy of co-operation and alliances with some selected partner firms. In the following we focus on these two series of changes, because they not only underlie SGS-Thomson's recovery but also show clearly the potential offered by a clear commitment to appropriate innovations in organisation.

The 'Lab-Manufacture' at Crolles

One of the main illustrations of SGS-Thomson's spirit of innovation is provided by the analysis of what has been carried out at Crolles, Isère, near Grenoble. By bringing R&D activities closer to manufacturing - something approaching what might be called a 'lab-manufacture' has been created. This is now one of the major assets of the Group in its growing competitivity. Inaugurated in September 1993, Crolles is regarded widely as the most advanced European centre in microelectronics. This unit indicates an important step forward in semiconductor production methods. Indeed, there are only five research and production centres in the world able to produce 200-millimetre diameter silicon wafers (among these are IBM-France at Corbeil-Essonne and Intel in Ireland).

From the beginning it was decided to conceive and settle a manufacture that would be both flexible and evolutionary, capable of following the evolution of semiconductors after 2000. This required a number of innovations. The basic concept that was finally chosen consisted of combining in the same place a research centre, a pilot line (for experimentation and the development of new products and processes) and a mass production manufacturing line. As one of our respondents observed, 'R&D invested in sub-micron silicon technologies, process assembling on pilot lines and mass production are integrated in the same unit, in the same facility'. This represented a major shift from the 'sequential model' that traditionally prevailed in the management of innovation in which the commitment to specialisation led to the separation of these three stages.

The integration of research and development activities into other functions of the firm was a response to the need to react to the specific challenges in the semiconductor industry where time to respond to customers' demands and strict conformity of products to the required specificities were key competitive elements. By doing away with the strict separation between the different functions and tasks which were characteristic of the traditional organisation, and by organising the exchange of information between the different services involved to satisfy an order (from R&D to manufacturing) in a more systematic way, development time could be considerably shortened while quality was noticeably improved. A total quality approach was also utilised, the essence of which consisted of 'producing without defects at the first attempt'. As will be shown below, another advantage targeted in this integration between functions was to increase capacity utilisation, and hence profitability; this was especially important given the heavy capital requirements of this industry. In the previous phases of specialisation, actually, each function focused only on its own equipment, and capacity utilisation was uneven.

This integration is organised from a 'Common Centre' included in the industrial area and governed both by SGS-Thomson and the CNET (Centre National d'Etudes des Télécommunications) within a formal alliance (typically under the form of 'Groupe d'Intéret Economique') formed in 1989. Philips semiconductor researchers joined this initiative in 1992 (see below), resulting in a 'hub' of co-operation and partnership. The research programme focused on the adjustment of high-performance CMOS and bimodal BICMOS technologies as well as on the development of the science and technologies required in production. It was in the joint process/product dimension that research was being led.

The advantage of such a 'Common Centre' lies in the fact that research is being led directly in an industrial context[4]. The making of prototypes of complex ICs is then immediately possible on the pilot line and these can be continually transferred to SGS-Thomson's production line to the required quantity. Management described this centre in the following manner: 'We had to develop a research centre that would be able to make prototypes of advanced circuits in an industrial environment, both to ratify LETI[5] and CNET's research and to enable users to have quickly manufacturable prototypes.'

Another advantage of this Common Centre is that both the R&D and the qualification of technologies on pilot lines and mass production are carried out with the same equipment[6]. As we were told, 'the machines are standardised within the firm so as to avoid readjusting the process each time, as is the case with different equipment. They are fit for mass production use and thus operators share the same machines and the same resources in all the plant. Mostly, and this aspect is important, all of them work in the same room, which allows rapid and intense information exchange. They can use the machines both for research and production.'

Working on the same machines offers numerous advantages. As it is 'a close application of research designed to achieve mass production, it is essential to be able to undertake experimentation and production on the same machines': Important time saving is achieved and learning occurs more rapidly and systematically. Not only are know-how transfers difficult to accomplish in the separate and successive sequential organisation, but the risks in the path from research to production are diminished.

Thanks to the Common Centre, interaction between actors is almost immediate and solutions found are directly stored by the plant's technical staff, whatever the major occupation (R&D or manufacturing) of such a team. This new approach makes it possible to produce more quickly by shortening transfer times from R&D to production, to improve processes continually and to make better use of heavy investment.

Hence, for SGS-Thomson, Crolles represented the guarantee of quicker access to markets. 'It is much more efficient to insert research very close to production to allow a permanent transfer of the know-how acquired in research on the production line. And here lies Crolles' originality: we have both a research centre with a pilot line and a production centre working in permanent osmosis. This appeared to us as being the best way to make research as efficient as possible, in a field where time saving is very important.'

This series of organisational innovations is a key investment by the firm to maintain its competitive position at the frontier of technology and competition in this industry, in terms of product design policy. Relying on its innovative organisation, itself constantly improving, Crolles is determined to lead the way at the technological level. In December 1993, 0.5 micron technology was dealt with in terms of process and product qualifications and is presently being utilised in the manufacturing process. The 0.35 micron stage is also being studied and the required equipment will be installed before the end of 1994. The first ideas about new integrated circuits are being debated and prototypes are expected in 1995. Steps required for high volume manufacture would rapidly follow. In May 1994, 2,500 silicon wafers were produced. This will increase to 20,000 per month when the plant works to full capacity around 1995-96, by which time the whole investment will have involved $700m.

In order to be involved in the challenge with reasonable opportunities for success, the firm has also invested in another field: that of cooperations and alliances, turning Crolles into a 'hub'. As will be seen, this dimension of innovation - half-way between trade and research policies - is closely connected to the preceding one. In fact it represents a necessary complement.

A Hub of Collaborations and Partnerships for European Microelectronics

The policy of alliances and co-operation is both purposeful and systematic. The Common Centre was designed by both SGS-Thomson and the CNET (Centre National des Telecommunications) as part of a formal alliance ('Groupement d'Intérêt Economique') constituted in 1989, focusing on CMOS and bimodal BICMOS technologies for products as well as manufacturing processes. Thus research is being carried out by both approximately 200 CNET and SGS-Thomson's researchers (Box 2). This policy of co-operation has been developed further, and now about 20 Philips Semiconductor researchers work in the Common Centre, according to an agreement signed in 1992.

Philip's presence reflects the strategy of the Centre. As one respondent observed, 'it is a determination to bring competences together so as to come to a faster result, even if the results have to be shared. The average cost of R&D (equipment and manpower) is very high and as Philips could not afford to invest so heavily alone, they chose to sign an alliance with us.' Thus, Philips use the pilot line for prototypes manufacture and pre-production of circuits that are developed within common channels, and use them for their own requirements.

Thus, the unit set at Crolles represents a true hub of collaboration for microelectronics in Europe. Several countries are represented and researchers work together on ESPRIT and JESSI projects since part of the operation at Crolles are involved in a wider 'Joint Logic Project' (Box 3).

The policy of co-operation is also driven by customers, some of whom are present in the facility. They are of the utmost importance for SGS-Thomson. This form of co-operation is one of the important factors explaining the increase in the firm's market share and the fact that it has strong assets concerning numerous products linked to advanced applications. As our respondent remarked, 'the fields of applications of semiconductors are getting broader and broader and consequently we must increase our competence in "system architecture". We supply not only circuits but also other devices so that the users we work with can design their own circuits by using our most advanced technologies and processes.'

Box 2
Two essential Formal Alliances (Groupement d'Intérêt Economique) for SGS-Thomson

In 1989, SGS-Thomson and the CNET signed a formal alliance ('Economic Interest Pooling'), managed equally, for the realisation and creation of a research and development centre for sub-micron silicon technology. This was called the 'Common Centre' and was located at Crolles in France.

SGS-Thomson is also participates in another Alliance: GRESSI (Grenoble Sub-micron Silicon). This was established in 1991 as part of the JESSI programme, this involves CNET (at Meylan) and LETI (in Grenoble) researches for CMOS integrated circuit technologies. The goal to be reached by GRESSI as part of Jessi is the construction of basic technological requirements for future 0.35 and 0.25 CMOS micron technologies.

In May 1994 GRESSI managed to prove the feasibility of the new techniques dedicated to 0.35 micron CMOS technology. These are now being put together, and will be initiated in 1995 at the Common Centre of CNET/SGS-Thomson. The Franco-Italian firm signed a bilateral agreement with the EIP which will enable them to take advantage of the technological advances of CNET and LETI research.

The payback is substantial for SGS-Thomson since, in return for the facilities it offers its key customers, it is entrusted with circuit-assembling which, in addition, allows it to improve its knowledge of the increasingly sophisticated systems used by the most prominent users.

The systematic policy pursued in the building of strong partnerships with users can be explained by the fact that semiconductor suppliers are less and less able to design on their own the components required by their customers. Consequently, they must quickly have access to the latest technologies and deliver manufacturable prototypes in the key industries which the firm has targeted: telecommunication, video, data processing and automotive and professional electronic products. All this requires a particular organisation. As our respondent concluded, 'products and clients are here to fill the production line. Our strategy in the face of a fluctuating, difficult and cyclical market consists in trying to develop true partnerships with our major customers. It is not enough to have regular clients. We must ensure stable relationships with our most important customers so as to have some visibility on the market's evolution and to know what to do at the technological level. It is the only solution enabling us to keep on growing.' This notion of 'visibility on the market's evolution', entailed by this partnership policy is judged decisive by SGS-Thomson's administrators, given the speed of evolution and the often unpredictable feature of the demand and use of semiconductors.

Box 3
SGS-Thomson and JESSI

SGS-Thomson plays a key role in European research programmes, including in JESSI (Joint Sub-micron Silicon Initiative). The facility at Crolles is part of this programme. The 'Common Centre' dedicated to advanced sub-micron technologies is the result of the operation called 'Grenoble 92 ' initiated in 1989 by SGS-Thomson and CNET with support from the European Commission and the French state. This resulted in 0.5 micron CMOS process technology in December 1993.

SGS-Thomson participates in numerous JESSI projects together with The CNET and the LETI, as well as Philips and IBM. SGS-Thomson and IBM - both recipients of financial support under JESSI - currently collaborate in a FF100m project exploring new manufacturing processes for Ics.

The following table shows SGS-Thomson's participation (central R&D) in JESSI in 1993:

Area	Projects	SGS Participa-	Person/years of SGS Staff
Technology	10	tion	365
Applications	20	7	83
Equipment	31	11	15
Advanced	1	10	2
R&D	62	1	465
TOTAL		29	(50% in France)

Source: SGS-Thomson.

JESSI is a project launched by industrialists and labelled EUREKA in 1989. It comprises of four subprogrammes: Technology, Applications, Equipment and Materials, and Advanced Research.

In order to respond to all the needs of users and the market, SGS-Thomson has invested in technologically advanced computer-aided-design tools which are available for customers, 'who in turn give them access to their markets and know-how in the design of more and more sophisticated system architectures'. This supports Dauvin's idea that 'R&D will make tomorrow's winners. The winners will be the ones able to provide system solutions stored on a chip, mass production capacity being no longer a decisive element in itself.'

It is in this state of mind that SGS-Thomson, working together with Philips and Alcatel, and providing them with the silicon wafers their applications require, has recently signed a joint venture agreement with Northern Telecom, linking Crolles and Ottawa facilities for design and manufacture of special circuits. Such alliances permit regular information exchange between the different actors and make it easier to take technological options for future common markets. The firms take risks for the future and they take them together.

Today SGS-Thomson administrators are aware of the fact that the needs emerging from the market (which they keep in touch with through their alliances with users) require an innovative organisation, like the one designed and realised at Crolles. The latter makes it possible to adjust process/product interactions, that is to say, between the design of a product itself and the required new technologies. Owing to this set of measures, SGS-Thomson, with the centre at Crolles, can offer their customers more competitive complex and dedicated circuits for present and future important markets, such as telecommunication and data processing industry. So, the firm geared itself to the market transformation that thoroughly changed the bases and determining criteria of competitivity in this trade, transformation - 'if 15 years ago competition used to depend exclusively upon price, we have to note that today the first criterion is no longer the price but the quality of the service we bring our customers as well as the technologies we provide them with.' This relationship to the market, practically carried out thanks to a policy systematically drawing in semiconductor users with their suppliers, is a powerful mover of organisational evolution which brings it closer to customer needs and better prepares it to respond to their demands in shorter time. Thus it becomes possible for technical innovation and organisational innovation to stimulate and reinforce each other.

So by integrating R&D and manufacturing, the shift from the traditional sequential model appears clearly and forms a central part in the Group's latest success.

NOTES

1. For a recent estimation of competitivity of European firms in this sector, see Catinat in Coriat and Taddei [1994].
2. EPROM (Erasable Programmable Read Only Memory) are a kind of non 'volatile' memories also called 'dead' memories. They are read only memories the content of which is inscribed by the memory maker and based on data given by the user. They are saved even when electric power is off.
3. EEPROM (Electrically Erasable Programmable ROM) are memories programmable by the user and electrically erasable. The data stored in digits can be individually erased and reprogrammed.
4. As the whole environment is a potential source of pollution (water, air, fluids, waves, vibrations, humans, machines and even partitions which are suspected of conveying damaging particles 'sanitary rooms' responding to quality and cleanliness criteria are used for the development, pilot production and mass production of components.
5. The LETI (Laboratoire d'Electronique de Technologie et d'Instrumentation) is an important research centre of the CEA (Commisariat à l'Energie Atomique) with which research agreements have been signed.
6. The equipment is sourced from America (75 per cent), Europe (20 per cent), and Japan (5 per cent).

10

ORGANISATION AND INNOVATION IN RESEARCH AND DEVELOPMENT: A COMMENTARY

Giovanni Dosi

In these notes, I shall start from some remarks on the general linkages between innovation, forms of business organisations and competitiveness, and then move to more specific considerations highlighted by the case studies.

I. RESEARCH AND INNOVATION

It is not possible to discuss here the scope and limitations of the empirical proxies typically used to measure innovative efforts (most often, Expenditures) and innovative outputs (frequently, the number of international patents). Notwithstanding their limitations - related for example to the neglect of the informal learning activities in Statistics, or to the different sectoral propensities to patent in output measures - I shall assume here that these proxies do reveal some core feature of each national system of innovation. In partial modification to the analysis of the introductory chapter, the evidence appears to suggest an approximately linear relation - in cross-sectional estimates amongst OECD countries - between business-performed and international patenting [*Dosi, Pavitt and Soete, 1990*].

Where does the impact of organisational specifies come in then? In my view, it is reflected primarily in the ability of different firms to exploit a given innovative output commercially and, in the longer term, in the differential commitment of diverse organisational forms to innovation itself.

II. INNOVATION AND COMPETITIVENESS

An indirect but highly revealing evidence of the country-effects, with respect to organisational nature, emerges from estimates of the dynamic relationships between competitiveness on the one hand, and innovation and production costs on the other hand. For example, in Amendola, Dosi and Papagni [*1993*], we test with pooling techniques the determinants of the changes in competitiveness - proxied by variations of world market shares - for a group of OECD countries: both international patents (a measure of 'disembodied' innovation) and fixed investments in machinery and equipment - a proxy for capital-embodied technical progress. Both display a long-term positive impact while labour costs, denominated in an international currency, show only a short-term impact that fades away in around three years. Equally interesting for our purpose here is the importance of country-specific fixed effects which, so to speak, 'shift' up or down the influence of technical progress upon competitiveness: these effects have, interestingly, a magnifying nature in the case of, for example, Japan, and a relatively dampening one in, for example, the USA or the UK, with many European countries somewhere in between.

My conjecture, perfectly in line with the thrust of this project, is that indeed, these national structural effects have to do with, at least partly, the forms of organisation, patterns of behaviour and strategies of business firms in each country.

III.   ORGANISATIONAL FORMS AND COMPETITIVENESS

To begin with, note that the conjecture is quite a demanding one and requires three additional hypotheses, namely:

(1) Specific forms of corporate organisation exert a long term impact on the opportunities, constraints and revealed performances of individual firms;

(2) These organisational forms are not randomly distributed across countries, but rather are shaped by some systematic country- (or region-) specific determinants;

(3) Notwithstanding the apparent 'superiority' of some organisational forms there are equally systematic factors which prevent any quick international diffusion of the former and account for inertiality and persistence.

Let me also add a fourth, more dynamic hypothesis, that is, in the long term, organisational forms and innovative capabilities co-evolve so that current organisations in a sense 'shape their own technological future' by their own current behaviours and strategies and collectively lock in within particular directions and rates of learning.

All four hypotheses in my view are justified by an ambitious research project, an obvious relevance from a policy point of view as well. To provide some scattered supporting evidence, think of the importance, extensively argued by economic historians and *in primis* by Alfred Chandler, of the role of the archetypical 'American' multidivisional corporation in the establishment of American leadership in terms of technological innovation and, also, of the income-generating possibilities in the first half of this century [*Chandler, 1990; Chandler et al., 1995*], or of the more recent debate on the differential performance of the 'Japanese corporation'. This argument, however, has got to match the puzzling evidence on the long term persistence of national specificities even when performance may appear systematically weaker. Here, one may foresee an explanation in terms of *embeddedness* of the incentives, opportunities and constraints facing each firm within the network of institutional relations specific to each country, ranging from user producer linkages to the forms of governance of the markets for finance and labour. (An interpretation along these lines is found in Zysman [*1994*]). Furthermore, one may also start to gather convincing evidence on the co-evolution of technologies, organisational forms and supporting institutions (see Nelson [*1994*]).

The issue of national (or regional) specificities of organisational forms and their relatively inertial reproduction over time is entangled with the identification of organisational and behaviourial elements that make one firm 'more competent' than another at doing something, whether in the efficient exploitation of an innovation, the penetration of foreign markets, or the search for new products. In my view, these differential competencies entail more than simply the quality of the discretionary decisions of the strategic management: if it were so, one would observe much less persistence of inter-firm asymmetries and less country-specificity, given the abundant supply of international management consultants! Rather, in tune with several like-minded colleagues, I suggest that differential competencies are also hidden in the diverse sequences of organisational routines and rules of interaction with customers, suppliers, workers, bankers and so on.

All this is to say that the general conjecture that 'organisational forms matter for competitiveness' (and, via that, growth) is beginning to find some corroboration, but many pieces of the puzzle have yet to come into place: progress in this field can be made only through extensive comparative investigations, covering both broad statistical aggregates concerning the distributions of characteristics and performances of firms in different countries and regions on the one hand, and detailed case studies at the level of individual sectors and firms on the other.

IV. EUROPE: TECHNOLOGICAL STRENGTHS AND
ORGANISATIONAL WEAKNESSES?

In greater detail of analysis when interpreting the European technological and organisational capabilities, an initial question comes to mind immediately, namely, to what extent one can talk of a 'European way of doing things', as opposed to an 'American' or a 'Japanese' one? Is there any evidence that the intra-European variance in modal organisational forms and institutional set-ups is any lower than the inter-regional one? Are there any distinctive European features that cut across all EU countries?

A second issue regards the distinction between organisational and technological factors as determining the strengths and weaknesses of European industries. Ideally, one would like to achieve some sort of combinatorial matrix, mapping sectors and countries along the double axes of technological and 'organisational' capabilities (once they are properly defined in terms of some measurable proxies as well).

The two foregoing chapters are good cases in point. The case of Renault illustrates the painstaking process of organisational learning in a sector (automobiles) where European industry has been traditionally strong in technological terms. Here, fundamental analytical issues include, for example, how the new organisational set-ups influence longer-term innovative abilities, the degree of transferability of organisational innovations to other firms, the compatibility of such new organisational routines with other pre-existing institutional arrangements concerning for example, labour training, incentive governance, career structures, and so on.

Conversely, the case of SGS-Thomson presents a rather unique success story (at last) in an industry (semiconductors) where Europe has been historically weak on every account. Why has one not observed more SGSs? (Incidentally, note that the past state subsidies that allowed both SGS and Thomson-Semiconductors to survive for a couple of decades through heavy losses must now be considered as part of the essential conditions: many more firms, now mostly defunct, have been publicly and imaginative in top management - which certainly SGS has - compared with the accumulated technological competencies that the firm embodies? What are the broader reasons for a general European lag in semiconductors (or for that matter in computer technologies)? How do European weaknesses in the production of microelectronics devices affect the general competitiveness of industry, given the serendipity of the technology? What is the importance of organisational arrangements in all this?

V. EFFICIENT PRODUCTION AND EFFICIENT INNOVATIVE SEARCH: A POSSIBLE TENSION

The last point I wish to raise - emphasised also in Nathan Rosenberg's intervention - concerns the criteria upon which particular organisational set-ups are evaluated, and the dilemmas that they are likely to engender. In particular, tensions might arise between 'being good at doing what one is already doing' versus 'being good at searching for new things', that is, what

James March suggestively calls 'exploitation vs. exploration' [*March, 1991*]. For example, in an extremely rough comparative evaluation, the failures of many American big corporations seem to be at least partly compensated for by institutions supporting 'exploration', such as the linkages between university and industry, and venture capital organisations (Incidentally, note in this respect that seemingly 'inefficient' entities - when evaluated from the point of view of individual corporations - such as Bell Labs, Xerox Park, or IBM central labs might well have been crucial institutions supporting major innovative externalities.) Conversely, the fact that Japanese organisational forms were shown to be highly conducive to 'exploitation' and incremental innovation but have yet to prove their merits in terms of producing original microprocessor technologies, computer system architectures and software might hint at a more general problem.)

In this respect, Europe appears to be falling dangerously in between, sharing, albeit at a lower extent, the weakness of both systems with, for example, forms of organisation of production which might out-compete the American, especially under the 'German' arrangements, but seemingly not the Japanese. At the same time, while 'exploration' is stifled by the scarcity of large 'bridging institutions' between pure and applied research of which America is so rich in, venture capital markets are still at only the embryonic, stage. Further, there are feudal restraints on university life, at least in continental Europe, that are only second to Japan. In conclusion, the diagnosis of the long-term impact of these European specificities is, in my view, another central element of this research.

REFERENCES

Amendola, G., Dosi, G. and E. Papagni (1993), 'The Dynamics of International Competitiveness', *Weltwirtschaftliches Archiv*.

Chandler, A. (1990), *Scale and Scope*, Cambridge, MA: Belknap Press of Harvard University Press.

Chandler, A. *et al.* (eds.) (1995, forthcoming), *Big Business and the Wealth of Nations*, Cambridge: Cambridge University Press.

Dosi, G., Pavitt, K. and L. Soete (1990), *The Economics of Technological Change and International Trade*, New York: New York University Press.

March, J. (1991), 'Exploration and Exploitation in Organisational Learning', *Organisation Science*.

Nelson, R. (1994), 'The Co-evolution of Technology, Industrial Structures and Supporting Institutions', *Industrial and Corporate Change*.

Zysman, J. (1994), 'How Institutions Create Historically Rooted Trajectories of Growth', *Industrial and Corporate Change*.

PART IV:
ORGANISATION AND INNOVATION IN HUMAN RESOURCE DEVELOPMENT

Human resources lies at the heart of modern competitiveness, where the labour force (at all levels) is now seen as a primary asset in production rather than a cost to be minimised. The task confronting the industrial sector is how to maximise participation so that the capabilities of these human resources are most effectively utilised. This involves new approaches not only to the development of this key resource, but also to the integration of human resource management into the spheres of production and R&D; moreover, it also requires new patterns of relations with education and training institutions external to the enterprise.

The five Dutch firms described in Chapters 11 and 12 are notable for their integrated approach towards the optimum utilisation of knowledge in these information-intensive sectors and the development of personal career paths. By combining these two objectives, significant improvements have been achieved in responsiveness to market conditions, allowing these firms to move from a supply-push to a demand-pull trajectory. The Danish hearing-aid firm, Oticon, is similarly distinguished in its attempt to promote innovation through the sweeping away of traditional functional specialisations and managerial hierarchies. The final enterprise in this Part is distinctive because of the potential link between participation in ownership (for this is an employee-owned enterprise) and in processes of continuous improvement. In this latter case, the social context of innovation (a traditional manufacturing area with craft-union industrial relations) shows that intra-enterprise organisational changes are significantly influenced by the external environment within which the firm operates.

11

MANAGING KNOWLEDGE FLOWS: A KEY ROLE FOR PERSONNEL MANAGEMENT

J. Friso den Hertog and Ed van Sluijs[*]

KNOWLEDGE AND COMPETITIVE ADVANTAGE

Firms are becoming increasingly knowledge-intensive. The competitive ability is determined more and more by the effectiveness with which firms innovate their products, services and processes. The character of the chain of values is thus changing: from a sum of labour and capital to an increase of added available and new knowledge. Particularly in the case of the modern industrialised countries, competitive advantage and employment depend on the way in which they manage to exploit the knowledge intensity of their firms and institutions. The way back to pure price and quality competition seems to be cut definitively by the turbulently growing Eastern industry.

This increased knowledge intensity presents a firm with new problems and challenges. Firms are confronted with the task of bringing tailor-made products and services of higher quality on to the market more rapidly. However, the available knowledge extracted threatens to become obsolete at an increasing rate. The 'half value time' of available knowledge is shrinking all the time. If policies remain unchanged, the 'obsolescence' of knowledge workers threatens to become a kind of epidemic-sized Pfeiffer desease. Continuous development of new knowledge is needed because stagnation means, in fact, deterioration. The problem here is that new knowledge must be made effective: good ideas must be converted into hard currency [*Van de Ven, 1986*]. This is the obstacle for European firms. Investment in R&D does not guarantee success. Even firms such as Philips and Unilever are forced to reduce their R&D budgets. The challenge that thus arises is to find new ways of improving the entire knowledge system,

---

* The authors are at MERIT (Maastricht Economic Research Institute on Innovation and Technology), University of Limburg, Maastricht.

to acquire a better grip on the process of knowledge development, knowledge transfer and the use of knowledge.

Upstream in the knowledge chain, developers must take more account of the implications of their choices for those who must work with them downstream. Those working downstream must anticipate better what is thought out upstream. The implication of this development is that firms must search for new strategies in order to control the effectiveness of knowledge flows. The existing management techniques are particularly directed at the control of routine production processes. Firms have attempted to use traditional planning and organisation techniques to control innovation trajectories. Meanwhile [*Cobbenhagen, den Hertog and Pennings, 1994 Cooper, 1994, Van den Ven, 1986*] it has become clear that such a mechanistic approach does not suffice to function faster, better and cheaper. Innovation processes are too complex, uncertain and chaotic for that. An important key to this control problem is provided by the personnel management. Within the modern vision of personnel management, *Human Resource Management*, the factor labour is thought of as an asset rather than a cost. This approach can be applied especially to knowledge-intensive firms, where the personnel primarily carry, transfer and Pink use knowledge. Each intervention with the workforce can be viewed as an intervention with the knowledge flow. An absolute requirement is that personnel management should be an active factor in company policy, and does not stop with filling vacancies and transferring those who have dropped out in the innovation trajectory. Additionally, the approach to personnel development must be directed much more strongly towards the business strategy of the firm. Thus, personnel policy assumes a double face: both as an effective means for improved development of individual talents and as an instrument to better knowledge flows.

This chapter reports on the practice of four knowledge-intensive firms. All these firms have recognised the importance of the knowledge enterprise and have developed new approaches derived from personnel management that may contribute to that. Two of the firms are from the services sector: Moret, Ernst & Young, the biggest Dutch accounting firm, and Pink Elephant, a Dutch firm that focuses on the management of large computer centres. The two industrial firms participating in this study are Raychem, the Belgian daughter company of the American chemical firm, and Océ-van der Grinten, the Dutch producer of copiers. Before going into the practice within these firms, we will first look at the characteristics of the knowledge enterprise. The last section of this chapter will concentrate on the implications for company policy.

Managing the Knowledge Enterprise

Economists that study technological development use a remarkable concept: embodied knowledge. They mean the knowledge that is laid down in matter in one way or another: patents, software, expert systems, archives and equipment. Strangely enough, disembodied knowledge is defined as the knowledge carried from ear to ear. Economic research focuses particularly on the factors one can count with: patents, licences, investments in research and process development. Factors that are less concrete do not attract their attention. The same phenomenon may often be found in firms. Things that are hard to quantify or to express in money terms threaten to be neglected in policy. Like economists, firms steer on the basis of numbers. The disembodied (tacit) knowledge is difficult to express in numbers, as a result of which it is often given too little attention in company policy. During harder times, they easily give in to the temptation of reducing expensive knowledge staff. After all, it quickly shows what savings may be made by retrenchments in knowledge staff. It is easy thus to cut down on a firm's core competences, but rebuilding them may take years.

Throughout the last 20 years, most firms have become fairly successful in managing the cost of their stock and the use of capital. The key to that control has been sought for, particularly in terms of processes and flows: the flow of material and that of money.

Control becomes process control. This means that firms first map out how their resource and material flows run, try to recognise the bottlenecks and check to see which shortcuts may be made. Next, the process is regarded as an input/output system [*cf. Nonaka, 1994*] and points of measurement are set up before and after the critical links of the process that help them to adjust policy during the process. Applied to the flow of knowledge, such an approach is increasingly employed by a number of knowledge-intensive firms. They evolve from a production to a knowledge enterprise that is understood here as the process wherein:

- information is acquired in such a way that knowledge is developed;
- knowledge is classified and integrated;
- knowledge is stored;
- knowledge is updated;
- knowledge may be retrieved and transferred;
- knowledge may be applied.

However, we have no clear map of knowledge flows within firms at our disposal. After all, these flows do not constitute a static given. They may best be compared with strongly changing currents and tides in sandy basins off the coasts of Britain and the Dutch and German Wadden Sea. Such flows constantly vary rhythm of time and the limits of space.

Complexity of Knowledge Flows: Time and Space

While pressure on the control of the knowledge enterprise has grown throughout recent years, its complexity has increased correspondingly. Two characteristics of the innovation process play a role here. First, the *spacial dimension* of innovation which, in a figurative sense, becomes visible in the organisational boundaries and distances inside a firm. When a firm innovates, it calls upon a variety of groups. An important part of these groups is based on a certain discipline (chemical engineering, physics, power current), and others are based on functions to be filled inside the firm (purchase, quality control). In firms, these functions and disciplines are also accommodated in different areas. This holds true equally of the organisational units, which operate in different places on the basis of the mere geographical spread of the firm. In the end, innovation is increasingly the result of co-operation between suppliers and clients. Organisational boundaries are concerned not only with the inner boundaries, but with the outer boundaries of the firm as well. Knowledge is not a static given, but 'flows' right through the organisational boundaries. Thus, innovation increasingly requires breaking through these organisational boundaries and reducing organisational distances. Multidisciplinary teams [*Nonaka, 1994*] are the logical answer in many firms. Such teams are under great pressure. They have to develop a common language in order for the different disciplines and functions to be able to communicate effectively within the boundaries of a team.

The second characteristic of the innovation process is concerned with the *dimension of time*. The development of a product or process is an activity consisting of a beginning and an end. It is a temporary activity which requires a temporary kind of organisation. The project team that operates within clear time boundaries is an appropriate type, but it is under a great deal of pressure. Projects follow one another increasingly rapidly and overlap. As a consequence, time boundaries tend to fade away. Additionally, the time dimension becomes manifest in the sequence of operations marked out on the time axis. Previously, innovation was thought of as a purely sequential process. One might compare it with a relay race [*Nonaka and Takeuchi, 1986*], where one races in a fixed direction without sidetracking or returning. In actual practice, innovation cannot be straitjacketed. Processes are iterative rather than sequential in nature. Process phases must overlap. Once in a while it is necessary to go back. Choices made upstream in the innovation trajectory have important consequences for those working downstream, and *vice versa*. Constant feedforward and feedback is needed to implement timely processes that 'function', and to introduce products and services that match market demands. Thus, 'concurrent engineering' is focused upon the development of both product and process within a single (mostly temporary) organisational context. Formal procedures and planning techniques are just a limited solution to this control problem, and sometimes even an obstacle. In the case of team work, groups are made responsible for all matters that are difficult to handle in the regular organisation. All sorts and conditions of people are brought together, given a certain independence, and it is expected that this leads to a motivating environment in which creativity may flourish.

Personnel Management

In the knowledge enterprise, a new perspective for personnel management arises. After all, practically all interventions carried out by personnel management, such as acquisition, selection, career guidance, training and rewarding, can be viewed as interventions in the knowledge flows. In the case of acquisition and selection, not only is new personnel brought in, but new knowledge as well. In the case of transferrals, knowledge and experience are transferred from one sector inside the firm to an other. Career guidance results not only in individual development of personnel, but also provides a path along which knowledge may be integrated and accumulated. Of special interest is the transfer of knowledge across functions. Training programmes not only cram personnel for a function, but also serve to spread new knowledge within the firm. Rewards are an important factor in this respect - they provide an instrument to stimulate the acquisition of knowledge and development of competences.

THE MANAGEMENT OF KNOWLEDGE IN ACTUAL PRACTICE

The management of knowledge is still in its infancy. Nevertheless, there exist numbers of firms which have made important steps forward in this area. They have used the available instruments derived from personnel management to achieve a strategic goal: accelerating and improving knowledge flows right through the inner and outer boundaries of the organisation. The following four cases are illustrative here. Although they are no 'glamour cases', they concern the 'work in progress' of successful firms that have been serious about putting personnel management into active service in the company's development.

Moret, Ernst & Young

Innovation is not likely to be associated with the services sector by outsiders, and this probably holds true even more for the offices of accountants and tax advisers within that sector. However, this image of conservatism has been superseded by reality in many service firms. Throughout recent years, the accountancy sector has been forced to set a new course in a radical manner. First, because offices have internationally operating clients, and must operate on an international level themselves. Secondly, because its clients demand a full range of services: internal control, external auditing, the laying out of the administrative organisation, automation, tax and organisation advice. The role of the accountancy firm has thus become much more varied than it used to be. The application of information technology (IT) is a third factor. IT has made it possible to tap directly the necessary accountancy information from the client's administrative organisation. Finally, accountancy firms are increasingly able to offer new services in numerous areas, for example, advising firms when they invest or settle abroad, establishing environmental care systems, advising about property taxes, and advising about and monitoring mergers and takeovers. As a result, the modern accountancy firm has evolved into a multinational enterprise that continuously converts new experiences into new services, innovates internal processes, and transfers and supplies knowledge to its clients. No wonder then that communication, the management of knowledge, training and education are the basic elements in the business strategy of many large accountancy firms.

Moret, Ernst & Young (MEY) is the biggest Dutch service firm in the area of accountancy, tax advice and 'management consultancy'. MEY is part of Ernst & Young International, and resulted from a merger of a number of Dutch accounting firms. In 1993, about 4,200 people were employed by MEY, while its turnover was approximately 750 million guilders. Seven to eight per cent of turnover is spent on training programmes, in which two streams may be distinguished. The first and the most dominant stream is focused on the regular professional development of its employees. The emphasis in MEY's personnel policy is on personnel development. This dynamic perspective is central to the acquisition of personnel. New employees know that they land in a firm in which they will have to continue studying and be retrained constantly. This process keeps going on until the end of their careers, and applies to all echelons of the organisation. For example, the partners and certified accountants and tax advisers are obliged to spend at least 40 hours per year on their own education.

The second stream that can be discerned in training is concerned with the innovations in the firm's most important products and processes. The size of the firm and its links with E&Y International allow for the use of shared knowledge and the development of common products. MEY therefore pursues a clear innovation policy, which has the following features:

New Ideas Usually Originating from the Market

Like its colleagues in the same line of business, MEY is strongly and regionally organised and maintains long-term contacts with its clients. As a result of this interaction, ideas for new services arise frequently. These mostly start as a problem faced by a client. The initial phase of the development is that such a problem is translated into a rough sketch of a product. Let us take a property tax problem as an example. In discussions between MEY tax advisers and a client, the idea is brought forward of developing a new product which enables the latter to make better policy choices and to control better his or her expenses. Regional advisers then make a rough outline of the product, resulting in what might be referred to as a guide. The product is actually developed after consultation with the central MEY organisation and, locally, with colleagues from other regions. The product then is brought on to the market once it has proved its usefulness in actual practice.

New Ideas that must be Successful within the Firm

The regional offices, and thus those people employed there, are the ones that are eventually charged with the introduction of new services. In that sense, an accounting partnership operates just as a medical partnership: in the end, the doctors are the ones that decide what medication is prescribed. Before MEY invests in the development of a product, it must first be 'sold' internally. Each new product requires intensive communication both in the trajectory in which the specifications are set and in the trajectory in which new expert knowledge must be transferred. MEY has a system of specialist meetings that constantly communicate at different levels of the organisation the new needs for services in the market, proposals for product development, and the implementation of new products and services. In that sense, innovating means continuous communication for MEY.

Innovation in a Decentralised Firm Requiring 'Orchestration'

MEY is a highly decentralised organisation. The development of a new service takes place in close conjunction with clients. One might speak of 'lead users' (*von Hippel, 1986*) here: clients are only interested in the new products to the extent that they are also willing to make extra efforts in test fields. However, the knowledge thus acquired must subsequently be made available to the rest of the firm. This interaction between local practice and general use within the partnerships demands a central 'linking function'. One of the tasks of such a function is to make budgets available to support the local development. More important is the 'drive wheel function', which reinforces local developments. In addition, this process requires a kind of quality control. However, the orchestration of communication between the product developers and the users of the product within MEY is most vital. MEY has chosen to integrate both the development of professional skills and transfer and training in the orchestrating of this central function.

Innovation which Means Training, Training, Training

It is of the utmost importance that new products are made operational as quickly as possible in the regional organisation. This is only possible by directly connecting development with training. The training of MEY employees and clients is directly linked to product development. When a product cannot be transferred effectively, it is not a full-fledged and mature product. The MEY approach shows that innovation of products and services, the acquisition of local practical experience, the transfer of experience, and personnel policy are all part of one single fundamental process in the organisation.

Pink Elephant: People are our Capital

Pink Elephant is part of the RCC group. The company was founded in 1980 in order to support computer operators and system managers. In the very beginning, the company worked with work students of technical universities who wanted to earn some money or had not (yet) completed their studies. At present, the company employs 650 people and among its clients are numerous large multinationals. Years ago, Pink Elephant was a job shopper that filled the gaps that arose in the internal computer services of its clients. It developed as a firm which has set the professional norm for the management and exploitation of computing and information centres in The Netherlands. The firm supplied a broad range of services, varying from the management of computer systems, consultancy, audits, training programmes and interim management to the complete care of automation infrastructures. It increased rapidly over the last five years: In 1988 it had a staff of 385, which rose to 629 in 1993. During that period, its turnover increased from 15.8 million guilders to 48.0 millions guilders.

A Changing Technology in a Changing Market

The growth of Pink Elephant kept pace with the development in which firms focus on hiving off activities that do not belong to their core competences to specialised companies, which are able to carry them out more efficiently and more professionally. These firms have become aware that 80 per cent of automation costs are spent on its management. Through Pink Elephant, they have given a more process-like meaning to management. At the start of the company, this development was still in its infancy. The computing centres operating in this market served particularly as the suppliers of capacity to fill the gaps in the workforce of the continuously operating computing centres. In the first place, they offered their clients flexibility in its ability to stand in unexpected moments. In the second place, they offered efficiency, because they were able to supply the services lower costs compared with in-house management. This opportunistic approach proved to be successful during a period in which the operation of a computing centre was particularly a routine matter. Up until the mid-1980s, it looked as if the technical development of computer systems would only simplify this further. The management of computing centres has become a professional affair which places high demands on the operators, systems managers and their managing staff. This sector can be compared with the processing industry. The systems they work with are extremely complex and costly. Minor mistakes can have serious consequences. Although there is only a slight chance that such faults may occur, if they do, immediate and adequate reaction is required.

System Management as Core Competence

Pink Elephant was the first firm in The Netherlands to recognise these developments: a growing market due to the focus on outsourcing and the necessity of making the system management professional. Soon it was clear that the rapidly growing firm would not be able to survive based on the factors of price and flexibility alone for long. After all, such policies may be copied. This holds true especially of an undisciplined market without norms and standards, where competitors run about as 'cowboys'. In the longer run, the firm would be able to service only when it would set the norm for the development of system management. This means that the firm which started as a supplier of workforce, soon changed into an innovative enterprise, a leader in its own area. This example shows the focus on core competences (*Prahalad and Hamel, 1991*), and the skills that can be used in a creative manner to provide products and services that other firms cannot supply and which are used to *create* new markets.

The market in which Pink Elephant operated lacked a professional norm. There existed no leading and accepted vision of the field. Nor was there a tailor-made building of training programmes. The moment the market offered a new perspective and the technological development demanded that, there was a gap for Pink Elephant to readily leap into. It introduced a method which described all systems management processes in a systematical fashion: ITIL. ITIL stands for the Information Technology Infrastructure Library, developed by CCTA, the body advising the British government in the area of information technology. ITIL has been given further shape by the implementation experiences that Pink Elephant has gained in its contacts with clients. Once again, this is an example of 'lead users' [*von Hippel, 1986*].

Steering by the Development of Knowledge

Pink Elephant's success cannot be attributed only to the way in which it seized the moment. The decisive factor here was the way in which Pink Elephant linked its innovation strategy with an integral vision of the management of the knowledge flow. The instruments of personnel management played an important role here. From the outset, Pink Elephant had recognised that the management of the 'Human Resources' provided the basis for its company policy. This was reflected by the firm's mission which was formulated in 1989: Pink Elephant's ambition was 'to become the quality market leader in the full management and exploitation of IT on location', and 'the best firm to work for'. Looking at the development of Pink Elephant, it seems that this mission was not an empty slogan. ninety per cent of the activities was performed at the premises of the clients, which meant that the firm had constantly to invest in maintaining a good relationship with them. Additionally, Pink Elephant had chosen to train its own staff. Approximately ten per cent of the gross income was spent on the development and maintenance of the knowledge organisation.

Good vocational training. The philosophy of Pink Elephant is not to keep the experience gained for themselves, but to set a standard in the area. In other words: a market was created to transfer their knowledge as effectively as possible. In order to make a trade of systems management, Pink Elephant, in conjunction with the Rijkshogeschool IJsselland (a type of college), set up a HEAO training programme with courses focused specifically on systems management (HEAO/BI/Management of Automation Means). Together with Pink Elephant, this Hogeschool established a training programme for systems management, and the programme's application-oriented component is taken care of by Pink Elephant staff. The training programme is also used for the professionalisation of the firm's own (young) workforce. As mentioned previously, Pink Elephant invests large amounts of money in its staff's training: ten per cent of its gross income. A large part of the training programmes developed in-house is sold off again by bringing them into the market.

The link between development and training. Once the firm introduces a new service into the market, the firm's own staff must be able, of course, to carry out that service. Fast and sound transfer of experience from the development stage to normal business management is therefore of the utmost importance. This has led the firm to accommodate the development and training functions in a single organisational unit: the Education & Development subsidiary. This has led to two types of results. First, transfer is taken into account the moment new services and processes are given shape. In addition, new routines and instruments could thus be transferred rapidly within the firm.

To this end, Education & Development also designed simulators which allow for a quite natural simulation of practical problems by means of large mainframes. Education & Development is able to fulfil this function because it plays a central role in 'orchestrating' the numerous development work-groups and subgroups, including about 100 staff members.

The 'pilot' system. Pink Elephant developed its own, clear standard for its services, which was to be filled by relevant staff. This was the reason for Pink Elephant to plot clear career development paths for individual staff members. A pilot from the personnel department was appointed to each employee. Twice a year, career interviews are held with this pilot on the basis of a so-called skills map. This map keeps track of the knowledge and skills each employee possessed and of ones he is expected to develop. The latter is partly a matter of training. More importantly, on the basis of the skills map, a desired experience path is plotted which serves as the basis for the participation of employees in projects. This meant that the allocation of staff to projects is used as an important steering device in order to stimulate employees' personal development and thus to anchor the firm's core com-petences in the human resources.

In late 1993, a start was made with a career development plan that provided a link between the services to be offered on the one hand, and the capacities of staff, their career opportunities and guidance instruments on the other. This plan gave clarity to the employees, their pilots and to the organisation as a whole.

Raychem: Managing Personal Growth

The chemical sector was capital-intensive. When wandering through the extensive company property between a labyrinth of pipes, one encountered personnel only occasionally. Nevertheless, the chemical industry was of strategic importance for the economy and employment. First, it offers a link in the network of suppliers and clients. Second, it is a knowledge-intensive sector. This knowledge intensity concerns each link in the chemical firm: from research and product development in the lab, engineering and the design of production processes, to maintenance, production and the market-ing and sales departments. In each link of activity, the skills, knowledge and experience must be constantly adapted to the state of technology and the wishes of clients.

This certainly holds true of market leaders, who want to increase the distance from their pursuers because of their headstart in knowledge. Raychem is such a knowledge-intensive forerunner. One of the areas in which Raychem is market leader is in heat-shrinking protective materials. These materials are used in all kinds of varieties in telecommunication, pipe systems and construction. The core of Raychem technology consists of netted and conducting polymers, materials with shape memory, ceramics, adhesives, thin films, liquid crystals, optical glass fibres and electrochemicals. In other words, the firm is concerned with an intelligent combination of chemical and physical disciplines, with material sciences at its centre. The company philosophy is focused on keeping the firm in motion, or as the former CEO van Raychem Paul Cook put it [*Taylor, 1990: 104*]: '*For an organization to remain innovative it has to be willing - even eager - to obsolete itself as fast as it can*'.

Raychem has a large establishment in Belgium (Kessel-loo), which is responsible for its own R&D, manufacturing and marketing. The establishment has 1,050 employees, including 250 academics. Like most other chemical firms, Raychem has passed through a difficult period in the market. This was related particularly to the dip in the defence industry and the construction sector. However, the firm has managed to recover from this recent economic slump and is once again the leading firm in its line of business. In 1993, the turnover in the Belgian branch was 10.3 billion Belgian francs, while its profit before taxes amounted to 1.2 billion francs.

Core Competences

Raychem's core competence lies especially in combining new technological and scientific knowlege from various disciplines. This has two major consequences for the management of Raychem's knowledge flows. First, knowledge must constantly be innovated, and the knowledge of its personnel must be updated. Second, the crossroads problems in the knowledge flows must be kept manageable. The discipline or function-oriented supply of knowledge constitutes the vertical axis of the organisation. Along this axis, the state-of-the-art technological and scientific knowledge is transported and diffused. In the traditional organisation, this vertical flow has priority. Raychem, however, gives priority to the knowledge flow along a horizontal axis, where concrete products and processes are developed and connected.

The horizontal axis is directly linked to the market, and the pressure is highest here. Disciplines and functions co-operate in close conjunction in multidisciplinary teams. Giving priority to the horizontal rather than the vertical product stream also involves a risk; due to the dominance of the project and the product, one loses contact with innovations in specific areas. Raychem's strength is in the management of this crossroads of knowledge. For the organisation and personnel management, this mean that the link between functions (disciplines) and projects (products) must be constantly safeguarded. Personnel management offers some vital instruments to achieve this:

HRM must create a learning climate: Personnel management at Raychem certainly has an operational task, and Raychem does not differ from other firms in this respect. However, the personnel management fulfils yet another stimulating role: Raychem wishes to create a learning climate in which people continue to develop. This also involves a working environment in which knowledge and experience is shared with others, and this can be achieved only by an effective transfer of knowledge and experience within, and particularly between, teams and departments.

Acquisition of 'moving' employees: Raychem's vision can be clearly recognised in its acquisition policy. What Raychem wants is not only technicians and scientists who are good at what they do. In interviews, it is made clear to the candidates that their future added value for the firm lies in their ability to translate their knowledge into applications in other areas. This implies that they will not work at one single function for a long period of time, and that there is no fixed discipline-oriented home base within the firm.

Managing personal growth: Raychem's personnel policy follows a dynamic perspective. At the individual level, this manifests itself in career coaching. Two starting points are selected here: first, the need for knowledge originating from business development, which serves as input for acquisition and personnel development. Not only are the firm's current core competences concerned here, but also its future core competences. The current and desired development of knowledge and skills of the individual are the second starting point. Interviews are conducted with each employee about this several times a year. This confrontation of the knowledge needs of both the firm and the employee results in a so-called analysis of gaps.

The gap analysis allows for an indication of current and future shortcomings in functions, jobs and skills. The resulting image is the basis for plans at the level of the firm, the department, the team and the individual, pertaining to acquisition, training, career development and rewards. Raychem's goal is to make these plans 'hard' in terms of responsibilities, objectives and expected performance. Interviews are conducted with the employees several times a year to adjust objectives, set norms, follow progress and establish concrete criteria. The latter are concerned to a large extent with the ways in which the knowledge and experience of employees may be broadened and deepened. These can be achieved through:

- an appropriate training programme;
- working under the guidance of a mentor during a fixed period;
- outlining an experience path (projects in which one can subsequently gain experience);
- secondments of developers to the corporate R&D lab;

- traineeships in other departments;
- individual studies monitored by an internal coach;
- visiting other companies, fairs, field trials, benchmarkting activities;
- break-out meetings of functional specialists throughout the organisation world-wide;
- cross-divisional and cross-site project groups;
- studying cross-divisional and cross-site state-of-the-art approaches.

It is important that the development of knowledge is also confirmed in the rewarding of employees. For this purpose, elements of 'skill-based pay' have been included in the reward system.

Figure 11.1.: Competence Development

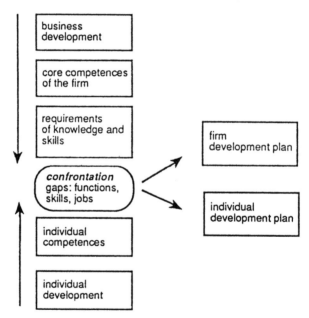

Cross-border flows: Rather than functions or disciplines, the flow of knowledge from development to application is central to Raychem's policy. In recent years, the firm has undergone a radical change in the development organisation. Its R&D organisation is now separated from the dominance of the functional knowledge domains. Knowledge flow in the client's direction has priority.

Multidisciplinary teams are operating in new product development. The marketing, production and engineering departments are involved in the organisation of a project from the very beginning, both to bring in their know-how and to be able to anticipate new developments. In other words, they draw on the knowledge from a 'later' stage of the development process 'sooner'. This reversal cannot be introduced as a formal structural change. In particular the behavioural and communication patterns need to be shifted. Such a change in culture demands a clear formulation and confirmation of norms and values. This works better in one department than it does in another. A relapse into the old patterns must be constantly guarded against.

Océ-van der Grinten N.V.

Océ-van der Grinten N.V. supplies products and services for the reproduction and representation of information on paper. Its product range consists of copying, printing and plotter systems, including the necessary materials, for both the Office Systems and Engineering Systems markets. Founded in 1877, the development of products and procedures has always been one of the firm's major strengths. Since the 1950s, more attention has been given to production and sales, and the company has grown significantly, through the establishment of subsidiaries and the acquisition of other companies. Océ-van der Grinten is the Dutch parent company of the Océ Group, which is active in about 80 countries. Most of its products are developed and produced by Océ itself. Direct contact with clients is considered as being of the utmost importance by Océ. Sales and Services are therefore dealt with by their own companies. In this way, Océ assures the necessary knowledge about the market. Its aim is to deliver products and services which are recognised for their high quality, reliability, productivity, durability, user friendliness and environmental friendliness. With respect to the Office Systems market, Océ focuses mainly on the high-volume segment (more than 10,000 copies a month) and in Europe, Océ has a market share of more than ten per cent. On the Engineering Systems market, Océ has a market share of about 30 per cent in Europe and 20 per cent worldwide and is market leader. Its overall annual turnover is around 2,6 billion guilders. Around seven per cent of the annual turnover is invested in research and development. Worldwide, Océ employs around 11,000 people, some 4,000 of whom work in The Netherlands. Around ten per cent (1,100 people) of its total workforce is active in research and development, practically all of them in Venlo, The Netherlands.

Océ is a relatively small company when compared to its competitors, such as Xerox, Kodak and Canon. Due to the trends towards digital and colour applications, both the Office and Engineering markets are rapidly and constantly changing. In order to sustain its position as a relatively small company, Océ makes strategic choices, pertaining particularly to the out-sourcing of around 95 per cent of the production of parts. A number of strategically crucial parts, such as toners, are produced by Océ itself. In addition, Océ's activities are aimed mainly at the medium and high-volume segments. Systems for the low-volume segment are produced according to Océ specifications by suppliers.

The relatively small size of Océ has also consequences for research and development activities. It is not able to deal with all the new developments itself, but has to make strategic choices with respect to research and development projects. Project selection is therefore one of the crucial points in the R&D of Océ. Besides, it is becoming increasingly important for Océ, being a relatively small player in this market, that development projects are successful from the outset. This requires close co-operation between R&D and the various business units responsible for Marketing and Sales.

R&D: Changing Organisation in a Changing Market: Until 1992, Océ had structured the R&D activities in a matrix organisation. One side of the matrix consisted of projects being executed and the other line of functional departments, grouped according to the phases in the R&D process (Research, Development and Engineering). Employees from the Development and Engineering departments used to work under the supervision of a project leader 65 per cent, and later 75 per cent, of their time in projects. The remaining time was devoted to the development and acquisition of new knowledge by working on defined subjects, supervised by the head of the functional department. Within the Research Department, people worked mainly individually on defined subjects.

With the growing necessity to develop and innovate more efficiently, effectively and more quickly, the R&D organisation was reorganised in 1992 and connected more closely to the Marketing, Sales and Service Business Units. At present, there are three product-oriented business unit R&D teams within R&D (BU teams). These BU teams are headed by Business Development Managers (BDM), which are at the same time deputy directors within the Business Units. Each BU team has a similar matrix organisation, with projects on one side of the matrix and departments on the other. The departments are Development, Mechanical Engineering, Electronical Systems and Engineering Processes. They function as capacity groups: all employees belong to a department and are allocated to one project at a time within their BU team. Thus, each BU team consists of more or less the same departments. The transfer of knowledge between departments and the prevention of double activities become important issues (see below).

In addition to the three BU teams, two other teams were formed: first, the Group Research & Technology team (GRT), which is aimed at more fundamental research, acts as a buffer between the application-oriented BU teams and the generally available knowledge, and second, the R&D Resources team (RDR), which executes all R&D-supporting activities.

Internal Acquisition, Exchange and Transfer of Knowledge

As mentioned previously, because of the overlap in functional departments within the R&D organisation, the acquisition, exchange and transfer of knowledge has to be properly co-ordinated, in order to prevent knowledge gaps arising or double activities being carried out. To this end, Océ uses a complex system of secondary structures. For instance, the so-called 'cross-linkages' are disciplinary-oriented groups of department heads from all the BU team, which discusses the development of the field (for example, mechanical engineering), external recruitment and the internal labour market. Further, there is a large number of working groups which focus on specific technologies (for example, toner group), and which all employees participate who work with this technology in their project participate in.

Department heads as 'people and knowledge managers': Departments within the BU team are actually empty departments. All personnel work constantly in projects and are also located physically near the project leader and the other members of the project team. The most important tasks of the department head centres around the management of knowledge and, thus, the management of people. With respect to the management of knowledge, the department head must assure a proper balance between long and short-term development and research. Also, he is responsible for the sufficient supply of new ideas for projects and for making sure that the department functions as a platform for the exchange of technical knowledge.

Of course, these activities concerning the management of knowledge coincide directly with the management of people. Formally, department heads have the following tasks with respect to the management of people: the allocation of employees to projects; the long-term development of employees and the long-term development of knowledge. The allocation of employees to projects also implies the function of sustaining the development of people, even though department heads vary in the extent to which they give attention to this long-term aspect of project allocation. With the increasing emphasis on short-term results of project work, project leaders become much more demanding with respect to the quality of team members. Consequently, there is the risk that some staff members may not be accepted in some projects. Department heads, together with the coaches within the projects, give increasing attention to the supervision and coaching of individual employees.

Using 'Classical' Personnel Management Instruments by Department Heads

In addition to the above-mentioned tasks, department heads in fact act as personnel managers, using well-known personnel management instruments. With respect to recruitment and selection, it is important that Océ selects people not only on the basis of their technical skills. At least as important are characteristics such as professional attitudes, affinity with application, teamwork, independence, flexibility and quality consciousness. Additionally, department heads have annual performance appraisal interviews, as well as so-called 'manager-employee interviews'. The last type of interview is future-oriented and has an explicit two-way nature between head and employee. Both these interviews are used as input for personnel planning and personnel development activities. With respect to the latter, a Human Resources Review has recently been introduced. Department heads must draw up a department resources plan, a career development review and a management development review on an annual basis. In this way, explicit attention to the progress of departmental and individual development is fostered. Considering all these tasks, it is remarkable that the personnel department operates mainly in a supportive, information-gathering and information-supplying manner.

Tension Between Short-Term 'Profits' and Long-Term Development

Océ used to have what might be called a 'sandwich strategy' for the development of competences. Project members used to be involved in direct project-related work 65 per cent, later 75 per cent, of their time. This more or less guaranteed the development and acquisition of long-term oriented knowledge and skills. With the necessity to devote more attention to short-term results, this percentage has now been increased to 90 per cent. This leaves employees with only ten per cent of their time in which they may be able to update their skills and competencies or develop new ones. However, even this ten per cent is under high pressure; in many cases it is simply impossible to achieve other things than strictly project work. Also between consecutive projects, there remains little time for employees to recover from the strains and stresses of project work and to refuel their energy and competence tanks. Consequently, the risk arises that there will be insufficient time and opportunities to supervise employees who are performing less well, let alone pay attention to the long-term development of employees and knowledge. Océ is well aware of these risks, and is in the process of developing a system by which the allocation of people will contribute both to short-term results as well as long-term development and innovation.

STRATEGIC PERSONNEL MANAGEMENT

Personnel management has long been considered and practised as a control function. The implementation of personnel management was part of a separate staff function, whose task was to assure that questions asked within the firm were adequately answered: filling vacancies, refresher courses and retraining, transferrals, training and education, and rewarding. The increased knowledge intensity of firms, however, requires more than an operational use of personnel management. After all, the firm's employees are the most important developers, carriers and users of knowledge. The challenge for personnel management is to reinforce the knowledge enterprise within the firm and the exchange of knowledge with the environment. The four examples in this study show what patterns have been developed by firms that take HRM seriously. Remarkably, these patterns are based upon the well-known instruments of personnel management. They are not new, but the way in which they are used is new: to support the business development. Four fundamental elements can be distinguished within these patterns:

(1) Knowledge management is related to the business development

   Most firms are becoming aware that knowledge management should be focused on core competences. These can be described as the knowledge and skills reflected in the firm's core technology which are at the base of the firm's competitive advantage in the market. When formulating and implementing personnel management, one continuously asks oneself the following question: what is the added value of policy and decisions regarding the reinforcement of core competences? The firms that have been reviewed in this chapter are not directed only towards their current core competences, they also try to translate the core competences that they consider to be desirable in the future. Further, they start from a clear strategic mission that is endorsed by top management and is constantly transferred.

(2) Knowledge management starts with acquisition and selection

   Acquisition and selection are an essential link in knowledge management in each of the four firms; firms are interested not only in filling vacancies and hiring professional people. The future is already involved at the time of selection. The knowledge and skills one has to become familiar with is at least as important as today's givens: the characteristics of the current functions and the candidate's current capacities.

(3) Personnel development is a responsibility of management

   Each of the four firms uses a method for the monitoring of personnel development; personnel development is steered. This means that interviews are conducted with employees on a frequent basis, in which the development of the individual is compared with the company's development. When calling upon personnel in new projects, not only is their available knowledge and experience taken into account, but also the knowledge and experience they still have to acquire. This process is formalised in order for it to be planned, followed and adjusted. Personnel management provides the instruments, but the responsibility lies with the line management. The importance of personnel management increases when links have to be made surpassing the boundaries of knowledge areas. Additionally, personnel management is clearly related to 'personnel maintenance': in other words, the knowledge and skills of employees should not be worn out by their intensive participation in projects. Instruments that are suitable for this are: traineeships, participation in professional development projects, training programmes and sabbaticals, and temporary secondments to corporate development centres.

(4) The link between development and training programmes

Particularly in the service companies mentioned in this chapter, a direct link is made between development and training functions. This has two advantages: first, it allows for a quick introduction into the market of a new product or service. After all, the knowledge developed in the firm must be transferred to the client. The firm's employees are the vital vehicle in this respect. Second, a direct contribution is made thus to personnel development. Employees are directly and continuously fed with new knowledge gained inside the own firm. This trend will become increasingly relevant to industrial firms in future years because they tend to develop more and more from producers to suppliers of services.

Knowledge management will develop into a real professional area in the years to come. The need for that already exists in actual practice. The tools of this area (discipline) can be found to a large extent in personnel management. This chapter has shown that a number of firms have managed to make use of these instruments in a strategic manner. However, these instruments are not the primary issue here. What is much more important is the partnership that has originated in the above-mentioned firms between the line organisation and the personnel function: the joint responsibility for the development and use of people from a strategic perspective.

REFERENCES

Allen, T.J., 1977, *Managing the Flow of Technology*, Cambridge: Massachusetts MIT.

Assen, A. van, 1990, *Technologie en Personeelbeleid: De Draad van Ariadne in het Technische Labyrint*, inaugural speech. Nijmegen: University of Nijmegen.

Cobbenhagen, J., J.F. den Hertog and J.H. Pennings, 1994, *Succesvol veranderen: Kerncompetenties in bedrijfsvernieuwing*, Deventer: Kluwer.

Cooper, R.G., 1994, 'Third Generation New Product Processes', *The Journal of Product Innovation Management*, Vol.11, No.1, pp.3-15.

Diepen, B. van, 1994, *Engineers, Project-to-Project Routes and R&D Effectiveness: Effects of Different Career Paths*. Maastricht: MERIT.

Florida, R. and M. Kenney, 1990, *The Breakthrough Illusion: Corporate America's Failure to Move from Innovation to Mass Production*, New York: Basic Books.

Hertog, J.F. den, E. van Sluijs, A. van Assen and B. van Diepen, 1991, 'Innovatie en Personeelsbeleid: De Beheersing van de Kennishuishouding', *Bedrijfskunde*, Vol.17, No.2, pp.103-27.

Hippel, E. von, 1986, 'Lead Users: A Source of Novel Product Concepts', *Management Science*, Vol.32, No.7 (July).

Nonaka, I., 1994, 'A Dynamic Theory of Organizational Knowledge Creations', *Organization Science*, Vol.5, No.1, pp.14-38.

Prahalad, C.K., and G. Hamel, 1990, 'The Core Competences of the Corporation', *Harvard Business Review*, Vol.68, No.3, pp.79-91.

Rothwell, R., 1992, 'Successful Industrial Innovation: Critical Factors for the 1990s', *R&D Management*, Vol.22, No.3, pp.221-39.

Sluijs, E. van, A. van Assen and J.F. den Hertog, 1991, 'Personnel Management and Organisational Change: A Sociotechnical Perspective', *European Work and Organizational Psychologist*, Vol.1, No.1, pp.27-51.

Sluijs, E. van and J.F. den Hertog, 1993, *Praktijkverkenning Personeelwetenschappen*, Tilburg: University of Brabant.

Takeuchi, H. & I. Nonaka, 1986, 'The New New Product Development Game', *Harvard Business Review*, Vol.64, No.1, pp.37-46.

Ven, A.H. van de, 1986, 'Central Problems in the Management of Innovation', *Management Science*, Vol.32, No.5, pp.590-607.

12

ENTREPRENEURSHIP ON THE SHOPFLOOR: NATIONALE NEDERLANDEN

J. Friso den Hertog[*]

Nationale Nederlanden (NN) is an insurance company with a well-established name in its home market. Management and workers are proud to be working for a market leader in The Netherlands. They are proud of their knowledge and experience of the sound revenues of the firm and, not in the least, of the splendid new building NN moved into in the summer of 1994. However, this removal from NN's old into its new home marked more than a spatial change. The removal date also coincided with what NN's management described as a 'rotation' of its organisation. After an intensive, three-year preparation, NN implemented a basic redesign of the organisation of its general (property/casualty) insurance company.

(Hans Richaers, managing director of NN general company division): *'We are absolutely not forced with our backs to the wall. We still had an excellent return on our insurance portfolio and a good market position. It's just that we are looking at our markets and our customers with new eyes.'*

This study goes into the question of why and how a strong, profitable and well-respected firm in the services sector managed to put so much energy into the innovation of its organisation from top to bottom. NN's general insurance company changed from a product to a market-oriented firm with a flat hierarchical structure. Self-managing teams with an optimal attainability were regarded in this set-up as an effective vehicle for close co-operation with NN's intermediaries. NN's management laid down the broad lines within which the actual redesign was to take place, leaving much room for its employees to shape the new organisation. The key to answering the

* We are very grateful to the management of the general insurance company of Nationale Nederlanden and to the consultants of KOERS Consultancy Group for their active participation in this study.

leading questions in this study is to be found in the change in the commercial and social environment in which competitive advantage had to be retained and improved. This study focuses on the changes in NN's environment, the implemented organisational changes, the change strategy followed and the early lessons to be learned. It is based on intensive interviews with NN's management, theconsultants involved and on the project documentation.

FROM A COMPLACENT TO A TURBULENT MARKET

Markets are changing, even those known to be stable, prosperous and complacent fields of business such as the insurance market. During the last five years, the insurance market has been essentially transformed into a turbulent market where firms have to fight to survive. A well-established name that inspires confidence and sound investment strategies is no longer sufficient to retain and gain competitive advantage. As in many other fields of our Western economies, the suppliers market has been changed to a demand market. The direct effect of this shift is that insurance firms are being challenged to reduce their costs while offering better services to intermediaries and end-customers at the same time. Other developments faced by these firms originate from changes in the social environment in which they operate. In The Netherlands, as in many others Western countries, there is a strong societal necessity to reduce the costs of health care. This has created a new market in which buyers (the insurers) and suppliers of health services have to create new conditions to ensure that the customers (the insured, the patients) receive the best value for their money. The pressure on the social security system is yet another main trend that insurance firms must anticipate. The firms have to deal not only with the continuous stream of changes in the system, but also with new target groups in the market which have to be approached in the most effective way. Finally, both insurers and the insured are confronted increasingly with the effects of diminishing social control in our society. As a result, both groups are faced with a rise in damage claims. The increased instances of car theft, burglary and so on, place strong pressures on the margins of general insurance.

To date, insurance firms have increased their efforts to fight for the favour of independent intermediaries. Firms working with intermediaries are faced with strong competition from the direct writers over market share. The former are confronted with the necessity of reducing costs and increasing their flexibility, while the latter are becoming aware of the need to offer better service to their customers.

This market change has also urged insurance firms to look more intensively for new markets, whether it be a market abroad or new market sectors or niche markets at home. During the last ten years, most firms have followed two main strategies in this effort. The first was directed at economies of scale. This resulted in a long list of mergers and take-overs. This concentration of activities was regarded by most firms as a necessary and self-evident step. However, it also confronted most firms with new problems. The merger of firms with strong but traditional cultures was far more difficult than expected in most instances. Not only did new, more open and 'hands-on' cultures have to be built, but the old deep-rooted patterns had to be broken down as well. For many firms, the integration of various computer systems after merger caused even further worries, not only for insurance firms, but also for their intermediaries and end-customers.

The introduction of information technologies (IT) has been the second main strategy. In the late 1970s, it was generally expected that the services sector, especially the financial services, would benefit from the new IT. While the introduction of IT is now regarded as inescapable, huge investments have often failed to lead to the desired results. This is well illustrated by a study from the Massachusetts Institute for Technology [*Roache, 1986*]. The researchers in this study point out that during the 1970s and 1980s the steep rise of IT investments in the services sector was accompanied by a decline in labour productivity. Stephen Roache, the principal investigator of this study, envisaged a drastic change, particularly in the financial services. He predicted a transformation process similar to the one the industry had undergone in the 1980s, a transformation characterised by a higher quality of services, the breakdown of heavy corporate structures, higher flexibility, a sharp reduction of costs, and more effective use of IT. In other words, he sketched out - four years before the publication of another well-known MIT study [*Womack et al., 1990*] on the position of the automotive industry - the profile of 'lean production' for the services sector.

THE FIRM

NN is The Netherlands' largest insurance firm, employing 4,000 people with an annual turnover of eight billion guilders. In 1993 NN merged with Post-bank/NMB to form the International Netherlands Group (ING), the second largest financial service firm in The Netherlands. NN consists of two main divisions: life insurance and general insurance. The firms works with a network of 9,600 independent intermediaries. These intermediaries are regarded as NN's primary market. NN is competing with the other insuring firms in the Dutch market for their favours. The intermediaries differ stongly in turnover. The 20/80 rule can well be applied here. About 20 per cent of the intermediaries bring in 80 per cent of the turnover. Throughout recent years, NN has realised a substantial international expansion. To date, the firm has substantial interests in countries such as Belgium, Spain, Italy,

Greece in Europe, as well as the USA, Canada, Australia, Indonesia, Japan and Hong Kong. The general insurance company of NN employs (1994) about 1,950 people. The division has a yearly turnover of about 1.8 billion guilders. The design of the organisation followed primarily the main product differentiation (Figure 12.1).

Figure 12.1.: The Old Organisation

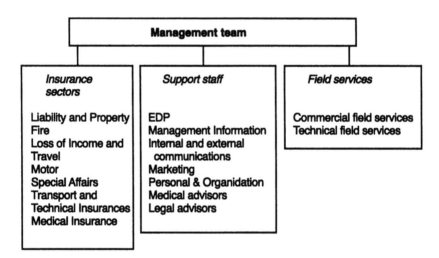

The technical know-how of the firm was concentrated in these product sectors, or product groups. These were responsible for the operation (acceptance of risk and the assessment of damages) and for the product policies. However, the products groups were strongly dependent of two other main groups, situated at the divisional level: the marketing department with its extensive field service and the actuarial department, responsible for 'translating' risks into premiums.

Division management installed a task force in 1990, which was charged with the task of finding out: 'whether and how the organisational structures and work processes had to be adjusted in order to safeguard continuity and normative return, seen in the perspective of market changes and other important developments in the environment of the firm'. Rather than the profit level, the reason for this study was the threat of the division's market share, particularly from the side of direct writers. The report of the group became available in 1991, and underlined that fundamental changes were needed in order to retain the firms strong position. The firm had to be transformed into a more flexible and market-oriented organisation. It had to know its customers better and improve the service quality.

Division management took the report seriously. Management was aware that major changes in the structure and culture of the firm were needed. However, it was also recognised that these changes would only become effective when managers and employees at all levels would support the direction of change. This change should not only focus on formal internal and external boundaries, but also on behavioural patterns of managers and employees, as well as improvement of co-operation with the intermediaries. This implied that the redesign of the division should be carefully prepared, making use of the knowledge and experience of the NN staff. This required a participative approach to the redesign process. Division management made use of the assistance of a consulting group which is specialised in organisation redesign and, particularly on the implementation of redesign (KOERS Consulting Group). A steering group was set up to guide the process.

THE CHANGE PROCESS

The steering group decided to follow the five-phase approach proposed by the consultants (Figure 12.2). The approach can be characterised in three ways. First, it has a strong architectural or design element, which means that certain design rules, principles and procedures are followed to guide the process. Second, to a large extent the approach is to be considered as a form of participative design or 'self-design'. The organisation redesigns itself and does so by an active involvement of its employees and managers. The integral view on the organisation is a third characteristic. The interrelationships between function are viewed as being crucial in this respect [*cf. Roberts, 1993, de Sitter, 1994, Dankbaar and Den Hertog, 1991*].

The first phase is referred to as the strategic orientation round (SOR). Division management, product group managers, and department heads were brought together in nine work conferences. The articipants were given the task to make an ('SWOT') analysis of the firm's strengths and weaknesses and of its opportunities and threats. During this process it was also decided to organise two conferences for the intermediaries. The argument was that the implementation of a market orientation is only feasible on the basis of open dialogue with the customers. The objective of this SOR was to list the functional requirements for the organisation's redesign. However, the work conferences served other aims, that is, they also were an important exercise in communication. The served to start dialogues across the hierarchical and functional boundaries of the firm. The main result was in fact a shared perception of the position of the firm and a shared awareness of the need for a fundamental change.

Figure 12.2.: The Change Process

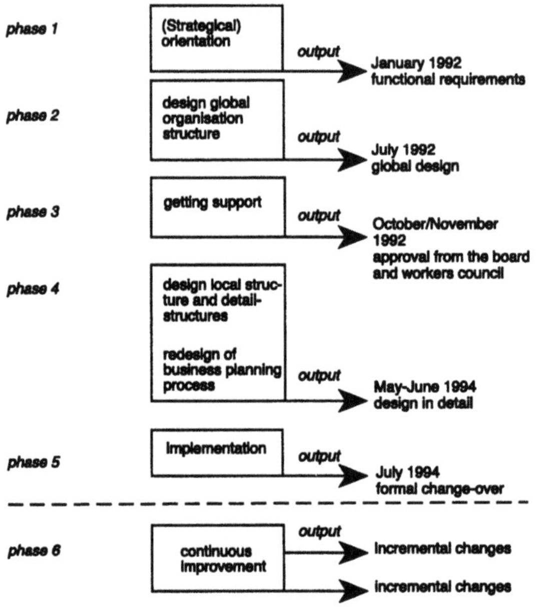

phase 1	(Strategical) orientation	output → January 1992 functional requirements
phase 2	design global organisation structure	output → July 1992 global design
phase 3	getting support	output → October/November 1992 approval from the board and workers council
phase 4	design local structure and detail-structures / redesign of business planning process	output → May-June 1994 design in detail
phase 5	implementation	output → July 1994 formal change-over
phase 6	continuous improvement	output → incremental changes / incremental changes

Parallel to the SOR, in-depth analyses were made of the primary process in each insurance sector. These analyses were carried out by group leaders and operational staff, coached by the consultants, and strongly focused on the interrelations within and between product sectors and, between the product sectors and the functional groups in the division. The findings of both studies were reported during a evaluation conference in which division management and the product group managers participated. During this conference it was decided that a design group be formed consisting of managers from different levels: the division, the product group, and field services. This group was given eight weeks to present the global design (phase 2) of the division. This design had to provide a picture of the new organisation from the division level to the levels of the unit and the work team. The more detailed design of tasks on group and individual level was to be made at a later stage.

From the beginning of the design process, it was considered essential to obtain support from the most important stakeholders involved: the board of NN, the works council, the intermediaries and the employees of the division. The third phase was introduced to communicate the findings of the analyses and discuss the ideas that were at the basis of the global design. Throughout the process, the objective was to involve NN's employees very actively in the analysis and design work. This was not only meant to get their support, but also to make use of their knowledge and experience. A broader direct

202

involvement of the operational staff became especially relevant during the phase in which the design of the work teams had to be filled in (phase 4). This is the level where the direct consequences of the redesign for the work of most employees becomes visible. The redesign did not stop with the formal implementation in July 1994. Much had yet to be done at the unit level. In fact, the new design (phase 5) is meant to create the conditions for continuous improvements. The units and the work teams are given the room to develop their own initiatives in this respect.

THE ROTATION OF THE ORGANISATION

The first important structural choice was a change-over from a product towards a market and region-oriented organisation. The general insurance companya division was divided into a personal and a business division (Figure 12.3). The divisions are organised into regional units. The regional unit is the 'fighting unit' of the firm in the new concept. It is the level where the firm's main functions with a shared business responsibility are brought together. The manager of the regional unit is expected to make his own business plan and is held responsible for his unit's market performance. With this rotation, the product specialists of the former product groups are allocated to the regional units. Furthermore, the inspectors of the commercial field service are also divided over the regional units. In this sense, the regional unit is a complete, flexible and transparent insurance firm within the context of a large firm. The district managers (who do not have their own staff) are particularly important during the transition period in which the new regional units have to grow into their new role.

TEAMWORK

A market-oriented organisation is not realised alone by the change-over from a product into a market or region-oriented formal structure. Patterns of behaviour must change at the actual interface between the firm and its customers, that is at the work level where acceptance of risks and the assessment of damages claims take place. That is also the level where the objectives are to be fulfilled: better, faster and more effective service to NN's customers, the intermediaries. At this interface, an effective 'business-to-business' relationship was to be established. This objective is reflected in the internal design of the regional units (Figure 12.3). The regional units of the 'private customers' division now consists of four groups. The inspectors, dealing with the commercial contacts with the intermediaries, are reporting directly to the unit manager. The integration of the commercial function in the unit offers the possibility for the unit manager to formulate and realise his or her own business plan. The direct inputs from the market are essential in this respect to bring entrepreneurship close to the shop floor.

Figure 12.3: The New Organisation

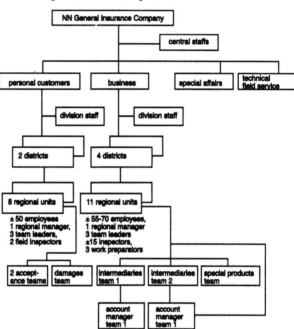

Two groups are held responsible for the acceptance of risks and one for the assessment of claims. The reasoning here is that at this stage it is far easier to integrate product domains both in the acceptance and assessment than to integrate acceptance and assessment. Procedures, systems and practical experiences can be more easily transferred in this way. At a later stage, the latter integration might be a feasible option. However, of importance was that team members should first acquire sufficient knowledge and experience to make this step.

Furthermore, it was essential in the new set-up that the inspectors work closely together with the operational staff of both the acceptance and assessment teams. For the first time, members of these groups were systematically confronted with the real requirements of the market: the needs, problems, suggestions and considerations of the intermediaries. The feedback between the commercial and operational functions became short. The teams became part of a single business. This change offered a new perspective on a process of continuous improvement for the benefit of both the intermediaries and the firm.

The design of the regional units in the business insurance division took a different direction. In this sector the acceptance and assessment are strongly interlinked. Far more knowledge about the context of the end-customer (the firm) is required to do the job effectively. Experience with handling the damage claims is very useful in acceptance, and *vice versa*. The units in this division are composed of two teams serving a fixed group of intermediaries. The inspectors are also linked to these groups.

Design groups were aware that know-how over the full product range could not be incorporated in each team. They can adequately deal with the mainstream. To remedy this problem certain teams were appointed as 'focal points' for the more specialised products. The other teams could call in their assistance when they were faced with questions on these fields.

INFORMATION TECHNOLOGY

The insurance business is information-intensive and must rely on a sound information structure. The developments in this domain have been far-reaching in the last decade. However, it has also introduced new problems. Firms are being confronted with the necessity of investing heavily in the maintenance of the existing infrastructure. Additionally, integration of systems becomes increasingly important once the firm has decided to integrate its main work flows. At the same time, management is becoming aware that the effectiveness of information systems is not only to be measured in terms of internal efficiency, but rather in terms of the quality and speed of its service for the customer. This change in perspective can be well recognised in NN's redesign process. NN tried to find the right mix of sound long-term policies and effective short-term measures. For instance, a number of direct measures were needed for supporting the implementation of the new organisation. The old product groups worked with different systems having different user-interfaces. However, it was not realistic to expect that the team members in the new organisation would be able to work with five or six different procedures. In order to temporarily remedy this problem a new shell had been developed under which the different systems could operate. Another measure is the introduction of 'helpdesks' in the regional units for solving urgent operational problems and for supporting the introduction of new packages. NN also invested in the development of knowledge systems which enabled the intermediaries to take care of a substantial part of the acceptance of risks and the assessment of damage claims.

At the same time, long-term policies have been critically discussed. To date, NN's IT policies were based on the following objectives:

- a more effective maintenance, streamlining, integration and monitoring of the firms' 'central' information infrastructure;

- a sharper focus on the development of systems which are crucial for the continuity of the business;
- a more effective support of the people who have to 'work' with the systems: both the members of the regional teams and the intermediaries.

These policies have to be viewed against the background of an important development: the NadNet, a network which mutually connects the NN teams, as well as the NN teams with their customers (the intermediaries).

MANAGING KNOWLEDGE CYCLES

Knowledge about the specific insurance products is considered by NN as belonging to the core assets of the firm. In the old organisation, this knowledge was developed, stored, safeguarded and transferred by the product groups. In the redesign process, it was clear from the outset that under no circumstances should this rich body of accumulated knowledge be allowed to leak away. The change-over from a product to a regional or market-oriented organisation could create this risk. Who would be held responsible for safeguarding NN's product knowledge in the new organisation and how could this knowledge be made available to NN's employees in the regional organisation? It was recognised by the steering group that management knowledge flows had to be regarded as a basic function to be incorporated into the redesign. One of the design group received the assignment to develop a systematic approach for this function in such a way that it fitted into the new organisation. Figure 12.4 gives an impression of the design option that was finally agreed upon.

Figure 12.4.: Managing Knowledge Cycles

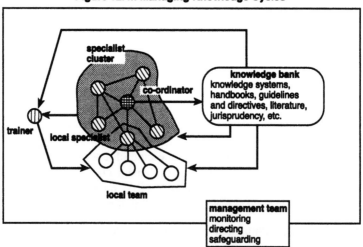

In this design three main functions can be distinguished:

The specialist. Each regional unit has a number of specialists with their own field of interest and competence, whether it be a certain product or cluster of products, acceptance or damage claims. They act as 'information points' in their unit. They inventory questions, problems and new ideas and discuss these matters on a regular basis with their colleagues from other units.

The co-ordinator. He or she is a member of the division staff and chairs the specialist meetings. The co-ordinator is responsible for the adjustment of the directives and guidelines for acceptance of risks and the assessment of damage claims. These, in turn, are transferred to the members of the regional teams. The co-ordinator is furthermore responsible for updating the knowledge as well as for the development of knowledge. This means that he or she is expected to provide an important input in the development of new products. In addition, it is also his or her task to inventory the training needs in the regions and to work together with the training department in the development of new courses.

The trainer. The trainer works closely together, both with the specialists in the regions and the co-ordinators. He or she operates primarily in a professional support role.

The management teams of the divisions have the explicit task of directing and monitoring the development and safeguarding of existing and new knowledge cycles.

The implementation of the described system of knowledge cycles management is to be regarded first as a direct consequence of NN's redesign. The existing body of knowledge must be secured and made available to the regional units in an effective manner. However, the system also introduced a new important element into NN's management practices. The management of the knowledge cycle was regarded explicitly as a new function within the firm. In this approach, knowledge development and transfer were not regarded as being a sum of specialist capacity and adequate training courses. It was viewed as a flow of meaningful information throughout the organisation, a flow that linked people together in their efforts to adequately serve the customer.

EDUCATION AND TRAINING

Education and training is of crucial importance in insurance firms, as in most other professional services. NN had already possessed an elaborate system of professional training. Nevertheless, NN's redesign had important implications for the education and training functions which went beyond its usual role. Employees in the regional teams had to be able to handle, in principle, most of the products rather than just one. This clearly required an enormous extra investment in education and training. The same applied to the preparation of managers and team leaders in their new roles. Furthermore, the introduction of new information tools had to be supported by intensive training.

More important in the long run was the changed position of the education and training function within the firm. Previously, this function had acted as a kind of school in the backyard of the company. Nowadays, it is increasingly integrated with the development of the business, particularly in the management of the knowledge cycles in the firm as outlined above.

A DIVE INTO DEEP WATER

After a preparation of three years, the new organisation was implemented formally, in July 1994. It might be too early to be able to assess the costs and benefits. This did not mean, however, that no important lessons could be drawn from the experiences of the last years.

The Organisation as a Whole

The redesign was grounded on an integrated approach of the organisation as a whole. One might ask whether a more sequential and less complex approach in which design problems are set apart would not have made the job easier.

(A district manager):

> 'We chose to dive into the deep. We've made the decision to tackle the organisation as a whole and not part after part. We did not choose for a piecemeal approach. This means that our information systems have to be operational in the changed context, that team leaders and team members had to be trained, the intermediaries had to be informed, the new management positions had to be filled in, and so on, and so forth. And at the same time the business has to go on as usual. Once we decided to pursue along these lines, we were well aware of the fact that we did not have the time and the means to do everything perfectly. For example, in the field of training. We did a good job, but more training is certainly required. Nevertheless, we did the best we could. More important is that we kept the right momentum in the process. The process has become irreversible. It is not completed, it has just started. We have now the right insight into the functioning of the business and this insight is gradually spreading from the top to the shop floor and back up again. That means that we have created the basis for continuous improvement.'

Self-Design

NN made use of the assistance of a consultancy group, but never let the initiative slip out of its own hands. NN redesigned itself. Employees from division level to the shopfloor were actively involved in the analyses, design and implementation throughout the process. That process took three years. It has freed the energy on which the process is kept going.

(A district manager):

> 'We had never been aware of the full potential of our work force. During the past few years it has become clear that most employees have capacities we never envisaged. Their active involvement made it all happen. However, this also means that a new style of leadership is required. We want to introduce entrepreneurial attitudes on the shopfloor of our new units and do not need to be surprised when our employees are starting to behave as entrepreneurs.'

REFERENCES

Dankbaar, B. and Hertog, J.F. den, 1990, 'Labour Process Analysis and Sociotechnical Design: Living Apart Together?,' *Technology, Work and Employment,* Vol. 5, pp.122-134. [*Roache, S., 19*].

Roberts, H., 1993, *Accountability and Responsibility: The Influence of Organisation Design on Management Accounting,* Maastricht: UPM.

Sitter, L.U. de, 1994, *Synergetisch produceren*, Assen: Van Gorcum.

Womack, J.P., Jones, D.T. and D. Roos 1990, *The Machine that Changed the World.* New York: Rawson Associates.

13

DOES PARTICIPATION IN OWNERSHIP FOSTER PARTICIPATION IN CONTINUOUS IMPROVEMENT? THE CASE OF BAXI PARTNERSHIP

Raphael Kaplinsky*

I.   INTRODUCTION: CONTINUOUS IMPROVEMENT - THE ROUTE TO COMPETITIVE EFFECTIVENESS

In this chapter we chart the process of introducing Continuous Improvement (CI) into a British firm manufacturing gas-fired central heating fires and boilers and industrial air-conditioning units. The distinctive feature of this firm's performance is in part the very considerable progress it has made in the endogenisation of processes of CI. But more unusually it has made this progress within the context of a relatively unique form of ownership relations, for the firm is wholly-owned and controlled by its workforce. We begin with a brief discussion of the principles of CI, before providing a brief history of the evolution of employee ownership. Thereafter we explore the evolution of the CI programme and its positive impact on the firm's competitiveness. However, in recent years the Baxi Partnership has begun to experience a number of difficulties, some of which relate to problems with its process of organisational renewal and some to its particular ownership structure; these issues are discussed in the concluding discussion.

Technological progress has frequently been seen as comprising a series of jumps in performance. Often this perspective is closely associated with an approach in which technology is seen as being embodied in capital equipment. However, there are two problems with this traditional approach. First, in reality incremental changes - a process of 'crawl' - have often

---

*   The author is grateful to Eddie Gartside and other staff at Baxi for their co-operation with this
     research. Errors and misinterpretations are his responsibility alone.

outweighed the importance of step-function jumps in performance [*Enos, 1962; Hollander, 1965*]. But secondly, the very belief in step-function improvements has undermined the ability to achieve incremental crawl; hence 'technological change' has been seen as being the within the purview of scientists and technologists rather than 'unskilled workers'. The Japanese - building on a long, albeit neglected western tradition of incremental change - have shown that a sustained process of 'small step, high frequency, small cycle of changes' [*Bessant et al., 1994: 18*] provides the key to rapid overall progress in competitive production. Moving to this particular path of technological progress has necessitated the involvement of all the labour force in production, so that the traditional distinctions between 'head' and 'hand' have been removed.

Organisational structures to ensure CI are imperative both because they permit the sustained accretion of marginal improvements in operating effectiveness, and because they prevent a process of back-sliding in which hard-won gains (achieved by overturning the custom and practice of mass production organisation) are lost. The key to CI thus lies in new forms of social relations and in the fostering of a culture in which all of the labour force participates in innovation, not just those specialised and highly trained workers working in the R&D department. It is in this context that the importance of ownership relations arises. The hypothesis to be explored in this chapter is whether employee-ownership which, by its very nature focuses on participation, is likely to be particularly conducive to sustained CI; in the words of Philip Baxendale (the former private owner of Baxi - see below),

> I have recently read the book *Road to Nissan* and liked the slogan 'Flexibility, Quality and Teamwork'; that appeals to me because it describes what we should be able to achieve as a Partnership better than a conventional company.

II.   THE BAXI PARTNERSHIP - A BRIEF HISTORY

In 1866 the Baxendale business was begun as a foundry, with a particular speciality in castings for railway wagon and then textile machinery. The recession in the textile industry led the family-owned enterprise to search for new markets and in 1935 a simple, but effective design of coal fireplace was patented. This catapulted Baxendale on to a national market, and after the fireplace-design was extended to allow for solid-fuel central heating (by placing a back boiler inside the chimney), the firm gradually expanded to employ 60 people. But during the late 1960s Britain began to gain access to North Sea gas; in addition per capita incomes were rising and consumers wanted a more convenient form of heating. Hence Baxi made an important - and very successful - transition by complementing its solid fuel fires and back boilers with gas-fired units; by 1973, these gas back boilers accounted for 40 per cent of the total UK gas central heating market.

By the end of the 1970s, Baxendale remained in family ownership, with effective control lying in the hands of the founder's grandson, Philip Baxendale. He faced a problem, since he did not believe that it was right that his four children should inherit the company. He was therefore left with three alternatives - to sell Baxendales to a competitor; to float it on the stock exchange; or to pass it on to the workforce. It was in the belief that worker ownership was the only way to maintain long-term employment - rather than a strongly-held commitment to co-operative ownership - that led Philip Baxendale to 'sell' this profitable enterprise to its workforce. In 1983 Richard Baxendale and Sons Ltd. was sold to an employees trust and became Baxi Partnership Ltd. The selling price (£5.25m.) was less than its profits in the previous year (£5.84m.) and contrasted with an estimated flotation value of £40m; the purchase was made from company reserves, so no cost accrued to the employees.

Thus the workforce inherited a firm not only unencumbered by any debt, but with money in the bank. Moreover, it also had a history of relatively good industrial relations and a Works Council had been introduced in 1961 (a rarity in the UK) which had the authority to raise any issues, not just those related to wages. Philip Baxendale was an enlightened employer and morale was high, as was confirmed by attitudinal surveys conducted by the Tavistock Institute in 1979 and the London School of Economics in 1983. Finally, there was a strong tradition of re-investment, and dividends had historically been low.

As the 1980s progressed, Baxi recognised that the chimney breast boiler was a mature market. It therefore widened its central heating product portfolio to include both floor- and wall-standing boilers. In addition, through acquisition, it diversified into environmental control in 1988 (in the process building one of the most modern foundries in the UK), industrial heating in 1989, and into Denmark in 1993. All of these firms became employee-owned and Baxi moved to a new Group-structure (see below).

III. ENDOGENISING CONTINUOUS IMPROVEMENT THROUGH ORGANISATIONAL CHANGE

Pressures to Change

The decision to engage in a series of thoroughgoing changes in manufacturing organisation emerged during 18 months of intense discussion in 1986-87. Baxi management had come to recognise four major problems:

- rising overheads were eating into profitability;
- the market was fragmenting and the product range was extending, both in the number and variant of different products; there were 25 variations of the major product family;
- despite holding large levels of stock, it was frequently unable to meet customer orders for specific products; and
- there were recurring problems with quality, requiring costly reworking, entailing high levels of scrap and undermining its reputation amongst customers.

The Company Improvement Plan and the First Pilot Cell

In the early 1980s, the sheet metal shop (pressing boiler and fire bodies out of flat metal) had taken the advice of the engineering faculty at the nearby Manchester university and reorganised itself into five 'cells' (although as will be shown later, these were grouped sub-optimally into types of machines, rather than families of products). Partly because of this experience, partly because of Baxi's growing familiarity with Japanese organisational techniques (it had sent a senior manager to Japan), and partly because of advice offered by a Consultant, the decision was made to experiment with a JIT in 1987. Under the banner of a Company Improvement Plan (CIP) seven key elements of production were targeted:

- balanced production, that is producing in smaller batches rather than building for stock;
- quality improvement;
- reduction in throughput time, that is, the period taken for materials to pass through the plant;
- reductions in set-up time to facilitate balanced production;
- the development of cooperative relationships with supplier to facilitate inventory reduction and quality improvement;
- the utilisation of a 'pull system' through the factory through the use of 'kanbans'; and
- better housekeeping practices.

The first concrete step in the CIP was taken in 1988 with the establishment of a pilot cell for the manufacture of floor-mounted boilers, a relatively small contributor to total sales. This introduction of this pilot plant took four months. Instead of producing a single design for seven weeks, a mixed-model assembly programme was utilised. In addition, purpose-built pallets (which they called kanbans) were introduced to limit the build-up of WIP, and attention was given to set-up time reduction. The results were stunning:

- throughput time was reduced from seven weeks to two hours, and the savings in WIP were consequently enormous; in one factory, 35 per cent of WIP was stripped out in two days of consultation with the labour force;
- the space required in production halved (from 30,000 to 15,000 sq. ft.); and
- scrap and rework fell dramatically.

Reorganisation of Company Structure: The Key Role of Team Working

Although this pilot programme was successful, Baxi's profits were falling (Figure 13.1), despite rising sales. In early 1989 the Director charged with promoting employee participation undertook an attitude survey from which it was clear that despite six years of employee ownership, equity-participation meant little to the labour force; there were low levels of trust between management and the shop floor, and industrial relations were worsening. This occasioned intense discussion, not only amongst senior management, but also in the Council which represented the employee owners. It was concluded that the cause of this malaise was that both the company and employee ownership were too remote from the individual 'partners' and management and lines of communication had remained hierarchical, operating in a traditional functional structure.

Consequently Baxi decided on a major organisational restructuring. It moved from its four functional divisions (manufacturing, sales and marketing, finance and R&D) (Figure 13.2) to a new system based on seven strategic business units (SBUs) (Figure 13.3). These SBUs were based on product groupings - the traditional back boilers; wall and floor boilers; space heating; the foundry; sheet metal and painting; and environmental systems. Each has its own functional units plus access to corporate-wide support in marketing, central engineering, personnel, purchasing, distribution and information technology. The key to the operation of these business units was to be the team and the managerial structure was pared down to three layers - the Board at the centre of the organisational wheel, the seven Business Area Managers in the middle and the self-governing teams (each with a Team Leader) at the edge. The intent was to introduce 'fast-response, customer-focused, and profit-conscious development teams to create a common sense of ownership of the business issues, greater harmony, and more direct employee involvement and participation' [*Annual Report, 1990*].

Figure 13.1.: Profits, with and without interest income, 1984–1994 (£1986)

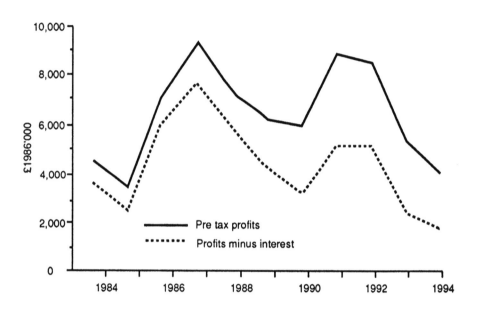

Figure 13.2. : Organisational structure, 1989

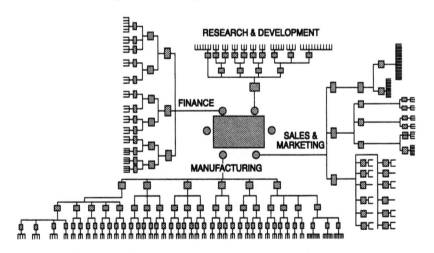

Figure 13.3. : Organisational Structure, 1990

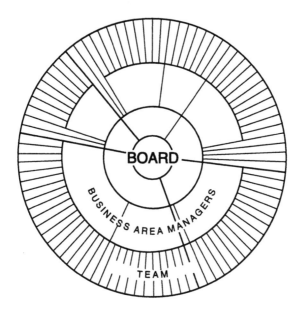

Thus in so far as our concern lies with the confluence between CI and employee ownership, it is at the level of the Team that the important issues arise. Each of these teams is designed to comprise eight to ten people, although some teams are in fact larger; in fact, as the self-managing capabilities of the teams has grown, the average size of the teams has increased. To facilitate flexible working, a programme of cross-training was introduced and each team member is expected to master four to five different tasks. The teams are provided with a daily or weekly output and are left to define for themselves the sequence of building and the division of tasks. Indeed, quite often, the teams adopt different manufacturing procedures and in the newly laid-out fire and back boiler cells, each approaches the sequence of assembly in very different manner - some build sets of sub-assemblies in lots ('kanbans') of five and others manufacture on a single unit flow basis. The teams thus have the capacity to compensate for illness and vacation, as well as to facilitate the use of the Open Learning Centre (see below).

In addition to these manufacturing functions the teams have responsibility for first aid, health and safety, data entry and environmental impacts (in addition to housekeeping functions). More importantly, though, they are expected to assist in the design of layout changes. For example, in the new back boiler assembly room, the decision to split production into five cells and the layout of the new flexible transfer line was decided together by the

217

business area manager together with the teams. However, the teams are excluded from some areas of decision-making, specifically with respect to terms and conditions of employment, wages and salaries, grievance and disciplinary procedures, and individual targets and personal problems.

The 20 Keys Programme

Although much was achieved through breaking up Baxi into teams, an attitude survey concluded that morale was low. It was also increasingly obvious that the pace of change had begun to grind to a halt. For both these reasons the teams were given the additional remit of achieving CI throughout Baxi's operations. This was an important step since the experience of many companies has been that unless an infrastructure is created to endogenise CI, the commitment remains an ideological one, and the resulting implementation is poor. However, also in keeping with experience elsewhere [*Bessant et al. 1993; Kaplinsky, 1994*], the creation of this institutional infrastructure alone was not adequate. The teams need to be provided with specific tools if a *process of change* was to emerge. Initially this was seen as a challenge of training and Baxi employed a battery of consultants building expertise in communication and teamwork skills (for example, all senior and middle management and all supervisors were put through a five-day course). But after initial success, and after the glow had died down (the well-known 'Hawthorne effect'), CI ground to a halt in most areas of the firm and the lunch-time team presentations were discontinued since the medium (that is, the glossiness of the presentations) were outweighing the message (that is, the substance of change).

Searching around for a solution to these problems, one of the senior managers who had been sent to Japan stumbled upon a book outlining a process designed to endogenise CI. It involved the identification of specific objectives which each team would use through a process of regular team meetings to ensure that progress was maintained. This new scheme became known as the *20 Production Keys to Workplace Improvement*. Twenty corporate-wide objectives were identified, including, for example, good housekeeping, quick changeover, elimination of non-value added operations, production scheduling, quality assurance and supply chain management. Levels of achievement were specified for each of these Keys, and the teams were given the task of setting themselves goals, and charting their performance through the utilisation of radar charts; Figure 13.4, for example, shows both the target and achieved performance of one of the teams in manufacturing. At the height of the teamworking initiative in the first half of 1992, 80 per cent of the labour force were involved and there were 112 teams with an average membership of 10; teams involved both blue- and white-collar workers.

Figure 13.4. : 20 keys chart for continuous performance

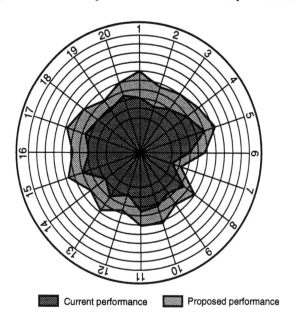

Current performance   Proposed performance

Human Resource Development Underpinning Organisational Change

In support of its process of organisational change, Baxi has made very large investments in training, adopting a scatter-gun approach. As one of the beneficiaries of this programme remarked it involved a 'stunning investment in the life of the company and in people and the organisation'. This began in 1988 with a company-wide awareness programme - all shopfloor workers (and subsequently all the office staff) were introduced to the principles of JIT through a stickle-brick simulation of factory production. The implementation of the new organisation and the introduction of teamworking (which, for example, required workers to make presentations on the results of their team meetings) occasioned some concern amongst the labour force, and when one of the trades unions were approached by an educational consultancy firm specialising in communications skills for industry, it in turn addressed the problem to Management. A steering committee was established, comprising of the Production Manager, the Human Resources Manager, trades unions shop stewards, the educational consultancy and the local college for further education. The first step was to undertake a needs' survey and 150 randomly chosen employees (about 15 per cent of the labour force) were interviewed, looking at both job-specific and unrelated skill requirements. The primary assessed needs were for communication skills (82 per cent) and proficiency in mathematics and English (44 per cent). But an

219

additional 7 per cent were identified as having more severe problems with basic functional literacy and elementary mathematics. A number of specific job-related skill needs were also identified (for example with metrification), but it was notable that one-quarter of the labour force felt the need for prolonged training as a route to further promotion. The idea of 'learning for life' (which was subsequently adopted as a motto in Baxi's HRD) was thus in part stimulated through the process of enquiry itself..

Baxi responded with three initiatives. The first were those offered on-site in a purpose-designed Open Learning Centre (OLC). This provides courses in information technology, English, mathematics, French and Business German, as well as one-off advice on training needs; it is open 24 hours a day. With the agreement of the team, workers can attend these courses during working hours; hitherto there have been no cases in which the teams have prevented participation. The 'costs' of this training in terms of lost-time are borne equally by the central training budget and the team, who are required to make up time lost in training. Within two years of the OLC being established, 180 employees - 22 per cent of the total direct labour force - had undertaken at least one course of a four-week duration, with 60 per cent progressing to more advanced courses. In mid-1994, 10 per cent of the labour force were either actively utilising the OLC, or were on a waiting list for a course

The second initiative was to fund the fees of anyone who wanted to take any course at the local further educational college in their own time, irrespective of the subject chosen. This voucher scheme included courses on Chinese cooking, arts and crafts, health care, languages and business skills. In 1993-94 122 employees (12 per cent of the total labour force) participated in this scheme. And, third, Baxi invested in longer-term training pro-grammes such as the NVQ (National Vocational Qualifications) scheme and also funded a number of staff on MBA courses at local universities. The key theme running through this programme on HRD was that in the context of the previous low levels of skill development in Baxi (and elsewhere in UK industry) there was a need to substantially alter the trajectory of learning. This required recruiting more graduates, as well as a concerted programme of continual training available to all staff.

IV. ORGANISATIONAL REFORM AND CORPORATE PERFORMANCE

There are many a priori reasons why these investments in organisational change, teamworking and HRD should be commended. But ultimately it is the bottom line of corporate profitability and survival which must be used to judge their suitability.

Sales, Margins and Profitability

The UK recession of the early 1990s was reflected in a particularly severe downturn in the construction industry and hence in the central heating market, where demand fell from a high point of 930,000 units in 1990 to 650,000 in 1993. The level of sales and profitability in this industry are closely connected, partly because some of Baxi's operations (notably the foundry) are scale-intensive and partly because in a declining market, unit prices have been falling with discounts rising from nine per cent in the early 1990s to 30 per cent in 1994. The decline in Baxi's turnover (11.9 per cent) was substantially smaller than that of total industry sales (28 per cent), but this has been at the cost of profits; market share has been maintained. It is striking, however, that despite these adverse conditions Baxi has managed to sustain profitable operations, even when its investment income on its vast accumulated profits is excluded.[1] It is also striking that investment levels remained high throughout the 1980s after the employee takeover whilst Baxi equipped itself with a state-of-the-art aluminium foundry; after falling sharply in 1989-90, the investment has began to grow again in 1993-4.

The strengths and weaknesses of Baxi's employee ownership is evident from this performance. All of its rivals are part of large groups and have managed to contain the impact of collapsing prices within group financial strength. On the other hand, the conservative financial behaviour and the long-term perspective of management is reflected in very large accumulated profits which have provided an investment income to buffer cyclical downturn. It is widely recognised - both within Baxi and by industry observers - that had Baxi been taken over by a public company, the accumulated reserves would have been distributed as dividends or be utilised in other group activities.[2]

This maintenance of profitability despite extremely adverse market conditions arises directly from the organisational reforms described in the previous section. The impact of these reforms on overall manufacturing operations - building on the extension of the principles implemented in the pilot cell described above - can be seen in overall stock control in boiler and fire assembly (Table 13.1). This improvement has led to Baxi's enhanced ability to satisfy its customers more rapidly and to deliver in smaller batches (hence assisting the attempts by its customers to reduce their own levels of stocks).

Product Innovation

By the late 1980s, Baxi had managed the transition to employee ownership, but had come to realise that its product portfolio was 'mature' and offered little room for growth. One of the three major responses was to introduce new product designs (the others were to move into industrial heating and to diversify into Europe) and to improve linkages with customers. Thus two new teams were introduced, cutting across the SBU structure. One concentrated on new product innovation (in the process breaking the traditional isolation of designers), and a second on Customer Satisfaction. Modifications were made to the traditional gas fires, which became available in increasing varieties; given Baxi's new production flexibility this enhanced product variety was associated with a fall in production costs. But more fundamental changes were made to the design of central heating boiler units. This achieved the desired effect and sales of boiler units grew very rapidly. However, the innovativeness of this design and the pressure to introduce new products quickly meant that a design error had been introduced, and in early 1994 Baxi had to recall a number of units and rectify the errors. Although this dented its long-lived tradition of reliability, Baxi appears to have recovered from this problem and sales have grown strongly since the product recall. By late 1993 a survey of users by the British Consumers Association recorded Baxi as one of the two most reliable makes of central heating boiler [*Which? September, 1993*].

TABLE 13.1
STOCKTURNS IN MANUFACTURING

	1991/2	1993/4
Bermuda boilers	9	38.5
Convectors	8	22.7
Brazilia boilers	5	16.9
Floor and wall boilers	9	18.5

This unusually rapid development of a major product can be directly traced to the organisational reforms outlined above. In particular, the introduction of a cross functional design team - integrating marketing, design, production and vendor development - was the driving force in product development; cross functional teams were also important in the rapid response to the design error and the assuaging of customer concerns.

Working Conditions

Labour turnover - aside from the two programmes of retrenchment (see below) - has been exceptionally low, at less than one per cent p.a. This arises from a combination of factors, including the relatively high levels of wages, where Baxi has consistently paid above the industry average. For example, in 1992, its average remuneration level (£17,581) was 47 per cent higher than the median for the top quartile of the heating and cooking appliance sector [*Oakshott, 1993: 29*].[3] But it also reflects policy towards training (see above); health and safety (where its performance has been consistently better than the UK average for over 20 years); its policies towards the employment of disabled (Baxi has twice won national awards for this); and its purpose-built surgery (where workers are provided with comprehensive medical check-ups every three years). Baxi has also won two awards for environmental impact (one from the EU).

All of these working conditions can be directly attributed to employee ownership. But it should be recognised that they do not only reflect distributional considerations, but also an investment in the skills and commitment of its labour force.

V.   EMPLOYEE OWNERSHIP - WEDGE OR BRIDGE?

Following the sharp fall in the heating market in the early 1990s, Baxi was forced to consolidate the organisational restructuring it had begun during the late 1980s. However, the adverse external environment has meant that it faces considerable difficulties in the future and is fortunate that its employee ownership has left it with the banked resources to both cushion the cyclical downturn and to promote diversification out of mature markets. The extensive and ongoing investment in HRD provides the springboard for continued progress, particularly in relation to the pursuit of CI. But before considering the link between employee ownership, participation and CI, it is first necessary to recognise some of the major problems confronting Baxi during the second half of the 1990s.

Labour Productivity

Baxi's problems with labour productivity are evident from Figure 13.5. Although the labour force has fallen since its peak in 1990 (through one damaging period of 97 compulsory redundancies in 1990, and a further voluntary scheme for 115 in 1972), this has not kept pace with falling sales.[4] More importantly, and this suggests a characteristics of employee ownership, there has been no suitable mechanism available for compensating for the enhanced labour productivity arising from the organisational changes outlined earlier since market growth was constrained and employee ownership made further redundancies difficult. Taken together with significantly higher average wages, this poses a major challenge for balancing the interests of its owners (i.e. its workforce) with that of its management and long-term survival. But it is a problem which is not unique to employee-

223

Figure 13.5.: Sales and Output Per Worker, 1984–1994 (1986 = 100)

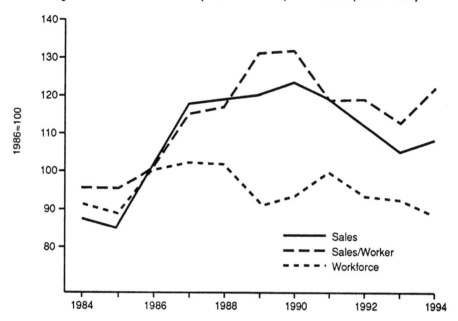

owned enterprises; moreover, in the context of heavy investments in training, the costs in labour displacement should not be under-estimated. The response of a voluntary redundancy scheme poses its own problems, since it is often the more skilled workers who take the redundancy payment and then pass on to further employment; Baxi is then left with the less trained and the less mobile.

Industrial Relations and the Incompleteness of Organisational Reform

Baxi makes widespread use of what it calls 'kanbans' in its production organisation. These kanbans were introduced in Toyota as signalling mechanism and were intrinsic to the introduction of 'pull' systems in production; workpoints only manufactured when the WIP was required by its internal 'customer'. However, in Baxi's case, the kanbans are often only utilised as pallets for storing WIP in an orderly manner; production continues to be pushed through the factory, and although WIP-control is far-improved from the classical mass production factory, the pull-system does not operate in a fine-tuned way.

The problem is particularly acute in the sheet metal plant. The performance of this unit was benchmarked against equivalent pressing shops and it is clear that its problems do not arise from out-dated equipment (to the contrary, investment has been high) or from an unfavourable product structure but from a combination of low levels of work-intensity and poor manufacturing organisation. Each of the 'cells' produces in large-batches and stores the output before it passes to the boiler-assembly plants. This occurs for classically fordist reasons - the changeovers of the large bedded manual presses take 70 mins., whereas the operating manual specifies 20 mins., but these could in fact be done in 5 mins. Similarly, the changeovers on the automated presses take 30 mins. rather than 5 mins. The reasons for these long changeovers (and hence large batch production) are to be found in an inter-union dispute where the 'skilled' workers union prevent the 'unskilled' workers from assisting with machine setting, despite the fact that almost all of the workforce have now mastered the full agenda of skills.

The optimal solution to this problem of manufacturing organisation is to rethink the location of metal-pressing. If the principles of cellular manufacturing are to be implemented properly, then the pressing capabilities should be integrated within the product divisions which are separate SBUs. Instead Baxi is boxed in by its earlier decision to make the sheet-metal shop a separate SBU, and has responded by forcing this area to become cost-competitive with outside suppliers (In fact, although the sheet-metal shop was designated as a SBU, it was in fact only a cost-centre). One option being considered - known to the labour force - is to reduce wages to reduce unit labour costs, but this is clearly a reversion to the mentality of mass production and is a sub-optimal response forced by management's inability to restructure social relations to foster reorganisation. The fact that this traditional dilemma occurs within an employee-owned enterprise is ironic; but it is also intriguing given the successful reorganisation of production in other parts of Baxi.

Slowdown of CI

After an initial success with the CI programme, facilitated by the establishment of teams and the use of the 20 Keys Programme, there has been a major slowdown in this initiative. Baxi is not unique in this (see Bessant in this volume), and if anything its problems are less substantial than most other British firms introducing CI programme. There is a combination of reasons explaining this phenomenon. In some parts of the factory - particularly that making the wall-heaters which demand has exceeded expectations - the teams were seen by the area business managers as an impediment to production. Workers were reluctant to have team-meetings outside working hours, and the 20 Keys were seen as a distraction. In this part of the plant, the CI has been put in abeyance. A second reason is that team leaders were chosen from the front-line supervisors of the previous functional organisation. Not all of these had the approach or the skills required, despite an intensive investment in training. Thirdly, heavy discounting and falling real sales have concentrated everyone's attention on labour productivity. But in the context of an effectively static/falling market, rising labour productivity is likely to lead to further retrenchment; workers in one area of the plant were explicit that this had led them to withhold suggestions which might reduce costs but reduce labour requirements. Finally, it was probably a tactical mistake that as one business manager put it, the CI programme 'rapidly degenerated into a cost-cutting programme' rather than focusing on product development and quality improvement. For example, of 35 CI projects in the space heating division in 1992-93, 22 were material cost savings and seven labour cost saving; only four were revenue generating, and two to improve marketing.

The evidence of this slowdown is visible throughout the plant. Twenty Key radar diagrammes (Figure 13.4) on display around the plant are frequently many months old; many teams meet sporadically; and one senior manager observed that in his view the '20 Keys are now part of the manager's toolkit' rather than being a driver of improvement throughout the firm.

The Problem of Low Morale

It is paradoxical that over the years all the attitudinal surveys conducted at Baxi have shown high levels of dissatisfaction, despite working conditions of relatively low intensity, high relative wages, good health and safety performance, and employee ownership. The reason for this is almost certainly that morale is more closely influenced by expectations than by the relativities with other places of employment. This is particularly apparent in a firm where many employees have worked in Baxi their whole working lives and do not know the realities of working conditions in other factories. Morale is further undermined by the fact that the high levels of internal information disclosure characteristic of this employee-owned enterprise have made everyone aware of the adverse market conditions and of falling labour productivity. Consequently most of the workforce feel extremely insecure, particularly as levels of unemployment in the Preston area are even higher than the national average. Thus, referring to the past, one worker responded that '[e]veryone wanted to work here'; another that '[s]ure they had an eye on profitability but the other one was on people's well-being too'. By contrast, referring to the current atmosphere, 'Baxi Heating's now just one of many little companies', 'these days its all about profit not people', '[w]e're just employees who hold shares', and '[o]ur councillors [employee ownership representatives] are just messenger boys for the Board'.

Wedge or Bridge?

Thus low levels of morale, the uncertainty of future employment levels and problems intrinsic to the adoption of CI have all led to the slowdown in innovative activity, at least with respect to shopfloor-based incremental change. In this respect there is little special arising from Baxi's special mode of ownership. On the other hand, it would be foolhardy to fail to recognise that employee ownership has conferred some special competitive benefits. First, there has been a very high level of commitment to HRD, which is the building block for sustainable CI. Second, despite the *belief* that Baxi has now become like a traditional firm, the level of participation is high. Third, the commitment of most of the labour force is strong. And, finally, without employee ownership Baxi would not have been able to maintain its independence. Its cash-hoard would have been distributed to its new owners, retrenchments would have been much higher, working conditions more intense and wages lower. Many workers are indeed aware of these facts and it is striking that there are distinct micro-cultures within the firm. Of the six production sites (including administration), three have levels of involvement and participation in change which are probably not easily observable anywhere else in the UK, particularly not in firms of Baxi's size. At least one of the other three plants has industrial relations that are typical of British manufacturing.

This suggests that with nuanced management, there is scope for considerable improvement in the future. In early 1989 Baxi's Director with responsibility for employee ownership wrote a document entitled 'The Partnership Dilemma'. He identified a distance between management and owners (i.e. the workforce) and considerable indifference and dissatisfaction. He attributed this not so much to employee-ownership *per se*, but to the specific conditions in which this had evolved at Baxi. It was operating in a geographical area with traditional British attitudes towards industrial relations and had achieved employee-ownership as a 'gift' rather than as a consequence of hard struggle. As a consequence many of the traditional groupings in British industry were evident, leading the Director to conclude:

> Baxi is heading into the 1990's with a 'negotiated' work environment which, I suggest, tends to reinforce the different roles of the various groups rather than enable an effective environment of collaboration. Instead of building bridges between groups, the behaviour of these groups in this negotiated climate will tend to drive 'wedges' between them. Is partnership a solution or a confusion? Is it a bridge or a wedge?

As evidenced by Baxi employee ownership thus provides the possibility of making significant progress with CI. But this is not an inevitable result of this ownership relation and is not independent of the specific experience of the individual firms. The rewards are there for the taking, but under what organisational scheme can this fruit be plucked?

NOTES

1. These accumulated profits reflect a combination of conservative dividend policy and the bounty obtained in the low price purchase price when Baxendales was transferred to employee ownership.
2. Unlike its competitors, Baxi has never taken advantage of Pensions Holidays.
3. In addition to these high wages, employees also benefited from the disbursement of profit-sharing. In 1992/3 this totalled £1.868m for a workforce of 1,062; the figures for 1993-4 were £1.227m 1,152. The number of shares held by each worker varies, depending upon their length of employment and their attitudes towards accumulating shares.
4. The first managing director after employee ownership had provided a 'Jobs for Life' commitment based upon Baxi's employee owned structure. Thus redundancies were a traumatic blow for everyone in the firm.

REFERENCES

Bessant, J., Caffyn, S., Gilbert, J., Harding, R. and S. Webb (1994), 'Rediscovering Continuous Improvement', *Technovation*, Vol. 14, No. 1, pp. 17-29.

Bessant, J., Burnell, J., Harding, R. and S. Webb (1993), 'Continuous Improvement in British Manufacturing', *Technovation*, Vol. 13, No. 4, pp. 241-254.

Dwer, J. (1993), 'Baxi Builds up a Head of CI Enthusiasm', *Works Managemet: Small Factories*, Aug., pp. 18-21.

Enos, J. (1962), *Petroleum Progress and Profits: A History of Process Innovation*, Cambridge, MA: MIT Press.

Hollander, S. (1965), *The Sources of Increased Efficiency: A Study of Dupont Rayon Plants*, Cambridge, MA: MIT Press.

Oakshott, R. (1993), 'The Winding Road to 'X' Efficiency: The First Ten Partnership Years at Baxi', Research Report prepared by Job Ownership Ltd. for Partnership Research Ltd., London.

Maddison, A. (1989), *The World Economy in the 20th Century*, Paris: OECD Development Centre.

Which? September 1993, London: Consumers Association.

14

OTICON: A CASE TO DEMONSTRATE A FLEXIBLE AND TRANSPARENT ORGANISATION

Lars Erik Andreasen*

INTRODUCTION

The 8 August 1991 is a date which will be remembered for many years at OTICON, a Danish company based in Copenhagen which manufactures hearing aids. It was the date when the '330' project was introduced. The project is easily defined. It means that over a three-year period OTICON's aim should be to improve its headquarters' productivity by 30 per cent. The objective was to change the entire organisation of the company's headquarters into a completely flexible organisation, what the president of OTICON Lars Kolind has called a 'spaghetti organisation'. 'We removed the entire formal organisation. We now have a tremendous competitive advantage, because we don't care about formalities' Lars Kolind, The Tom Peters Seminar, BBC 2, Spring 1994.

The project received financial support from the Danish government because of its creative and experimental features. Its focus was the overall white collar productivity, that is overheads: product development and marketing, service, distribution, management and alike. A change in the organisation of the production side had already been implemented during the years 1989-90.

OTICON represents a highly knowledge-based company and, thanks to the '330' project, the company is today a business where the interfaces between the main functions, research and development, production and marketing, have been successfully developed.

*   Lars Erik Andreasen, Commission of the European Communities, DG V. Employment Task Force.

THE COMPANY

OTICON was founded in 1904 by Hans Demont. It has always had its main domicile in Copenhagen. With almost 1,100 employees it is today the world's third largest company in the field of hearing aids. Before the Second World War it was essentially to operate as a trading company, importing hearing aids from the US for sale in Europe. It began its own production of hearing aids during the Second World War and remained a family owned and driven business until 1956 when a new management took over the company gradually took over manufacturing of all aids products and built up a network of sales subsidiaries in Europe, the US, Japan and New Zealand, and turned the company into mass production.

By the end of the 1970s the company had reached a number one position in the world market with about 15 per cent of the market and sales in over 100 countries. OTICON had established itself as a leader in miniaturiastion, and the technology that counted at the time which was used in the mass production of behind-the-ear hearing aids. The company, however, remained 'conservative'. The functional departments - production, marketing, financial - were headed by directors who, again, made up the top executive group.

OTICON was able to maintain its strong position up until the mid-1980s, all the time improving its financial records. This trend, however, came to an end. In 1986 and 1987 OTICON witnessed heavy financial losses. The declining value of the dollar against the Danish kronar was one reason, but much more decisive factor was the competitors' introduction of the custom made 'in-the-ear' products, which pushed OTICON into a highly threatened position.

After a management change the company went through a dramatic turnaround. The head office was downsided and it was decided to reorganise the production side of the company. Mr Lars Kirk, who had been criticising the way production was organised for some time , was given a free hand to change the production organisation. He had seen that the knowledge people had of production was not being fully exploited.

During the following two years the organisation of the production was changed and provided a strong basis when OTICON decided upon the '330' project in early 1990. This chapter intends to focus on this project. It is, however, useful here to give a short insight into the reorganisation of the production and the visions behind this reorganisation (see Figure 14.0).

THE '330' PROJECT

Despite the progress made through the reorganisation of the production system it became clear to the management of OTICON that the company was rapidly losing its place in the markets. In the year 1987, its share in the world market had dropped to half of what it was at the beginning of the 1980s. Management realised there were limited financial resources; the research and development activities were at a low level; and competitors had succeeded in developing better products. The company was therefore left behind in getting new products to the market.

FIGURE 14.0
REORGANISATION OF PRODUCTION

The main production site of OTICON is based in Thisted, a town of about 18.000 inhabitants in the western part of Denmark. Before the reorganisation of the plant, production was organised in a typical hierarchial way with about 30 people, divided in to groups of three or four teams, working in each department. The production process worked in a linear fashion with each person handling one or two operations. Communication between the departments had to follow the hierarchial way, passing several persons at different levels wasting a lot of time. What was worse, however, was the limited use of peoples capabilities. 'We knew there was a lot of knowledge out there on the shop floor that was not being used', Lars Kirk, the production manager, explains. The production had to be organised different-ly. After the change, each person was performing eight or nine operations in what Mr Kirk calls parallel production. A group of four or five people will be involved in the production of each product compared to some 25 people before the change. The change required an extensive training programme bringing peoples knowledge up to a certain level so they have almost the same efficiency in whatever part of the factory they are working. Flexibility and competence became the main characteristics of the employees.

As expected by the management there was no shortage of ideas on how to improve the changes. At a one day seminar in 1990, where the factory was closed, the 200 employees came forward with around 100 ideas which then were discussed in smaller groups - without any management involved. Afterwards a high proportion of the ideas were implemented.

A bonus system reflects how initiative is rewarded; the whole group receives a bonus, not a specific individual.

Some figures illustrate what has been achieved: the percentage of the workforce belonging to the management group in 1988 decreased from 11 to 4 or 5 per cent in 1993. People earning hourly wages increased from 200 in 1988 to 280 in 1993. Hours spent on rework dropped from about 6 per cent of total hours in 1990 to 3.5 per cent in 1993. Productivity, seen as the increase in the company's turnover, increased exceptionally. This is discussed further in the main chapter.

'We could not just carry on as we had done in the past: creating slightly better products. We had to do something out of the ordinary to break the mould', as Lars Kolind declared. 'We therefore turned to the overheads of the company. Not so much because they were the bulk of the total costs, but because changing the headquarters' organisation is the key to changing the whole company. Headquarters staff not only create costs of their own - they drive the competitiveness of the whole company. The key question was what could be done to move the barriers that prevent people from doing a far better job. It was not a question of reducing the number of staff.'

After about two years' preparation, involving everyone at the company, the '330' project was implemented on 8 August 1991. Its objectives were:

(1)   to create the right innovative working environment;

(2)   become more creative, action-oriented and more efficient;

(3)   reduce the time to market new products; and

(4)   to create 30 per cent growth in productivity in the first three years

There was no real change made in the business strategy of the company which had been updated by the end of the 1980s. OTICON would continue to focus its marketing efforts on key customers, who comprised the nearly 5,000 key hearing aid dealers and hearing clinics most committed to end-user satisfaction. These efforts would however be accompanied by a new product strategy to provide the dispensers with a full range of hearing aids. This strategy was to be developed within the new organisational set-up. Likewise, there would be no changes in the standards of the OTICON products; the company would maintain its focus on high quality and technical excellence, even though this would often imply demanding a higher price than its competitors.

With the introduction of the project '330' it was realised that four aspects of the way OTICON had organised its work in the past would have to be changed to achieve its aim of designing a company that would become much more innovative and competitive and be able to fulfil the above objectives.

First of all, OTICON's management decided that it was necessary to create a totally new perception of work for everyone in the company. As a consequence of this a complete change of the traditional hierarchical form of business organisation was to be replaced by a totally different type of organisation. This again led to the elimination of the old office concept for, in Lars Kolind's opinion, it is the office that exposes the organisation in its visible physical form and prevents people from doing a better job.

The fourth factor was to create a totally new information system which could provide the necessary back-up for the new organisational system. Organisation first, and then the technology to support it, was the philosophy.

Lars Kolind is today inclined to believe that all four points are a unique breakthrough in business management. This could be questioned. What cannot be questioned, however, is the determination with which all four points have been pursued at OTICON, and the complete understanding of the interdependence that exists between these points and that creates the conditions for becoming innovative and competitive.

Contrary to many other projects to restructure organisation, the '330' project did not allow for a step-by-step implementation. The vision behind the project was a total approach, that is, each part of the plan was an integrated element linked into an overall plan. For instance, it would not be relevant physically to create a flexible working environment if the organisation and the information system made it impossible to benefit from the newly created flexibility of the office.

The project covers two sites with only 140-150 employees in research and development, technology, marketing, services, administration and management. The major part of the overhead costs would be referred to these two sites, both of which were closed down on 8 August and all functions transferred to a new headquarters installed in an old brewery building.

JOB CONTENT

At the outset of the '330' project one of the aims was to activate human resources in the company much more than they had been in the past. OTICON's management believed that the employees had a range of capabilities that the old hierarchical organisation had prevented them from developing and employing. All the old traditional job descriptions and titles were therefore discarded; instead of setting up new job concepts and trying to fit people into the jobs, 'We', as Mr Lars Kolind stressed 'were doing the opposite. We were fitting a portfolio of jobs around the individual person.' The philosophy was that everyone had resources that were not used in a conventional system - a factor that the system was often very unaware of. Each employee at OTICON therefore had a portfolio of jobs. From the beginning of the '330' project the intention was that each person would be able to do at least three jobs. The first would usually be within his/her area of professional training; the other two would be in other fields chosen according to the person's choice, competence and interest.

The changes were welcomed by the majority of people and only a few left the company at the time the changes were made. This is somewhat surprising taking into account the average age of the personnel at the time was about 43 years, and that the changes presumed that everyone would have to engage in extensive training and in a very different working environment.

Of course, the general employment situation in Denmark with its high unemployment rate was a relevant factor to consider as well.

'Not everyone at OTICON has a job portfolio of 3-4 jobs. There are people who prefer to limit their activities to one, perhaps two fields. This is their own choice.' commented Helle Thorup-Witt, who was the employees' representative and had been working at OTICON for some years as assistant to the export manager.

When we visited OTICON we asked for information on the different jobs within people's job portfolio and the weeks or days spent on the different jobs to see how far this particular element of the whole reorganisation had been taken. Such information did not exist, however, and we were told that this could not be ascertained, as it could be seen as having control over people. However, from the information system available everyone could see who was working and on which projects, but this was to facilitate internal communication and ensure transparency within the company.

A career often creates problems for the staff of OTICON admitted Mr Sten Davidsen, who has a university degree in economics and occupies a post as director for human resources. Hierarchial layers have been removed and OTICON cannot offer promotion. 'What we can offer is personal challenge and development' declared Mr Davidsen and continued 'OTICON has shifted from an organisational structure of power to performance'.

We have no titles on the business cards at OTICON. This sometimes creates problems... When you are invited to dinner. Today's society expects you to have such a title.

Sten Davidsen

'This is not fully appreciated by everyone' commented Mrs Thorup-Witt, and added, 'to work at OTICON it is helpful to be determined'. She however, endorsed, the particular attitude taken by the management towards the staff and underlined this by making reference to the average age of the headquarters staff at the time of the implementation of the '330' project where, as mentioned, only a few left the company. Another factor that illustrates that people stay on at OTICON for a relatively long time is the average seniority, which is 12 years.

THE FLEXIBLE OFFICE

When the change took place on 8 August 1991 the staff took over a storeyed three floor brewery with one large office on each floor. An integrated working landscape was thus created. Staff members did not have their own desk, but they did have a personal mobile filing cabinet, a PC and a mobile telephone. Once coded into the information system the individual employee was installed. Laboratories and electronic test stations are also installed on each floor. So, when the technical staff had to work on a project, they would go to the laboratory and test stations. The result was total flexibility and mobility, with everyone being attached to whatever project and team at any place. Bars are strategically placed on all floors to encourage staff to meet and talk; there are no fixed hours for lunch and people on a project were often seen having lunch together. Throughout the building desks, filing cabinets and PCs were identical, including the president's desk which was identical to everyone else's and could be moved around when needed. Transparency and 'intentional disturbance' were therefore key conditions to be created in a new working environment.

THE INFORMATION SYSTEM FOR A FLEXIBLE ORGANISATION

From the very beginning it was clear to the people in charge of developing the information system that two aims had to be achieved: flexibility; and sharing knowledge. Flexibility was necessary in a flexible office environment where people's desks would be moved around without piles of paper. Working on sometimes several projects at a time also required that the employees had access to all information within the company without having to search in archives and so on for documents.

The task was to design and develop an information system which could provide everyone within the new flexible organisation, first of all, with unstructured information - reports, memos, documents, mail, and so on - whether external or internal. The aim was to create total transparency and ensure every staff worker had all information available on his/her PC.

The paperless office has thus become a reality, and OTICON has enjoyed the reputation of a company that has succeeded in creating such an office. About 80 per cent of all mail is scanned into the system on arrival and afterwards shredded; only legal documents or other material kept as originals are filed.

Lars Kolind's aims had been achieved. When he launched the whole project he was convinced that paper hindered efficiency, for paper hid information instead of sharing it. Paper makes communication formal and slow. Therefore, the solution was to be rid of paper and, instead, create an environment in which staff members talk to each other instead of writing memos to eachother. The basis for this was a computer information system with complete transparency which anyone could work anywhere by simply using a computer on any desk.

A training programme was not needed to implement the information system. Instead the company installed a PC in everyone's house about eight months before the change. This gave staff the opportunity to take care of their own training. Very soon after the information system was installed at the headquarters of OTICON it was extended to all the sites in Denmark and the more long-term aim is to link all the foreign subsidiaries to the system.

QUALITY OF THE ORGANISATION

The preceding sections have described how the organisation at OTICON has been changed to a system very different from the old hierarchical one with departments, procedures, papers, officers and titles. And already the reorganisation of the production plant at Thisted illustrates the vision applied at OTICON in the process of reorganisation. The implementation of the '330' project has fully manifested this vision. Right from the beginning of the project the objective was to remove all kinds of barriers at the headquarters which could prevent the development of the right innovative working environment conducive to continuous and spontaneous dialogue right across the company and including everyone. In the opinion of Lars Kolind, such an environment would inspire creativity, the innovation and productivity the company so badly needed at the start of the 1990s to regain its past competitiveness. OTICON has indeed succeeded in creating an organisational environment that has fulfilled these objectives. This is shown by the profit record, which is analysed below. The quality of the organisation confirms it as well. The working environment created has unleased individual capabilities to an extent which might rarely be found.

The organisation is completely flexible; now it could be argued that the only structure that exists is that provided by the projects themselves. The organisation has proved its ability to adapt to a changing market environment and develop new products and market these in an efficient way. A clear documentation of this is the MultiFocus series of products developed at OTICON and marketed over the past couple of years.

OTICON is a knowledge-based company with a very high level of competence within the organisation, be it in product development, production or marketing; and this competence is to be found in the individual employees. The knowledge-base is a common one in which the information system plays a crucial role in building up by ensuring access to all information for everyone. The high level of efficiency in this very flexible and transparent organisation can be attributed to a great extent to the level of common knowledge. Of particular importance might be the access to information on ongoing projects within the company for everyone, supplemented all the time by information about the strategy of the company.

> Our management used to have offices with blue carpet on the top floor and Jaguars in the garage. The company was functioning but not because of its organisation, but in spite of it.
>
> *Lars Kolind*

What has indeed also contributed to achieving this high level of efficiency is that the organisational structure has proved to have a particular capability to transfer inputs (information about the market, research and development results and alike) into output in a very efficient way, and to market these products through a network of dispensers who are continuously serviced by the headquarters. The time taken to market a new product has been reduced by half.

The organisation of a company is sometimes regarded as something mysterious and difficult to come to grips with. One talks of the black box or productivity box to be opened, but many companies have not really succeeded in opening this. However, people at OTICON have had a good deal of success in opening their black box, with the opportunity of unleashing their capabilities. Today OTICON has a dedicated staff working in an environment embodying a continuous learning process and an organisational social process, while the company itself has regained its previous competitive strength.

THE RECORD

1993 was the second full work-year after the fundamental changes in OTICON's organisation; its business value increased dramatically. Total sales, of which exports account for 92 per cent, grew by 23 per cent in an otherwise stagnant market. The pre-tax profit climbed from DKK 18 million to DKK 84 million. Employment remained almost unchanged reflecting a very strong growth in productivity. Table 1 shows figures for the company from 1988 to 1993.

The figures relate to the whole company, whereas the '330' project focused on the organisation of the headquarters. However, the changes have had an impact all the way through the company and have brought about a release of some of the potential created by the reorganisation of the production plant.

TABLE 14.1
KEY FIGURES (CURRENT EXCHANGE RATES) 1988-93, MILLION DKK

	1988	1989	1990	1991	1992	1993
Net Turnover	432	450	456	477	539	661
Profit Before Tax	0	22	13	5	18	84
R&D	12	14	16	30	40	44
Number of Employees	1064	1087	1049	1086	1069	1073

Source: Annual Report 1993, OTICON.

We can also see from the table that OTICON enjoyed a rather good profit in the year 1989. This was mainly due to cost-reducing actions in the whole company carried out in parallel with the reorganisation of the production system. However, the management felt that these efforts - although initially paying off - would not create any stable improvement in the medium and long term competitive position and that other changes were needed, changes that would help to explain the profit figures. Thus, in 1993 a marked improvement in innovation, one of the original goals of the new organisation, could be observed. The share of new products in the 1993's sales was about double that in 1991.

Behind this development lies a targeted increase in research and development efforts. Up until 1990 the resources allocated to research and development were rather modest. In 1991, however, these resources were almost doubled and 1993 shows an additional increase of 50 per cent compared to 1991.

In particular the development of the MultiFocus hearing aids programme has been costly. The first fully automatic hearing aids were marketed in 1991, and in October 1993 the second generation of this technology was introduced to the market. This fully automatic in-the-ear hearing aid is today recognised as a genuine technical breakthrough and is expected to dominate the market in the future. Within OTICON it is the general opinion that the marketing of this product has been particularly successful due to the complete reorganisation of the company which created the conditions for reducing the time it takes to market a new product by a half.

Another indication of success was that OTICON was the only European company to be nominated for the Computerworld Smithsonian Award in the

US in spring 1993. OTICON also received the IT award in Denmark in 1993 in recognition of its advanced application of information technology.

Administration expenses have been stable for the last five years as Figure 14.1 shows, which is surprising in light of all the changes and the huge increase in turnover of the company.

14.1.: Administrative Expenses

Below are the records for the first six months of 1994 compared to 1993. We see 1993 was not an exceptional year and at OTICON one would expect that the full year of 1994 will bring similar results.

	1st half 1993	1st half 1994
Net Turnover mio DKK	312	362
Profit Before Tax mio DKK	36	62

REFERENCES

Commission of the European Communities, 1994, *Options for the Union,* Luxembourg, Office for Official Publications of the European Communities.

Corporate Computing, No. 1, Feb. 1994.

den Hertog, J.F., 1994, *The Flexible Firm*, Maastricht: MERIT.

Peters, T., 1994, *The Tom Peters Seminar, Crazy Times Call For Crazy Organisation*, New York: Vintage.

Peters, T., *Liberation Management, Necessary Disorganisation for the Nanosecond Nineties*, New York: Vintage.

OTICON, 1993, *Annual Report 1993*.

Royal Danish Ministry of Foreign Affairs, 1992, *Business News From Denmark 1/92, Denmark Review*, Denmark: Publication Service of the Foreign Trade Relations Department.

15

HUMAN RESOURCES MOBILISATION: SETTING THE STAGE FOR ORGANISATIONAL INNOVATION

Ulbo de Sitter

The cases in session 3 represent a diversity of settings, problems and interventions. In such a variety of contexts, a common frame of reference might be helpful in order to understand their meaning and coherence. Before I go into the cases themselves, allow me to sketch briefly the organisation design perspective which might offer this frame of reference.

THE STRUCTURE OF ORGANISATIONS

Production systems produce added value by converting material and/or information into goods and services. Such conversions are called 'transformations'. The whole production process is a composition of operations carried out by people and material means (or: 'capacities'). Division of labour results from the division of operations over capacities and by their grouping and coupling. The production organisation is the product of such a division of labour. The division of labour has two main aspects: operations must be carried out, controlled and co-ordinated. The grouping and coupling of operations can be referred to as the 'production structure'. The 'control structure' is the allocation and coupling of control cycles. Production control implies a control object. A highly complex object requires highly complex control. Complex control raises the chance of disturbances and breakdowns occurring and diminishes the chance of effective and efficient control. Therefore, effectiveness and efficiency of production control are directly dependent upon the complexity of the production structure.

The Complexity of the Production Structure: Production Systems as Amplifiers of Variety

There are two dominant types of production structure to be found both in industry and in the services sector: the functional structure and the line structure. They share one basic characteristic: the concentration of functions. Basically, all capacities are linked to all orders. This is the reason why these structural types are so complex: there are so many (often variable) interfaces that have to be controlled. System losses result from co-ordination problems. Let us use the functional structure to illustrate this reasoning.

Suppose we are dealing with a system which produces seven standard products. Just the fact that all the capacities are potentially coupled to all orders means that the system has to deal with 127 ($= 2^n - 1$) possible order combinations. We call this: external or requisite variety. Each order combination requires a efficient and effective path through the production system. However, if the production is split up in two independent parallel flows (for three and four standard products), it becomes clear that the number of possible order combinations is drastically reduced with 84 per cent to 22 ($= 7 + 15$). This reduction can be even higher when the parallel flows are chosen in such a way that they match orders with common operational patterns, required skills, tools and materials. One speaks in this respect of 'homogenising'.

Looking at an order flow, the organisations functions can still be strongly concentrated. Take, for example, a production unit with four functional departments (Figure 2). In the case that the unit is producing only one standard product, 4^4 different routings are possible. We call this internal variety, because it is caused by the arrangement of the operations themselves. Internal variety grows both with the number of different departments and the number of capacities in each department. In the case of parallelisation as in the above-mentioned example of two flows with 16 different possible routings, each variety can be reduced with 93 per cent. It is clear that external variety is not only a function of the number of different products, but also of the number of different delivery conditions and of the number of different operational sequences. The total variety the production system has to deal with is thus an exponential function of the external and internal complexity. And because this variety is dependent upon the design of the production structure it has to be viewed as 'structural variety'. Structural variety is extremely high in a functional structure and minimal in a fully paralleled structure.

Controlling the Self-Induced Need for Control: Redundant Variety

The order flow seems to be invisible in structures which are concentrated around functions. One only sees the distinct separate operations. However, the invisible (or 'latent') order flows meet each other again and again at the crossroads of a workstation or department. This results in mutual interference. One order has to wait for the other and the stock grows as the queue becomes longer. One might state that 80 per cent of all the efforts in production control are spent on solving the potential traffic jams between the invisible order flows. Time is put into the co-ordination between orders rather than that of operations with regard to one order. In other words: why spoiling our time chasing orders when the sources of the interference can be solved in a structural way by creating parallel and homogeneous flows?

Segmentation

The paralleled homogeneous flow offers the possibility to use the available capacity for the precise co-ordination of operations of one order or order family. All the required capacities are available and can be directly co-ordinated without hierarchical intervention. Using flows, the number of interfaces can also be reduced in another way: by 'segmentation'. Different operations (or workers) are then brought together in a module (or team). The interactions take place on the level of these teams or modules rather than on the level of individual workers. This way, team production absorbs local disturbances instead of passing them over from capacity to capacity.

Integration

Variety is not totally of structural origin and arises also from the local circumstances in work stations, teams and departments, which are always changing over time. Local flexibility is required in order to cope with the local variety. The composition of individual and group tasks is decisive here. A strong division of labour has two effects in this respect. First, it strongly limits the capacity of teams and individual workers to solve problems which arise from local variety, and second, it is a source of disturbances which tend to be amplified all along the production process. The integration of closely related operations into complex and flexible tasks is in this sense an essential component of flow-oriented production.

HUMAN RESOURCES MANAGEMENT OR HUMAN RESOURCES MOBILISATION?

Flow-oriented structures offer the perspective of organisational learning. They are built upon integrated and meaningful tasks. People work closely together in teams. They have frequent mutual contacts and have overlapping rather than sharply demarcated tasks. This gives them insight into the process as a whole and opens a perspective on continuous learning, improvement and innovation of the work process. Continuous improvement becomes a 'built-in' organisational function. Practical experience in redesign projects working along these lines show what creative potential can be set free and provoked once the structural conditions for learning are created. In this respect, it might be better to speak of Human Resources Mobilisation rather than Human Resources Management. Creativity has to be mobilised and fades away when it is controlled. The essence is that conditions are created under which people can develop their own potential.

That is our message: reduction of the redundant complexity of the organisation is our key challenge. This offer the perspective of changing complex organisations with simple tasks into simple organisations with complex and challenging tasks.

Integration Can Only be Based upon a Structural Approach

The controllability of a production system can be expressed as the relation between the need for control and the capacity for control. Controllability can be drastically enlarged by the reduction of redundant variety and by increased flexibility. Flexibility is based on the integration of closely related partial functions and tasks in teams or segments. Such redesign options are structural because they are directly related to orders or the flow of orders. The structure of the production itself is the focus in this approach. Once the structure is changed, the relations between the parts are changed as well. That is the basis for integrated redesign, and that is the difference with partial changes in the field of logistics, quality control and personnel policy, which leave the structure of the system untouched.

Process and Product Innovation in a Structural Perspective

I use this frame of reference to draw the lessons from the cases of: Baxi (gas heating), Océ-van der Grinten (copiers), Oticon (hearing aids), Nationale Nederlanden (insurance company), Raychem (chemicals), MEY (accountancy and consultancy) and Pink Elephant (computer services). The presented cases deal with very different products, processes and markets. The firms also took different routes in their redesign process. However, the frame of reference has enabled us to point to remarkable common denominators.

De-functionalisation by Flow Production

The resemblances between the four larger firms are striking. These firms regained control by a drastic reduction of the redundant variety. This was accomplished by the creation of parallel and homogeneous flows and segmentation in units and work teams.

Baxi used a pilot project to show how the throughput time of seven weeks in the functional organisation could be reduced to a couple of hours in a flow-oriented set-up. The reduction of redundant variety made it possible to concentrate on the real problems of the firm. Improvements (for example in quality) became directly visible and concrete. Baxi used such experiences to move towards a complete de-functionalisation of the firm, by creating parallel flows of products and product families. These flows were brought together under the umbrella of Strategic Business Units, which offered the opportunity to create work teams and integrate tasks within teams. However, the case report also mentions the difficulty to anchor continuous improvement within the teams as an ongoing process. One of the explanations might be that the firm still has to make one other step: the decentralisation of planning, control and support functions closely to the work flow and the teams. The present case study did not go into that issue.

Océ-van der Grinten worked with a classical matrix organisation in its product development until recently. The functional units within R&D worked for the company as a whole. In other words: these functional units were not linked to a specific flow of orders (in this case: product designs). The case shows that the firm was urged to innovate in a more market-oriented manner and in close contact with both marketing, engineering and production. The firm decided to bind the functional R&D units closer to the three business units, and moved in the direction of parallel development flows. However, the functional set up was not left, although they were being given a quite less important status as capacity units. One impression one gets from the case is that the organisation still holds a high degree of complexity. This remaining complexity becomes specially visible in the flow of knowledge within functions and over projects. As a consequence, the firm had to invest in methods for knowledge transfer and diffusion. The department heads have been given a large responsibility in this respect. The personnel department acts here in an important support role in this process of knowledge transfer by offering and monitoring the instruments for training and career guidance.

The Oticon case shows that the firms started with the de-functionalisation of production. Teams of four workers were responsible for operations that were performed in the old organisation by 25 workers. This is a good example of the introduction of parallel flows and teamwork. The interesting thing in this case is that such a flow-oriented production proved to offer a platform for good dialogues with other groups which were brought into a flow later: production preparation and product development. This had been the second step in the organisation innovation within Oticon: de-functionalising of product development. The case report is not quite clear in this respect. The abolition of strong specialisation in product development indicates that the matrix organisation had been left and was replaced by small integrated and multidisciplinary design teams. Such teams at Oticon work with a minimal hierarchical interference and bring a market orientation within the development function. An open, unstructured and highly accessible information system reinforces the diffusion of knowledge. In this case too redundant variety originating from functional concentration is reduced by a structure based on parallel flows. In these parallel flows the relevant interfaces between projects are used for a fast and direct transfer of knowledge. The end result is a reduction of lead times in development and an significant raise in productivity.

The insurance case (Nationale Nederlanden: NN) deals with a comprehensive redesign process in which the functional structure is left and replaced by market-oriented parallel flows. NN's organisation was divided into product groups, dealing with fire, car and property insurance and the like. This gives an impression of a flow-oriented organisation with each product having its own flow. If one regards the flows not as goals in itself, but as a way to reduce redundant variety, then another picture comes up. The real issue here is the delivering of packages of services (risk acceptance and assessment of damage claims) tailored to the requirements of individual customers (the intermediaries). In this perspective, the products are not to defined in terms of comparable insurance polices, but as packages of different polices. The distinct policies are in this view to be assembled in an integrated insurance product. In this sense, the old NN organisation was functionally concentrated. As a result, there was a great need for co-ordination between the operations dealing with the various insurance polices for specific customers. More severe competition in the market urged NN to reconsider its organisation. The insurance company was split up into two divisions, one for the private and one for the business market. The regional units in these divisions are composed of insurance teams which serve their customers with complete insurance packages. Now, team members are starting to get an overview of the whole process and are beginning to understand the service needs of their customers. This has given them the possibility to work on continuous improvement. Again, the mobilisation of human resources is becoming manifest in concrete visible results.

The NN case also shows a danger that might arise in parallel flows. The new structure might block the diffusion of knowledge across flows. As a remedy, a combination of measures such as those introduced by NN is indeed necessary: organisational support structures for knowledge flows, training, career guidance, open information systems, cross regional development teams, etc.

The Raychem case provides a clear impression of the present management view on the traditional matrix organisation for R&D as being too complex, too slow and intransparent. Raychem reduced the redundant variety of its functionally dominated matrix structure by choosing organisation in which project flows always have priority at the crossroads of the matrix. Mobilisation of human resources is seen as a key factor for operating in a market-oriented context. The report gives an impressive list of measures by which knowledge development and diffusion are fostered. However, the case report does not show how the knowledge transfer between the product development flows is anchored in the structure of the development process.

Knowledge Maintenance

The introduction of lateral links between development teams and between development teams and the service (or: production) teams is the central issue in the accountancy (MEY) and the computer services (Pink Elephant) cases. The regional teams (MEY) and the local service teams (Pink Elephant) are the heart of the business. That is the place were value is added. They are strongly responsible for running 'their own business' within the framework of a larger supporting organisation. They act as parallel teams with a clear own responsibility. Product development does not take place aside of the ('production') process but within this process. That can be regarded as a typical characteristic of the service sector. Is this solution to the problems of an individual customer a potential new product for the market? Answering that question requires lateral links between the parallel units and extra measures for the transfer of knowledge and experience throughout the firm.

CONCLUSION

Human resources mobilisation is a key factor in product and process innovation. That is the basic conclusion one can draw from the presented cases. At the same time the cases show that human resources cannot be mobilised in a traditional partial manner, for example by the introduction of a TQM or HRM department. Human resources mobilisation is the combined result from structural measures which focus on the flow of products and services.

PART V:
CHALLENGES TO PUBLIC POLICY

It is clear from the case studies which have been presented in earlier chapters, that the competitive gains to the introduction of new forms of organisation are significant. yet the pace of diffusion remains too slow to meet the competitive challenge which Europe currently faces. There is thus clearly scope for appropriately-designed policies, at all levels - regional, national and supra-national. At the same time, it is evident that these forms of support are most effective when the state and the private sector act in collaboration, often including an active participation by the university sector in 'action research'.

The experience of small firm networking in both Bad-Württemberg and the UK continuous improvement programme illustrates clearly these various strands to effective policy formation. In both cases support is provided by a combination of government and the private sector; in the UK case, a critical role is played by the university system.

A further issue confronting government policy is what to do with those parts of the state apparatus which may benefit from changes to their organisational procedures. The case study of the Swedish hospital in Chapter 18 shows that the returns - both in terms of reduced costs and the improved delivery of services - may be substantial. But important problems of managing labour-displacing organisational change are highlighted.

16

NETWORKING AS A MECHANISM FOR ENABLING ORGANISATIONAL INNOVATIONS: THE CASE OF CONTINUOUS IMPROVEMENT

John Bessant

I. INTRODUCTION

The increasingly important role which technological change plays in determining competitiveness is now widely acknowledged. One implication of this is the need to explore better mechanisms to encourage the early adoption and transfer of technology, and this is of particular relevance in the case of small and medium-sized firms (SMEs). To rehearse the argument briefly (but see Rothwell for more detailed discussion), SMEs often lack the capacity for such technology transfer because of a lack of resources and capability [*Rothwell and Zegveld, 1982*]. Typically they have little spare manpower for the necessary search and scanning activities for identifying emerging technological trends, they lack internal experience in project management and implementation and have little capacity for absorbing costly failures. Resource limitations extend from financial and technological constraints to what may often be a serious gap in managerial capability in areas like firm strategy and project management.

To compound the problem, many sources of technology - universities, R&D centres, equipment suppliers and consultants - are not very experienced in bridging this gap to SMEs. The transfer of much advanced technology is predicated on assumptions about users who understand what they need, how to negotiate its transfer and how to make effective use of it within the firm. Arguably there is a gulf between these two groups which represents a weakness in the market and which may require some form of intermediary mechanism; examples include institutions [*Carlsson and Jacobsson, 1992*] and consultants [*Bessant and Rush, 1994*].

The persistence of this gap highlights a role for public policy in two directions; direct intervention to develop capability amongst SMEs and indirect support through creating a mediating infrastructure. There has already been some progress along this road; policies designed to promote innovation have shifted considerably over the past 15 years from a position in which the main resource gaps were seen as financial and technological to one in which the managerial gap is explicitly recognised [*Bessant and Rush, 1993; Vickery and Blau, 1989*]. In the past support was typically available in the from of a grant or loan for acquiring technology; implicit in this were a number of assumptions about the transfer process, including:

- that the firm knew about the technology;
- that the firm knew which particular configuration of that technology it needed;
- that the firm knew why and how its adoption would benefit the business in strategic terms;
- that the firm knew how to manage the process of transfer and implementation;
- that the technology was available in a discrete, neatly packaged and easily transferred form;
- that the supply side was experienced and competent, understanding both the technology and the particular needs of users.

By contrast, current policies increasingly emphasise support via information, advice and the development of learning opportunities. For example, many innovation promotion schemes employ some combination of awareness raising and information activities backed up by focused consultancy support aimed at helping adapt technological solutions to particular firm needs. In the UK, the new 'Business Links' programme offers SMEs a multi-level package of support; in the first stage an 'Innovation and Technology Counsellor' will work with the firm to explore problem areas, help articulate needs and formulate a basic strategy. This 'general practitioner' mode is followed by access to a range of consultancy advice and support which can be purchased via 'innovation vouchers' from a network of approved and experienced consultants and agencies. On a wider scale, the MINT initiative (Managing the Integration of New Technologies) which forms part of the EC's SPRINT programme combines basic diagnostic help for SMEs (in understanding their competitive position and formulating a strategic development plan) with access to consulting resources to help with implementation.

Common Themes in Innovation Support

An encouraging feature of this development in innovation policy has been the willingness of different state agencies to review and learn from successful experiences elsewhere. For example, the MINT programme built upon a successful Norwegian design, whilst there has been extensive learning in both directions between the UK manufacturing support and the German 'Projekt Fertigungstechnik' programmes. Common themes which characterise many policies and which are aimed at helping cope with market imperfections in this technology transfer process are summarised in Table 16.1.

The last group - actions designed to promote learning and capability development amongst networks of firms - is of growing relevance and it will be useful to look more closely at this policy option as a mechanism for enhancing the diffusion of innovation.

The Emerging Role of Networks in Technology Transfer

A number of studies highlight the potential of networks for dealing with some of the resource and capability constraints associated with SMEs [*Best, 1990; Piore and Sabel, 1984*]. Some experiments have been notably successful - for example, the Italian *consorzia* - and in countries like Denmark and Switzerland public policies have been explicitly designed to build networks as a key enabling mechanism through which SMEs can become more competitive. For example, the Danish Industrial Networks Programme supported the development of over 300 networks over a two year period from 1989 to 1991, whilst the Swiss CIM programme (designed to transfer advanced technical and organisational concepts in manufacturing) was based around a series of network nodes distributed in the various cantons.

The strengths of a network model for transferring technology to SMEs is that it offers a way of bridging both resource and capability gaps. In resource terms, much can be shared - for example, specialist equipment or R&D projects - where the costs to any individual firms would be prohibitive. And in capability terms the possibility exists for extensive self-help; through experience sharing and other informal mechanisms it is possible to bring up the level of managerial and organisational practice. A further advantage is the long-term development of strengths; by a constant process of informal comparison and experience-sharing, overall performance standards across a sector may rise.

Networks are also powerful mechanisms for communication. One of the key features of technology transfer is the extent to which it involves information flows and the possibility of success is enhanced through the regular use of multiple channels of communication [*Macdonald and Wil-*

TABLE 16.1
CONVERGING THEMES IN TECHNOLOGY TRANSFER POLICY

Mechanisms	Effect
Awareness-raising activities, especially those designed to take an *active* role in promoting an interest in innovation. Examples include the 'Strategy Roadshow' in the UK (which is a touring, interactive, high profile workshop designed to generate interest in competitiveness issues) and the 'CAD-Bus' projects in Sweden (again a touring exhibition and workshop facility designed to promote interest amongst remote SMEs).	Helps deal with the problem of passive SMEs by taking a proactive approach and taking the message out to potential user firms. Such 'missionary' work may be necessary to overcome what Carter and Williams term a 'parochial' approach and a consequent lack of technical progressiveness. [*Carter and Williams, 1957*]
Demonstration projects which create a wide range of opportunities for potential users of new technology to see it in action in firms of different sizes and in different sectors and markets. An example is the 'Inside UK Enterprise' scheme which now offers some 300 demonstration sites covering a wide range of technologies (including organisational innovations) (Department of Trade and Industry) [*1994b*].	Offers opportunities to exploit the 'observability' dimension in adoption behaviour [*Rogers, 1984*]. One of the main benefits is the opportunity to discuss some of the problems and to share experiences of implementation with early users.
Schemes designed to place graduates and other skilled human resources within SME user firms for an extended period, and to use these as a bridge between universities and other sources of technology and the user firm. Examples include the UK Teaching Company Scheme and the Irish Techstart programme [*Senker, 1994*].	Builds continuity of support over an extended period rather than assuming technology transfer taking place in a single transaction. Additionally such schemes have high 'bandwidth' in terms of what can be transferred across the bridge - information, resources, ideas, personnel - and they offer the possibility for learning and experiment.
Consultancy schemes which provide subsidised advice at a firm-specific level in areas ranging from general management through to specific technology issues. These may often be supported by a national register and/or some form of managed programme whereby users approach a single 'gateway' and are then introduced to consultants who best match their particular needs and problems	Provide intermediary support to bridge the technology transfer gap; of particular value is the firm-specific nature of much of the advice and information provided which is tailored and customised to suit individual needs.
Frameworks for auditing and measuring various dimensions of performance as an aid to diagnosis and prioritising of problems - for example, an innovation management audit (Department of Trade and Industry) [*1994a*].	Offer frameworks within which strategic innovation can be located and on which progress can be measured and mapped.
Self-help packages, designed to enable user firms to work through some form of development programme - for example, management workbooks on strategy development [*Gregory and Platts, 198*].	Offer low-cost learning and development of management capability
'Group help' activities which mobilise networks and groups in experience-sharing and mutual support activities around the development of capability	Creates a 'multiplier' on the learning process by mobilising and sharing experiences within many firms sharing a common interest in a particular set of innovations

liams, 1992; Rogers, 1984]. Networks offer a rich web of channels, many of them informal, and have the advantage of high source credibility; experiences and ideas arising from within the network are much more likely to be believed and acted upon than those emerging from outside. Similarly the demonstration effect has greater impact amongst groups of firms which are familiar with each other and against whose experience some direct comparisons can be made.

Networks are also useful in dealing with diversity. Firms, like people, come in a variety of shapes and sizes and exhibit widely varying characteristics. Designing policies which fit all these contingencies is clearly impossible, but an alternative is t o design flexible arrangements which can be modulated by a network which shapes and adapts them to suit the individual needs of its constituent members. The case of some of the *consorzia* oriented Italian technical institutes, for example, demonstrates the ability of networks to organise and articulate their particular needs at both a general level and to arrange for the delivery of firm specific inputs (resources and capability) to assist individual members [*Rush, Arnold, Murray, Hobday and Bessant, 1993*].

A number of variations on the basic model can be seen, such as the use of supply chains as a focus for developing a network with common interests. In Sweden one of the mechanisms whereby state innovation programmes have industrial impact is through using the large firms as engines for bringing on the SMEs which constitute their supply chains. In the case of advanced CAD/CAM where the issue is about encouraging widespread use of the technology for inter-firm design and development work, the supply chains around Volvo and Saab-Scania have been the focus of extensive work [*Arnold and Bessant, 1993; Bessant and Dodgson, 1994 forthcoming*]. Another variant is the sectoral one, in which the many SME representatives in a sector can obtain benefits of scale. It makes more sense to belong to the 'club' than to try and survive on an isolated basis; and the more members in the club, the greater the range of support - resource and capability - it can make available. The case of the German foundry industry is a good example here, where the overall level of technological competence is increased across a sector dominated by very small firms. Co-operation and participation in the network means that powerful technical and managerial support can be available on the end of a telephone; thus even small foundries can function in 'extended' mode as if they were much larger and better-resourced firms [*Appleby and Bessant, 1986*]. Some networks have common interests around which a focus can be built. In other cases it may be necessary to employ some form of catalyst or animateur to enable the network to form - for example, in trying to establish technology clubs or benchmarking groups.

One last point concerning networks is their potential role as a mechanism for enabling learning. The concept of 'action learning' has been successfully used in the context of management development [*Pedler, Boydell and Burgoyne, 1991*]. In this, groups of individuals meet regularly to share experiences, suggest alternative approaches, provide moral and resource support, and in other ways help each other to learn Arguably a similar approach can be applied between firms, using networks to enable experience-sharing, joint experimentation, inter-firm comparison and benchmarking and other learning mechanisms.

In public policy terms networks thus represent an attractive option for dealing with the challenge of technology transfer. As self-organising systems, networks can be relied upon to diffuse and modulate policy, and the task of the state becomes one of helping to construct and maintain networks and of designing robust and flexible policy which can be adapted effectively and used via networks. However, this is not as simple as it sounds; networks evolve organically and cannot be established to order. Understanding the conditions which lead firms to co-operate and share in this fashion is critical to successful network policy - and explains why 'manufactured' networks, set up from the top down may often be less effective than those which emerge naturally from the bottom up.

The remainder of this chapter reviews experience in developing a network of SMEs as part of a programme to enable the diffusion of a group of organisational innovations with the generic title 'continuous improvement'.

Problems in the Diffusion of Organisational Innovation

Continuous improvement (CI) can be defined as '... an organisation-wide process of focused and sustained incremental innovation ...' [*Bessant, Caffyn, Gilbert, Harding and Webb, 1994b*]. It is an attractive concept which has received considerable attention in recent years for several reasons, including:

- demonstrable success in Japan, and latterly, in Japanese transplant companies;
- extensive promotion of the concept on the back of total quality management (TQM) programmes;
- strong supply side drives for adoption of TQM (for example, government requirements for certificated standards such as ISO 9000, EC promotion for consultancy support in TQM, etc.);
- low capital investment requirement;
- low entry barriers in terms of skills and specialised knowledge;

- recognition of under-utilised assets - 'with every pair of hands you get a free brain'.

Not surprisingly, given this range of factors, the awareness of CI concepts is high. They are of particular interest to smaller firms, since they appear to offer an approach to improvement which is not particularly resource intensive. However these benefits only emerge when the CI activity is both *widespread*, involving a significant proportion of the workforce, and *sustained* over time such that the small increments of change can accumulate. Studies suggest a high failure rate; few of these are total disasters but in many cases, there is a gradual falling-off of effectiveness after a period of initial enthusiasm [*Kearney, 1992*]. This implementation problem reflects difficulties in organisational transition, requiring significant efforts in the re-design and re-shaping of organisations to enable participation and contribution on a large scale.

Issues in implementation of effective CI include the need to take a systemic view as opposed to a piecemeal approach and to locate such organisational change within a clear strategic framework. Within the CI system there is the requirement for appropriate infrastructure, monitoring, measurement and reward systems and to establish a formal problem-solving and learning process. In order to secure the commitment and involvement of a significant proportion of the workforce, extensive efforts are also needed in training and organisational development. It is unlikely that the specific needs of individual firms in this connection can be met with a standard 'off-the- shelf' package, particularly since the level of understanding about CI is still relatively underdeveloped and what experience there is, resides almost entirely in large organisations. Recognition of the complex nature of this problem, and the widespread experience of difficulties in introducing CI in SMEs in the UK led to the setting up of the CIRCA research project as part of the wider MOPS initiative.

The Manufacturing, Organisations, People and Systems (MOPS) Programme

In 1991 the UK Department of Trade and Industry launched a new R&D initiative entitled 'Manufacturing, Organisation, People and Systems'. This differed from earlier support for industry in that it focused explicitly on questions of organisational innovation which had been raised during a decade of strong promotion of advanced technology. MOPS aimed to provide a framework for research on a number of key organisational change concepts (such as team working, change management, inter-firm relationship development and continuous improvement) and a set of collaborative research consortia were established, involving universities, professional institutes (such as the Tavistock Centre), consultants, publishers and a wide range of industrial users. The objectives of the programme were to identify good practice in these areas and facilitate their widespread industrial adoption; to this end each consortium was required to produce a range of practical 'deliverables' from their project. MOPS supported a total of nine projects (including two pilot activities) which are outlined in the following table. For a relatively small programme (the total budget was only £3.5m of which industry provided around half), the level of industrial involvement was high; through the various networks and consortia developed during the programme, over 1000 firms became linked to the programme and many have continued to participate actively in follow-up work [*Gillis, 1994*].

TABLE 16.2
OVERVIEW OF MOPS PROJECTS

Project	Main focus
BESTMAN	Best practice in cell-based manufacturing - built upon autonomous groups and human centred systems design
TIM - Teamwork in manufacturing	Team working
DESTINY	Organisation design Communication networks
IMOCIM	Change management
OSISTEM	Personnel selection and development
CIRCA/CIGNET	Continuous improvement
SCMG (early pilot)	Supply chain management and inter-firm relations
Nottingham University (early pilot)	Inter-firm networking on organisational issues

II.   A NETWORK FOR ENABLING CONTINUOUS IMPROVEMENT - THE CIRCA PROJECT

One of the projects funded under this programme was CIRCA - Continuous Improvement Research for Competitive Advantage - which aimed to deliver a basic methodology for implementing and maintaining CI and a toolbox of resources to support this [*Bessant, Burnell, and Webb, 1992*]. The research design had two elements:

- action research on particular CI problem issues within a core group of companies (including both large and experienced CI users and SME users, beginning implementation for the first time);
- experience sharing and development of the CI field through a wider network of companies.

The core research led to the development of a series of models and guidelines for 'good practice' in design and implementation of CI systems; these are describe elsewhere but focus on an integrated model in which strategy, infrastructure, CI process, tools and supporting organisational culture are the key variables [*Bessant, Caffyn and Gilbert, 1994a*].

The original plan for the network was to offer access to these research results to a wider community via a series of dissemination workshops, but it has evolved into a much more extensive system. Membership has also grown from a planned group of 20 firms to over 70 organisations participating in some aspect of the Network's activities. Of these the majority are in manufacturing and although some large firms maintain an involvement, the network caters primarily for SME users; the main activities are described in Table 16.3.

There are a number of levels on which the effectiveness of such a network can be assessed. At the most basic, its persistence (and the renewal of membership) suggests that it is perceived as providing some support for CI implementation. This is borne out by anecdotal evidence, by the level of demand for membership, and by the take-up of services such as workshops, training and consultancy. The network has continued to develop in response to suggestions from members and now forms the prototype for a wider European version operating under the EUREKA programme.

However, feedback from members suggests that although formal network activities are useful and, on occasions, of specific importance in developing a CI programme, much of the benefit of membership comes through the general linking up with organisations facing similar challenges. Experience-sharing, often on an informal level, is of great value and the main contribution which the CIRCA network has made to this is by creating a forum to enable it to take place. There has certainly been significant growth in the extent and range of member-member interaction, from sharing problems and ideas through to inter-company visits, consultancy and even exchange of personnel. This suggests that the main benefits of such a network may be catalytic rather than as a direct input to intra-firm change programmes.

By the same token, it is difficult to relate output measures (for example, of improved competitive performance) to any particular aspect of network activity, especially across such a varied population of firms at different stages in implementing CI. There are certainly many examples within the

TABLE 16.3
OVERVIEW OF THE CIRCA NETWORK

Activity	Description
Workshops - average attendance is 70 people representing around 40 organisations, mostly at operating management level and often including those with formal responsibility for CI implementation. Themes emerge from the network membership and have so far covered setting up CI, measurement, creating a CI culture, developing infrastructure for CI, CI in inter-firm relations, and benchmarking for CI.	Regular (quarterly) 1-day meetings to explore a topic of concern in the area of CI. Typical format is: Introduction and scene-setting Industrial presentations (from network members and other firms) Research perspectives Discussion Group workshop activities exploring the main issue (often using / teaching CI tools) Summary
Conferences	Occasional large-scale meeting bringing all network members together with international experiences and key speakers
Special interest days - examples have included CI and the learning organisation, measurement in CI, mobilising CI at the individual level, and motivation systems for CI.	Limited numbers workshop meeting exploring a key issue identified by network members as significant. Format is typically a briefing paper, followed by presentation by each network member of their experiences in trying to deal with that issue.
Newsletter	Regular communication feature, containing items contributed by network members around useful tools and techniques, experiences in implementing CI, case studies, etc.
Library and materials support	Makes available key books, journal articles and other resources to members of the network
Consultancy	Tailored support for network members in training, programme design and other key areas. Significantly an increasing amount of consultancy is member to member rather than involving the CIRCA team
Resource 'toolbox'	Support package containing various resources to enable CI development. The toolbox is available via the CIRCA team and as a self-help system; contents include: •case studies of user experiences •route map of CI implementation •information packs on key CI issues such as measurement, reward systems, etc. •CI tools •diagnostic framework The toolbox is continuously evolving to take into account inputs of experiences and experiments within the network
Mapping and benchmarking	Independent assessment of CI programme against a diagnostic framework developed within the CIRCA project. This diagnostic allows a degree of inter-firm comparison and enables contact between organisations with complementary strengths and weaknesses, thus promoting learning opportunities

network of successful CI activity, ranging from individual projects to programmes saving in excess of £1m per year or contributing 20 per cent of annual profits, but it would be difficult to attribute these directly to network membership. Nonetheless, the facilitating role which it plays is recognised and can be seen more clearly through anecdotal data such as in the following examples:

- Company A is a large transnational firm in the computer industry which has been working in the area of total quality and continuous improvement for nearly ten years. Its main quality programme has been very successful but it has recognised that emphasis has been placed on various forms of error correction; arguably this has put limits on innovation and experimentation. It has also fostered the growth of relatively large, group-based improvement efforts at the expense of smaller, individual-driven activities. Its role in the network has been primarily as a source of experience and as a reference point for many firms at the early stages of implementing CI; however, it has also benefited from alternative perspectives which helped identify this gap in its own programmes and in learning from other organisations further down the road inexperience of individual-centred vehicles for CI. The result has been a broadening out of the range of 'vehicles' for enabling CI across the organisation and the development of a multiple-vehicle 'transport policy' for managing these efforts across the firm.

- Company B is a medium-sized food manufacturer operating an automated facility on a greenfield site. In the development and commissioning of the plant considerable attention was given to developing the teams to run it, with the result that a strong CI ethic was built into the organisation. In the short term this was extremely effective in enabling a rapid climb up the learning curve and the plant achieved high levels of performance; however, there has been a decline since then in the range and extent of improvement activities. Involvement with the network provided a number of external reference points (including a formal assessment of CI carried out by the CIRCA team), which highlighted the lack of a formal process for problem-solving and the possibilities of transferring a number of tools and techniques to support CI. Implementation of these changes has been done with extensive inter-firm involvement (including visits and the exchange of training materials).

- Company C is a small firm, also in the food industry, which is just starting out on the road to continuous improvement. It has made extensive use of the network as a mechanism for training a cross-section of staff through attendance at workshops, special interest days and via courses on facilitator skills, tools and techniques. The overall effect has been to develop a common language and to access a broad range of experience - both formal, and informal via various discussions and visits with other network members - to support the design and development of an appropriate CI system.

- Company D is a medium-sized firm in the electronics industry which was about to launch a CI programme developed in-house. Making use of the independent diagnostic/benchmarking service within the network helped them identify a number of areas which need ed further preparation work before launching the programme, and interchange with network members helped them identify various interventions which could help deal with the issues raised - for example, design of more appropriate reward systems. Their overall view is that these activities helped them 'look before they leaped' and avoided what might have been a high profile false start to their programme.

Other companies have used the network to validate their proposed CI activities, as a resource bank for expertise in particular areas (such as facilitator training), as a source of new ideas (for example, on different motivation and reward systems or on measurement approaches), and as a growing benchmark whereby they can compare how well their programme is doing with real and notional 'best' practice. A recent development has been the emergence of several consultants who have been working within member companies but who have left these organisations to offer their services more widely across the network.

III. DISCUSSION

The experience of the CIRCA project suggests that networks do represent a viable option in helping enable the transfer and adoption of organisational innovations. Their main contribution is probably in creating a forum which facilitates learning and experience exchange amongst firms sharing common problems and interests, rather than in direct provision of services or expert help. In particular:

- the network process mobilises many more active researchers than a single group (such as the university) could muster. As a vehicle for learning it is able to collect and process more data than an individual group. The emerging set of support resources for CI which the network has produced has much of the character of a 'hitch-hiker's guide' to a new country, with each traveller contributing his or her experiences and observations to an evolving knowledge base;

- within the network the diversity of experiences allows for 'comparing notes' at various levels. It also provides a mechanism whereby firms with different motives can congregate around a common theme. Organisations have a number of reasons for joining the network, ranging from access to basic knowledge and resources for those at the start of the CI implementation process, through to validation and extension of established practices for those with extensive prior experience;

- in terms of support for an individual organisation, the heterogeneous nature of the network means that there is a rich resource of experience to draw upon, ranging from expert help from organisations which have already learned to deal with a particular issue through to those in a similar position which can provide moral support. This model is similar to that of 'action learning' in which group support enables individual learning and development.

Our experience of the CIRCA network suggests, however, that establishing and running such networks is by no means an automatic process. The principles of learning also apply to network-building and there has been considerable experimentation and adaptation along the way. Amongst key issues which have emerged in the experience of the CIRCA network are:

- the need for common purpose and commitment - characteristic of the CIRCA network was a common concern with implementing CI, and this provided the motive for joining the network. Commitment was also encouraged through charging a fee to join, making it more of an investment on the part of member firms than simply a choice to attend workshops, etc.;

- the need for active network management - as with computer networks, simply connecting people together is not enough. Successful networks need a variety of activities, and a common node around which such activities can be organised; this role carries with it significant resource implications if it is to be played in tandem with research activity. In particular, there is a requirement for some form of 'animation', to ensure that the network develops and that less active members are encouraged and enabled to participate. Although networks can become self-sustaining, our experience is that there is a two-stage process in which much needs to be done from the centre during the building phase before sufficient member-member traffic takes place for some degree of self-sustainability to be achieved;

- diversity of activity - network activities need to be wide enough in range and scope to attract and motivate a heterogeneous population and also need to evolve to reflect a changing pattern of interests, needs and experience. Developing suitable mechanisms for feeding members' interests into the central organising node is also important here. The danger here is that in developing and offering too wide a range of services there may be capacity constraints in terms of people able to deliver them; this issue has been particularly relevant in the context of consultancy and training inputs which are relatively resource-intensive;

- neutrality - with so many different organisations, some of whom may be competitors, it is important to establish and preserve a neutral perspective, a role which can usefully be played by a university or similar group. This becomes particularly important as inter-company comparisons and benchmarking become an important feature, since diagnosing and giving feedback requires an independent perspective. (Similar experiences emerged in the de facto network which characterised the International Motor Vehicle Programme in which MIT and other academics took on this role of neutral catalyst [*Womack, Jones and Roos, 1991*];

- continuous monitoring and review - a key part of the network management task is to ensure mechanisms are in place for continuous monitoring and improvement. Developing and operating these systems is, once again, a major demand on resources.

In essence, effective networks represent complex systems in which there is considerable interaction but where the overall transformation is one of learning. And as systems theory suggests, maintaining effective systems requires considerable inputs of energy to organise and maintain such networks as more than simply a collection of firms with a common interest or problem.

Networks as a Tool for Innovation Policy

This chapter has argued that SMEs face a 'capability gap' in accessing technology, and this is likely to limit the effective adoption of organisational innovations, despite the considerable promise which these hold out for this particular group of firms. The gap derives from lack of managerial capability on the SME user side and a lack of experience or interest in dealing with the particular problems which this raises for suppliers of technology. Such a market failure requires adjustments which can be made through creating compensating mechanisms in the infrastructure - for example, through providing some form of intermediary support or through developing learning networks which enable a degree of self-help amongst SMEs.

One such intermediary model is that of consultancy, and this has been widely used in public policies designed to promote innovation. It works well under conditions where the technology to be transferred is relatively well-defined and embodied in equipment or systems; the technology transfer transaction is mainly associated with helping user firms identify their particular needs and providing expert help in the selection and implementation process. However, in the case of organisational innovation there are limitations to this model, not least because of the ill-defined and firm-specific nature of much of the 'technology' to be transferred. Concepts like 'total quality management' do not lend themselves to packaging up (beyond the basic awareness and conceptual level) as standard solutions and instead require individual firms to adapt and learn - to work out their own particular solutions to the general problem being posed. Evidence suggests that consultancy support is effective at helping firms meet specific targets - for example, attaining ISO 9000 certification for quality - but less so at facilitating the long-term learning process which innovations like building continuous improvement systems would involve.

This raises the question of the nature of consultancy required. Whereas most consultancy is organised on the basis of providing expertise or knowledge which a user requires, an alternative form is more catalytic in nature, enabling the client's own learning processes rather than intervening directly. This model has been termed 'process consulting' and is, arguably more relevant to the kind of learning needed in developing organisational innovations [*Schein, 1969*]. However, process consulting by its nature is a long-term, non-directive activity which is clearly incompatible with the working methodologies of many consulting firms.

A related problem in using traditional expert consultants lies with the need to separate out the diagnostic phase from the intervention phase in organisational development. Many consultants are concerned with promoting specific approaches, tools or methodologies which represent their intellectual stock in trade; consequently there is a potential conflict between the particular needs of a user firm and the set of interventions which may be offered. There are a number of ways of managing this, including separation of the diagnostic and intervention phases of consultancy work, but some form of independent management of the process is important.

For these reasons consultancy may not always be the most appropriate mechanism for diffusing organisational innovations, and instead some form of group self-help network may be worth exploring. As the CIRCA example suggests, this can be configured to offer process consultancy and to facilitate learning and development through a variety of mechanisms, including feedback and inter-firm benchmarking and development of shared models, methodologies and support resources. However it does require active management from the cent re, especially in the early stages, by some agency. Whilst universities and research groups may have the required level of neutrality and lack of vested interest in selling on consultancy services, they have limitations, especially in terms of resource al location, management experience and conflicts of priorities between network management and research.

However, it is also important to recognise the learning nature of such networks; they are not, primarily about transferring a stock of existing knowledge but rather about developing knowledge across a broad front through a process of experimentation. Other agencies (such as trade associations) may be better placed in terms of credibility amongst user firms and resource commitment to manage networks but they still need to develop a research, analysis and dissemination capability to enable the learning process to take place.

The experience of the MOPS programme - and of similar, network-oriented activities in other countries - suggests that these approaches are worth pursuing further. An important lesson from these programmes is that there is a need for some form of targeting and pump-priming from government; networks do not often evolve naturally but must be built up. Whilst they may become self-sustaining in the long term, there is a need for considerable organising and developmental work in the early stages, and this can be costly in terms of resources.

Learning networks of the kind described offer one route towards developing capability amongst SMEs and this may be particularly appropriate in the case of organisational innovations. However it is important to see such options as one part of a wider policy framework which also includes measures like awareness-raising and general promotional activity, consultancy and resource support, long-term in company development and self-help opportunities, etc. Networks are a comparatively new addition to the policy-maker's toolbox, and there is considerable excitement about their potential; this carries the risk that they will be used widely and not always appropriately. There is a need to explore further the strengths and weaknesses of this new approach; the learning process which characterises firms introducing organisational innovations, involving experiment and adaptation, is one which also needs to be applied to networks as a public policy resource.

REFERENCES

Appleby, C. and J. Bessant (1986), 'Adapting to Decline: Organisational Structures and Government Policy in the UK and West German Foundry Sectors', in S. Wilks and M. Wright (eds.), *Government-Industry Relations in the UK and West Germany*, Oxford: Oxford University Press.

Arnold, E. and J. Bessant (1993), *An Evaluation of the Nutek Action Programmes in Advanced Manufacturing Technology*, Brighton: Technopolis Consultants.

Bessant, J., Burnell, J. and S. Webb (1992), 'Helping UK Industry Achieve Competitive Advantage Through Continuous Improvement', *Industry and Higher Education*, Sept. pp 185-9.

Bessant, J. and H. Rush (1993), 'Government Support of Manufacturing Innovations: Two Country-Level Case Studies', *IEEE Transactions on Engineering Management*, Vol 40, No. 1, pp 79-90.

Bessant, J., Caffyn, S. and J. Gilbert (1994a), 'Continuous Improvement Research for Competitive Advantage: Final Report to the MOPS Programme, Department of Trade and Industry', mimeo, CENTRIM, Brighton: University of Brighton.

Bessant, J., Caffyn, S., Gilbert, J., Harding, R., and Webb, S. (1994b), 'Rediscovering Continuous Improvement', *Technovation 14*, (1), pp 17-30.

Bessant, J. and M. Dodgson (1994, forthcoming), *Effective Innovation Policy*. London: Routledge.

Bessant, J. and H. Rush (1994, forthcoming), 'Building Bridges for Innovation; The Role of Consultants in Technology Transfer', *Research Policy*.

Best, M. (1990), *The New Competition*, Oxford: Polity Press.

Carlsson, B. and S. Jacobsson (1992), 'Technological Systems and Economic Policy: The Diffusion of Factory Automation in Sweden', Working paper, Gothenburg: Chalmers University of Technology.

Carter, C. and B. Williams (1957), *Industry and Technical Progress*, Oxford: Oxford University Press.

Department of Trade and Industry (1994a), *Innovation - Your Move*, London.

Department of Trade and Industry (1994b), *Inside UK Enterprise*, Kempston: IFS Publications.

Gillis, J. (1994), 'A Review of the MOPS Programme', in P. Kidd (ed.), *Agile Manufacturing*, Manchester : Cheshire Henbury.

Gregory, M. and K. Platts (1988), *Competitive Manufacturing*, Kempston: IFS Publications.

Kearney, A. T. (1992), 'Total Quality - Time to Take Off the Rose-tinted Spectacles', *TQM Magazine*, March, pp 65-72.

Macdonald, S. and C. Williams (1992), 'The Informal Information Network in an Age of Advanced Telecommunications.', *Human Systems Management*, (2), pp 77-87.

Pedler, M., Boydell, T. and J. Burgoyne (1991), *The Learning Company: A Strategy for Sustainable Development*, Maidenhead: McGraw-Hill.

Piore, M. and C. Sabel (1984), *The Second Industrial Divide*, New York: Basic Books.

Rogers, E. (1984), *Diffusion of Innovation*, New York: Free Press.

Rothwell, R. and W. Zegveld (1982), *Innovation and the Small/Medium Sized Firm*, London: Frances Pinter.

Rush, H., Arnold, E., Murray, R., Hobday, M. and J. Bessant (1993), 'Benchmarking R&D institutes', mimeo, Centre for Research in Innovation Management, Brighton: University of Brighton.

Schein, E. (1969), *Process Consultation: Its Role in Organisational Development*, Reading, MA.: Addison Wesley.

Senker, J. (1994), 'An Evaluation of the Teaching Company Scheme', in J. Butler and A. Pearson (eds.), *Proceedings of R&D Management Conference*, Manchester: Manchester Business School.

Vickery, G. and E. Blau (1989), *Government Policies and the Diffusion of Microelectronics*, Paris: Organisation for Economic Co-operation and Development.

Womack, J., Jones, D. and D. Roos (1991), *The Machine that Changed the World*, New York: Rawson Associates.

17

PUBLIC SUPPORT FOR SMALL FIRM NETWORKING IN BADEN-WÜRTTEMBERG

Klaus Semlinger

I.   INTRODUCTION

The euphoria concerning the potential of small-scale enterprises in Europe during the 1980s has subsided as more has come to be known about the specific strengths and weaknesses of these enterprises. From recent research it is apparent that (a) the organisational advantages of small enterprises are neither general nor generic, but comparative and contingent, (b) it is not the potential of the individual company which is decisive for small enterprise development, but the interaction between (mutually) specialised firms, and (c) the main problem faced by many small firms is not their size, but their isolation.

However, inter-firm co-operation does not occur automatically, and to organise a network of more than just casual co-operative exchange is a demanding task, especially for small firms. In Baden-Württemberg, there is a long tradition of public policy designed to foster inter-firm co-operation between small firms. This chapter elaborates briefly the advantages and obstacles of 'inter-firm networking', especially with regard to small enterprises (section II) and describes a most recent, remarkable initiative of small-firm co-operation in Baden-Württemberg (section III). It concludes by attempting to assess the impact of public support and summarises the major elements of an effective programme for promoting co-operation between small firms (section IV) in areas which are germane to the new competition and involve organisational change in production.

II.   SMALL FIRMS IN NEED FOR CO-OPERATION

Recent research has shown that even in highly industrialised countries small firms play an important role in economic development [*Sengenberger, Loveman and Piore, 1990*]. However, their role is double-faced since their contribution does not derive solely from productive excellence. A closer look at the performance of small firms reveals that there are some severe intra-firm restrictions which, to be overcome, call for more inter-firm co-operation.

Strengths and Weaknesses of Small Enterprises

During the 1970s and early 1980s, in many advanced industrialised countries there was growing employment only in the small-firm segment of the economy. Accordingly, small business became a source of new hope for economic growth and full employment. Contrary to the pervasive image of their deficiency compared to big business today, small firms are praised for their flexibility, cost advantages, innovativeness and close customer relationships.

However, this positive new image of small firms does not apply generally: First, there are two alternative facets of small-firm flexibility, namely 'active versatility' and 'passive pliability'. The first type of flexibility derives from efficient internal information processing, quick decision-making, and is based on highly-skilled employees. With this type of flexibility, it is possible to recognise and exploit small and temporary market niches quickly and to respond quickly to rush orders. In contrast, the second type of flexibility is characterised by the submission to outside pressure and the acceptance of cutbacks to existing company aims and standards. Many small firms find themselves compelled towards this latter kind of adaptation by their inferior competitive position.

The same ambiguity applies to small-firm cost advantages. These only partially derive from a more efficient organisation with lower administrative, that is, internal transaction costs due to the informational economies of a small-scale organisation, and to a less fragmented division of labour. Thus, the cost competitiveness of small firms may not be traced to higher productivity but, rather, to smaller profit margins or to lower wages.

Correspondingly, many small firms also have low degrees of innovativeness. Apart from exceptions to the rule, their ability to innovate is restricted generally to the development of (customised) modifications of established products and proven processes, and to the investigation of further opportunities to apply new technologies; further their aptitude for more ambitious (basic) research is rather limited. Finally, the supposed close customer orientation of small firms in general only applies to simple structured (regional) markets, where personal acquaintance is possible and where the needs and wants of the demand side are easy to detect, but not to complex and diffuse (international) markets, which require costly distributive channels and extensive marketing efforts.

Accordingly, the praiseworthy features of small firms cannot be found in every single small enterprise. Where they do apply, they generally do not derive from really productive sources. Thus, as a rule, small businesses (in manufacturing) are strong in markets in which cost savings can be exploited from specialised skills, and in young and growing markets. They tend to be weak, where large-scale economies are obtainable, in export markets, in markets requiring a high intensity of investments in advertising and R&D, and, generally, in (mature) large markets [*Acs and Audretsch, 1991; Schwalbach, 1989*].

All in all, there are few structural advantages to small firms; instead there is evidence for the necessity of a productive division of labour between small and big enterprises. To this end, however, and to ensure that small firms might maintain, or even improve their competitive stance in the interaction with big industry, there is need for more inter-firm co-operation among small firms.

Advantages and Handicaps of Small Firm Co-Operation

The major conclusion from recent research in small business development is that small firms can overcome their weaknesses and magnify their specific strength through inter-firm co-operation. Research on 'industrial districts' [*e.g., Sengenberger, Loveman and Piore, 1990; Sabel, 1992; Pyke, 1992*] has shown that small firms profit from a (mutual) specialisation of competence, the (communal) pooling of capacities and the organisation of a (collective) orientation for development.

Exchange within networks offers many advantages with regard to effectiveness, efficiency, flexibility and innovativeness [*e.g., Sydow, 1992; Semlinger, 1993a*]: Networks of independent enterprises derive their special effectiveness from the access to external resources (joint ventures, outsourcing and so on) and the opportunity to focus internal resources on overcoming the restrictions of capacity and competence, which are necessarily limited within a single firm. Efficiency of co-operation within networks would then include economies in production costs as well as in transaction costs. Production cost economies, in comparison with internal procurement, are obtained by the effects on productivity of mutual specialisation (learning curve effects, economies of scale and so on). Transaction cost economies, compared with market-mode exchange, derive from the informational density of co-operation and the mutual familiarity of the partners involved, which ease coordination while at the same time rendering many common business investigations unnecessary (for example, with regard to quality performance, solvency and so on). Furthermore, co-operation within a network of independent firms increases flexibility by not only allowing quick access to external resources but also a quick withdrawal, since no capital commitments are required. Finally, networks improve innovativeness by encouraging inter-organisational 'interactive learning' [*Lundvall,*

1988], which becomes increasingly important when market development and new technologies call for a better coordination of 'complementary but dissimilar activities', exceeding the scope of competence of a single firm [*Richardson, 1970*].

Despite all these advantages, co-operation among small firms that goes beyond a sporadic and narrowly-defined collaboration tends to be the exception than the rule. Unlike big industry, small firms still have their subjective reservations and encounter objective difficulties with co-operative action. This fact is not surprising, since a comprehensive and continuing inter-firm co-operation between equally entitled partners is very demanding, especially for small firms. Some of the problems and obstacles that must be overcome in initiating and then sustaining co-operative exchange between small firms will be explained briefly.

First, there are ideological reservations and psychological impediments. Typically, many small businesses are run by a proprietor who appreciates his/her freedom of decision at least as much as deriving a satisfying profit. Thus, many small business entrepreneurs are reluctant to coordinate action and decision-making with someone else in advance. Co-operation, in turn, is thus defined by mutual *ex ante* coordination, even when it is designed intentionally to safeguard entrepreneurial independence, often entailing a loss of discretionary autonomy.

More important is the fact that co-operation begins with reasonable 'market investments' [*Johanson and Mattson, 1985*]. Successful co-operation requires (a) knowledge of the resources a potential partner might contribute, (b) a valid assessment of this contribution, (c) the ability to negotiate terms of exchange to ensure a fair share of the profits of co-operation, and (d) the ability to control and, if necessary, to enforce the agreement. Thus, building inter-firm co-operation entails transaction costs that many small firms, suffering from informational overload, cannot really afford.

These costs, however, can be reduced if co-operation does not rest on continuous negotiation but on a mutually shared set of aims and values, and if reciprocal control does not call for recurrent supervision and scrutiny but is guaranteed by mutual trust. Unfortunately, trust, defined as the experience-based expectation of co-operative and benevolent behaviour, cannot be unconditionally presumed. Accordingly, co-operation based on trust has to cope with a severe starting problem, as trust is a precondition of co-operative partnership while trust itself only grows in fair co-operation.

However, on the one hand, co-operation is only rewarding with partners of complementary profiles of performance. On the other hand, such partners should not be too similar as this would cause fear of competitive abuse. Nevertheless, the profile of activities should not be too dissimilar as otherwise the potential contribution of each partner would be of no relevance for a respective counterpart [*Van de Ven, 1976*]. The problem is that a small firm's scope of activity is normally quite limited. Accordingly, unlike large enterprises, small firms can hardly restrict co-operation to well-defined sectors of this activity and thus have problems finding and keeping the 'critical distance' for a co-operative partnership.

Finally, the returns from co-operation are not only a question of trustful and productive interaction. In the end, the decisive factor is whether the market will remunerate the improved performance. In markets with excess supply, and in so far as firms not succeeding in stimulating additional demand, whilst improved co-operation may level out a competitive advantage with regard to the partners in co-operation, it may not guarantee full capacity utilisation and profitable sales for each partner involved.

To summarise, there are many requirements to be fulfilled until co-operative partnership between independent small firms may emerge and continue to exist. Therefore, particularly for small firms, co-operation is unlikely to happen as an unconditional and unsupported act of self-organisation.

III. PUBLIC AID TO CO-OPERATE - SME-NETWORKING IN BADEN-WÜRTTEMBERG

To illustrate the problems of building up small-firm co-operation and to demonstrate the effectiveness of public support we will describe the development of a co-operative initiative in Baden-Württemberg which is remarkable not only for its organisational success, but also because it relates to one of the most urgent problems of small-firm development, that is, the requirement to introduce modern quality-control techniques.

Economic Background and Institutional Infrastructure

Baden Württemberg is economically one of the strongest regions in Germany. This position is due to the competitive power of its dominating industries, namely, machine building, electrical engineering and automobile production, which together account for almost 50 per cent of employment in manufacturing. Although large companies with more than 1,000 employees provide two out of five jobs in manufacturing, small and medium-sized firms (with less than 500 employees) contribute about 48 per cent of employment. While many of these smaller firms work as subcontractors to other, bigger companies, some of them, especially in mechanical engineering, are leading brand suppliers on their own.

The roots of the region's economic success, which took place mainly only after the Second World War, have to be traced back to the middle of the last century. Lacking the traditional requirements of industrial development - a local reservoir of raw materials - the region's industrial development was forced to lean on its human resources. This was built on a system of artisan production and cottage industry which, in turn from the beginning, sought the competitive niches of industrial markets for precision and quality goods. Today, when increasing demands world-wide for machinery, automobiles and electrical goods have turned the corresponding trades into big industries with large-scale production, Baden-Württemberg has developed the profile of an 'engineering economy' [*Cooke and Morgan, 1993*], concentrating on technologically advanced products for the top-end segments of their markets or for special customer needs.

From the outset, public policy has supported the path of development employing a 'synthesis approach of mercantilism and economic liberalism' [*Maier, 1987: 26*], designed to improve the ability of self-help for private economic initiatives and to foster inter-firm co-operative action. With this aim - apart from the financial support of the emerging system of local loan and savings banks and in addition to the educational services of a number of newly-founded vocational schools - regional governments started building up institutional infrastructures of informational and organisational support as early as 1848. This included programmes such as organising local trade exhibitions, encouraging resident firms to participate in international fairs, hiring foreign experts to work as travelling teachers, exhibiting advanced foreign technology in order to stimulate its adoption and reproduction, and providing selected artisans with advanced machinery from abroad.[1]

Today, economic policy continues in this tradition: in comparison with other German regions, public aid to private business in Baden-Württemberg is still committed to small and medium-sized enterprises; it gives prominence to the support of inter-firm co-operation, and it maintains the in-kind approach to promotion.[2] At the same time, its focus on human capital formation and the acceleration of technological innovation has been further emphasised [*Bernschneider et al., 1991; Hofmann, 1991*]. This it not the place to give a comprehensive description of the institutional infrastructure of private business development in Baden-Württemberg [*Semlinger, 1993b*], but it is necessary to briefly describe some of the programmes and institutions that form the background to the co-operative initiative presented in the following section.

To begin with - as it directly continues the tradition of public support to small and medium- sized enterprises - there is the Landesgewerbeamt (Regional Trade Bureau). In 1993, this agency disposed of a budget of about DM 111 million and a staff of some 300 employees for industrial promotion. The support it offered consists of consulting services, the operation of information centres (including databank facilities), the promotion of further training, and - last but not least - assistance with inter-firm co-operation. To this end, this agency provides subsidies for consulting and brokerage services of independent consultants engaged in the organisation of such networks, for travelling expenses in connection with network meetings, and for up to 50 per cent of costs incurred in the development of a network model or a concrete joint project. However, the impact of this support in cash should not be overstated. What seems to be more important is the in-kind support of organisational aid to corresponding activities. Until now, the Landesgewerbeamt was able to stimulate about 200 inter-firm networks of small and medium-sized firms.

As mentioned previously, the promotion of vocational education is one of the key features of public support of private business in Baden-Württemberg. During 1986-89 the regional government spent about DM 150 million to support the start-up and modernisation, as well as the running costs, of about 80 Joint Training Centres. In addition, the government supported the work of 59 Local Committees for Further Training which, since 1968, on an initiative of the Landesgewerbeamt, have been uniting all institutions engaged in further training to collectively promote the issue and to estimate (further) training needs. In 1983 a Regional Committee for Further Training was set up, which has since been developing concepts for this aspect of vocational education.

Besides introducing new subsidy schemes, Baden-Württemberg has been improving its scientific infrastructure to promote technological innovations since the late 1970s. Technology transfer received a new push when, in 1983, a Commissioner for Technology Transfer who became head of the Steinbeis Foundation was appointed.[3] The Foundation at the time had taken over the responsibility for technology transfer from the Landesgewerbeamt. Since then, it has set up a network of about 120 Steinbeis Transfer Centres which are mainly attached to the regional polytechnics and are run autonomously by professors of the respective schools. In contrast to technology transfer centres elsewhere in Germany, the Transfer Centres are not just brokering agencies but help directly with R&D support.

All in all, during the 1980s, the modernisation of industrial policy in Baden-Württemberg has led to further amendments to an already advanced institutional infrastructure of pan-enterprise support. Special emphasis was given to the improvement of knowledge and (mutual) information. Although the government explicitly committed itself to an active industrial policy, it also kept to the traditional maxim that public support of private business should restrict itself to improving the ability for self-help. This also applied to inter-firm co-operation. In this regard, the following section will give a more detailed illustration of the importance of (public) in-kind support in the process of network-building. This quality support project is also of interest since it addresses one of the key organisational challenges facing German industry (see Chapter 2 of this volume).

An Example: Co-operative Improvement of Quality Control in Small Firms

This is the history of the Steinbeis Centre for Quality Management (SZQ) in Gosheim.[4] Gosheim is a small village in the southern part of Baden-Württemberg. Although located in a remote area (the so-called Heuberg-district), it has become one of the regional centres of the metal-turning industry in Germany since the 1950's. Today, the area hosts about 400 independent small metal-turning firms, many of which use modern machinery and are specialised in high-precision processing.

The project began in 1988 through the initiative of the owner of a small supplier firm who found himself increasingly urged by one of his big customers to modernise quality control in his company. In fact there was no concrete quality problem with regard to the products delivered which caused this demand. Rather, it was due to the general increase in pressure to improve the quality standards of production processes, in turn derived from the inclusion in just-in-time production and from changes in liability law and international quality standards (ISO 9000-9004). Accordingly, traditional methods and equipment of quality control became inadequate. However, to cope with the new challenge the firm would have had to invest in new devices for testing and measurement which alone would have entailed costs around DM 300.000. At the same time, it was apparent that this investment could not be used economically, due to the small capacity of the firm on its own. Thus, forced into an investment which could not be afforded by a single firm, the initiator planned to purchase the new equipment collectively and to share it with other small firms.

With this in mind he approached fellow members of a local Association of Turnery Firms in Gosheim (GVD), which was founded in 1974 independently from the Federal Association of the Metal Turning Industry[5] in order to promote the local interests of resident firms, especially with regard to vocational education and further training in CNC-technology. Since this group, consisting of about 85 local firms, had experience as a collaborative organisation for promoting collective interest, it promised to be the appropriate forum for discussing the new initiative as well. However, the idea did not find general approval; some larger member firms rejected the proposal while many small firms did not realise the importance of the issue.

Subsequently, the promoter placed the matter on the agenda at a meeting of the municipal council of which he and some other employers were members. As a result, the mayor of the town took up the initiative and involved the county-chief (Landrat), who in turn asked the Steinbeis Foundation for support. Although the idea, which at the time was to build up a technical centre for measurement and quality testing, did not correspond with the standard proceedings of the foundation and the regular pattern of a Steinbeis Transfer Centre, the head of the foundation agreed to send a project manager to promote the initiative further. According to this manager, in the following weeks it was necessary to visit about 80 firms personally to obtain a sufficient number of employers interested in the project.

Finally, the GVD joined the endeavour as well. Together with another small local business association (which had interlocking membership with the GVD), it decided to set up a joint committee and split the costs for promotional activities and to commission a feasibility study, which was ordered from the head of an already existing Steinbeis Transfer Centre for Quality Management in the city of Ulm. The project progressed step by step. In order to elaborate the conceptual design of the project, experts of the Steinbeis Foundation, the local Chamber of Industry and Commerce as well as the regional Technical Supervisory Association (TÜV) were invited to join the discussion. However, this inter-institutional co-operation was not always as harmonious as the term implies: apart from the 'interests of domain' that implicitly or explicitly entered the discussions (at least partially), the Chamber had to take into account that its member firms, too, did not approve the project unanimously. Moreover, it had to push the interests of local private suppliers, who would be able to offer the same kind of services.

In the end, all objections were overcome - partly due to the fact that the profile of the intended centre was designed to fit into the landscape of the corresponding regional supply which already existed, and partly due to the institutional backing of the Steinbeis Foundation which had finally committed itself to the endeavour, declaring that it would assume full responsibility for the centre. Moreover, at the time of this official announcement, the Foundation was also of crucial importance in maintaining the commitment of the small firm entrepreneurs, since many of them had become disheartened when they realised how ambitious the initiative had become. Starting at DM 300.000 to DM 500.000 for a joint investment in some specific measuring machines, the calculated investment costs had increased to about DM 2.4 million, with additional annual running costs estimated at DM 0.5 million for a centre of comprehensive support in quality control with a reach beyond the local economy.

Meanwhile (in October 1989), about 40 firms founded a new association dedicated to supporting the project ('Förderverein'). Under the chairmanship of the head of the quality control department of a large local company, the association invited all the municipalities of the area in the bidding to be the home of the centre. The success of this call for tender was greater than expected: in addition to Gosheim, three larger towns applied, offering subsidised sites or buildings and further financial support. Finally (in January 1990), the tender of Gosheim, which promised to construct a new building according to the needs of the centre and to provide it rent-free for five years, was accepted. In addition, the project received subsidies from the state and the county as well as financial support from the Förderverein (subscriptions and revenues from fund-raising events). Own investments in measuring machines and testing devices could be substituted by equipment lent from corresponding manufacturers who had been canvassed with the idea that the centre would work as an effective showroom for their products.

Even before construction work on the building had started, the centre had already began to enlarge its consulting service which - offered by the project manager of the Foundation and the chairman of the Förderverein - had initially been free of charge to promote the idea of the project. Meanwhile, a number of firms, organised into six committees of the Förderverein, elaborated on the final design of the intended service programme. By spring 1993 the Förderverein has grown to about 160 member firms, and even today it still influences the work of the SZQ by its financial support and its statutory rights in personnel decisions and the planning of future activities of the centre.

In September 1991 the centre moved to its new home. Since then it has offered consulting and testing services as well as further training in quality control methods and quality management. Today, the SZQ has become a fully-developed, albeit somewhat special, Steinbeis Centre with a staff of 14. Its assets are worth DM 1.5 million, consisting partially of measuring and testing, but for the larger part as interest-free loans in-kind. However, contrary to the initial idea, there has been only a limited demand for 'hardware support' in quality control, while consulting and especially training have become the main tasks of the centre. Having a pool of about 80 instructors working on contracts has enabled the centre to flexibly adapt its programme to changing needs. In 1994, apart from its standard offer of courses in quality management that are licensed from and certificated by the German Society for Quality Management (DGQ), the programme includes around 100 other courses and seminars concerning quality control, office management and environmental issues.

Nevertheless, although the SZQ has continuously increased its services, the demand for training and consultancy has grown even stronger. Therefore, the regional Chamber of Industry and Commerce and other institutions have enlarged their corresponding services as well. It is worth mentioning a new approach of collective consultancy: on the initiative of a private consultant and its own technology adviser the Chamber has supported a new collective service programme of a couple of freelance consultants. This programme has begun with free information sessions for individual firms and has developed to joint change-projects to modernise the companies' internal systems of quality management.

The first of these projects which are designed to include one consultant and up to five firms, began in July 1994. The duration of each project and the methods applied will be decided collectively by the co-operating group. Each firm is obliged to assign an employee to the project who is in charge of managing the change process in his firm. The consultant supports these processes by advising firms individually. General information on the normative requirements of modern quality management and on respective organisational methods would be given in a series of individual plant visits and common workshops at the Chamber's premises and at the enterprises' sites. In addition, these workshops are intended to stimulate the mutual exchange of experiences. Thus, although each firm runs its own internal project, there is opportunity for co-operative action that can be restricted or enlarged in accordance with the development of mutual trust and consciousness of its productive effects.

IV. CONCLUSION: PUBLIC-PRIVATE PARTNERSHIP AND THE ORGANISATION OF INTER-FIRM CO-OPERATION

Inter-firm co-operation may be considered as decisively important for small firms to protect and develop their productive potential and to cope with the new challenges of markets and technology. Generally, however, small firms do not co-operate unless they are forced to out of necessity, and even then co-peration does not suggest and organise itself. Thus, to built up co-operation it is necessary to promote the idea, to establish and stabilise new relationships, to organise communication and to develop the scope of interaction. Many small (and even medium-sized) firms are inhibited in the involvement of such endeavours due to their restricted organisational capacity. Accordingly, the promotion of horizontal inter-firm co-operation amongst small firms has to become a priority issue for industrial policy.

This does not imply, however, that industrial policy has to provide ready-made answers to the problems of organising co-operative interaction. Rather its main tasks are to organise time and to provoke attention in enterprise decision-making to enable (continuous) reconsideration of standard practices and new opportunities. In addition, it has to provide information to overcome the propensity for 'simple minded search' and institutional support to stimulate and ease co-operative action.

In this regard, the example of inter-firm co-operation described in this chapter addresses some crucial points: (1) most importantly, co-operation among small firms does not only require financial aid by transfers in-cash but also in-kind support by organisational assistance; (2) organisational assistance is not just necessary to provide relief from the administrative burdens of organising a network of co-operative relationships, but to help with additional ideas and information; (3) the promotion of co-operation is to be oriented to a gradual development of co-operative processes and is to be implemented as a co-operative process itself; (4) apart from organisational assistance, small-firm co-operation will profit from institutional support, that is, from the provision of a 'neutral' organisation which may help to overcome distrust, fear of competition and the suspicion of unbalanced advantages; (5) the emergence of co-operative action does not follow well-established paths in detail and, thus, political support should be able to react in an adaptive way.

To summarise, there is evidence that a prosperous development of small firms and their productive role in advanced industrialised countries depends on a co-operative shift in inter-organisational relationships. This in turn does not only apply to inter-firm exchange but also to the interaction between private business and public policy. This is not a call for more public intervention but for a change in policy design: to effectively sustain small firm development and to protect (or even improve) the prospects of small firm employment, emphasis should be placed on enabling measures rather than on measures of relief. Industrial policy - not only with regard to small firms - should develop a new balance of service and guidance for private business [*Pyke, 1992*]. Again, this is not a plea for more normative regulation or monetary intervention into market prices by subsidies or levies. Instead, public policy should learn from industrial marketing and develop its reservoir of in-kind support [*Brusco, 1991; Semlinger, 1991*]. Finally, it seems necessary to enlarge and modernise the institutional infrastructure of private business but, again, neither by simple de-regulation nor necessarily by strictly public organisation. Rather, institutional reform should strive for a re-regulation which puts more emphasis on procedural norms and relies on the (competitive and adaptive) strength of institutional redundancy [*Schmitz, 1992; Grabher, 1994*].

Beyond the surface of structural change and technological progress that dominates the discussion on economic modernisation, there is a concealed process of institutional change that might be even more important for economic development. Europe is rich in dispersed experiences with corresponding experiments. They deserve more attention in research and public policy.

NOTES

1. Such a loan was conditional on the willingness to show the new tools and machinery to every fellow entrepreneur by request.

2. This applies even by comparison with other German states: during 1986-89, the regional government supplied SMEs with DM 3,716 million in loans, DM 1,273 million in securities and DM 249 million in grants. In total, grants and (interest) costs for loans and securities, that is expenditure for in-cash support to individual firms, totalled DM 562.7 million, while pan-enterprise (in-kind) support measures totalled DM 561 million [*MWMT, 1990*].
3. This foundation is a private organisation supervised by a board consisting of representatives from private business, the scientific community, political parties, regional ministries and the Landeskreditbank.
4. For a more comprehensive description of this history compared with the similar yet quite different development of an initiative of the same kind in Northrhine-Westfalia see Weimer and Semlinger [*1992*].
5. Some firms, however, were members of the Federal Association at the same time.

REFERENCES

Acs, Z.J. and D.B. Audretsch, (1991), *Innovation and Small Firms*, Cambridge, MA: MIT Press.

Bernschneider, W., Schindler, M.G. and J. Schüller, (1991), 'Industriepolitik in Baden-Württemberg und Bayern', in U. Jürgens and W. Krumbein (eds.), *Industriepolitische Strategien*. Bundesländer im Vergleich, Berlin: edition sigma, pp.57-73.

Brusco, S., (1991), 'Small Firms and the Provision of Real Services', in F. Pyke and W. Sengenberger (eds.), *Industrial Districts and Local Economic Regeneration*, Geneva: ILO, pp.177-96.

Cooke, Ph. and K. Morgan, 1993, 'Growth Regions Under Duress: Renewal Strategies in Baden-Württemberg and Emilia-Romagna', in A. Amin and N. Thrift (eds.), *Holding Down the Global: Possibilities for Local Economic Policy* (forthcoming).

Grabher, G., 1994, *Lob der Verschwendung. Redundanz in der Regionalentwicklung: Ein sozioökonomisches Plädoyer*, Berlin: Edition sigma.

Hofmann, J., 1991, 'Innovationsförderung in Berlin und Baden-Württemberg - Zum regionalen Eigenleben technologiepolitischer Konzepte', in U. Jürgens und W. Krumbein (eds.), *Industriepolitische Strategien*. Bundesländer im Vergleich, Berlin: edition Sigma, pp.74-97.

Johanson, J. and L.-G. Mattson, 1985, 'Marketing Investments and Market Investments in Industrial Networks', *International Journal of Research in Marketing*, Vol.2, pp.185-95.

Maier, H.E., 1987, 'Das Modell Baden-Württemberg: Über institutionelle Voraussetzungen differenzierter Qualitätsproduktion', Discussion Paper IIM/LMP 87-10a, Wissenschaftszentrum Berlin für Sozialforschung.

MWMT (Ministerium für Wirtschaft, Mittelstand und Technologie Baden-Württemberg), 1990, *Mittelstandsbericht 1990*, Stuttgart.

Lundvall, B.-A., 1988, 'Innovation as an Interactive Process: From User-Producer Interaction to the National System of Innovation', in G. Dosi *et al.* (eds.), *Technical Change and Economic Theory*, London/New York: Pinter, pp.347-69.

Pyke, F., 1992, *Industrial Development Through Small-Firm Co-operation. Theory and Practice*, Geneva: ILO.

Richardson, G.B., 1970, 'The Organisation of Industry', *The Economic Journal*, Vol.82, pp.882-96.

Sabel, Ch., 1992, 'Studied Trust: Building New Forms of Co-operation in a Volatile Economy', in F. Pyke and W. Sengenberger (eds.), *Industrial Districts and Local Economic Regeneration*, Geneva: ILO, pp.215-50.

Schmitz, H., 1992, 'Industrial Districts: Model and Reality in Baden-Württemberg', in F. Pyke and W. Sengenberger (eds.), *Industrial Districts and Local Economic Regeneration*, Geneva: ILO, pp.87-121.

Schwalbach, J., 1989, 'Small Business in German Manufacturing', *Small Business Economics*, Vol.1, pp.129-36.

Semlinger, K., 1991, 'A Marketing Approach for Public Intervention into Enterprise Decision-Making', paper presented at the 10th EGOS-Colloquium on 'Societal Change between Markets and Hierarchy', 15-17 July, Vienna.

Semlinger, K., 1993a, 'Effizienz und Autonomie in Zulieferungsnetzwerken. Zum strategischen Gehalt von Kooperation', in W.H. Staehle und J. Sydow (eds.), *Managementforschung* Vol.3, Berlin/New York: de Gruyter, pp.309-54.

Semlinger, K., 1993b, 'Economic Development and Industrial District Policy in Baden-Württemberg: Small Firms in a Benevolent Environment', *European Planning Studies*, Vol.1, No.4, pp.435-63.

Sengenberger, W., Loveman, G.W. and M. J. Piore (eds.), 1990, *The Re-Emergence of Small Enterprise. Industrial Restructuring in Industrialised Countries*, Geneva: ILO.

Sydow, J., 1992, *Strategische Netzwerke. Evolution und Organisation*, Wiesbaden: Gabler.

Van de Ven, A.H., 1976, 'On the Nature, Formation and Maintenance of Relations Among Organizations', *Academy of Management Review*, Vol.20, pp.24-36.

Weimer, St. and K. Semlinger, 1992, 'Kleinbetriebliche Zuliefererkooperation'. An den Grenzen der Selbstorganisation und Möglichkeiten öffentlicher Unterstützung, Teilbericht II zum Projekt 'Überbetriebliche Kooperation als Ansatzpunkt von Humanisierungspolitik', Förderprogramm 'Arbeit und Technik' im Auftrag des BMFT, mimeo, ISF Munich.

18

PATIENTS AS WORK IN PROGRESS: ORGANISATIONAL REFORM IN THE HEALTH SECTOR

Raphael Kaplinsky[*]

I. INTRODUCTION

Changes in organisational procedures have been sweeping though the manufacturing sector as firms attempt the transition from mass to flexible production. Initially the focus of change concerned the procedures governing the physical transformation of inputs into output, but in recent years increasing attention has been given to the relationship between individual firms and their external environment (both other firms and institutions in the public/quasi public sector). As firms have become increasingly 'lean' in the manufacturing operations, the focus of organisational reform has switched once again, this time to the procedures utilised in the processing of information (including in R&D), that is, white collar work. It is evident that an increasing number of European firms have begun making considerable progress in meeting these challenges.

But most of the attempts at organisational reform - and much of the literature on this topic - has been confined to the manufacturing sector (and indeed to the auto sector). It is only really in financial services and software that similar organisational principles have begun to be applied outside of manufacturing (see, for example, den Hertog, in this volume). Yet a cursory glance at output and (especially) employment statistics in any of the industrially advanced economies shows that the manufacturing sector accounts for only a limited share of total economic activity. Thus, insofar as organi-

*   The author is grateful to the staff at the Karolinska Hospital, to Michael Lovgren and Ulrika Dellby of the Boston Consulting Group, and to John Poulliér of the OECD for their assistance; errors and misinterpretations are his alone.

sational reform has the capacity to increase productivity (broadly defined to include product characteristics), its macroeconomic impact will necessarily remain limited if it is confined to industry.

The potential application of organisational change to the service sector has another important implication. Many activities in the service sector fall under the ambit of government, and hence the productivity of this sector is caught within the government expenditure/tax nexus. Increasing productivity in these sectors may enhance the capacity to control government expenditure without reducing welfare. Within this, health sector expenditure looms large, since it currently consumes almost 10 per cent of total OECD GDP (Figure 18.1). This chapter describes the application of principles developed in the manufacturing sector to optimise the flow of work-in-progress to the organisation of patient flow in a leading Swedish hospital. It illustrates that the principles underlying organisational reform in manufacturing are generic, and when applied successfully to the health sector, hold the potential to reduce treatment costs in hospitals significantly. Since the evidence presented below suggests that hospital costs could be reduced by around 15 to 20 per cent through the application of these organisational principles, and since in most OECD countries hospital costs account for approximately 50 per cent of total health costs (58 per cent in Sweden), the overall impact of a successful programme of organisational reform in hospitals would be to increase total GDP by more than 1 per cent per annum, and to reduce government expenditure accordingly (although the significance of this budgetary savings depends upon the extent to which health care systems are socialised). However, as will be seen, these gains are not free, and involve complex social trade-offs.

It is clear from Figure 18.1 that health expenditure is not only a significant portion of GDP in Europe and elsewhere, but is on a rising trend. It is not surprising therefore that a range of initiatives are being proposed to reduce these costs, particularly those that fall on the government exchequer. One avenue being explored is to promote the use of sophisticated information technologies in tracking patient requirements on a cradle-to-grave basis; this represents the embodied technological route, familiar in the attempts of European industry to promote competitiveness during the 1980s. A second avenue is that attempting to increase competition in health care provision by separating the functions of purchasing and care - it is believed that the introduction of market forces will promote greater efficiency. A third option is to lower the costs of drugs by utilising generic formulations and/or promoting bulk-purchasing. The fourth is to reduce costs by lowering the quality of and access to service provision, particularly that provided as part of a state health care system.[1] For example, a recent survey in Germany showed that 82 per cent of hospital managers believed that this programme of hospital cost-cutting would lead to a reduction in the quality of care [*Boston Consulting Group, 1993*].

Figure 18.1.: Health Expenditure as % GDP, 1960-92

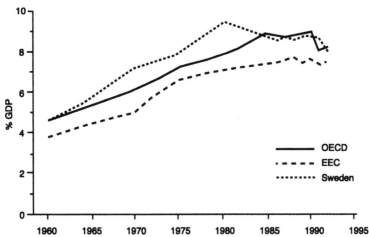

Thus the 'battleground' is clear. On the one hand politicians are required to provide adequate health care, a costly process given the increasingly ageing populations and the inherently labour-intensive nature of these services. On the other hand, the climate of opinion on taxation sets limits on the capacity to provide for this demand. The challenge is how to cap/reduce health care costs without sacrificing health care standards. This raises the possibility of a fifth, and more attractive route to containing health care expenditure. As is argued in this chapter, new forms of organisation in hospitals provide a partial resolution to this policy dilemma by simulta-neously lowering costs and enhancing service delivery. It is necessary to briefly review the relevant experience of the manufacturing sector before the process of organisational reform in this hospital is recounted.

II. FIRM-STRATEGY AND MANUFACTURING STRATEGY: THE CHALLENGE TO ORGANISATIONAL REFORM IN INDUSTRY

Either explicitly or implicitly, each enterprise has an overall firm strategic orientation and an underlying manufacturing organisation to achieve these strategic ends. In the era of mass production, the strategic focus was price competition; the manufacturing organisation required to meet this involved a fine division of labour, the hierarchialisation of managerial control and the use of special-purpose machinery to produce standardised products. In the post-Fordist era, the underlying basis of competition has changed - no longer is it adequate to be price-competitive, but it is also necessary to shorten product innovation cycles, to improve product variety and to enhance product quality. We have thus witnessed a reorientation of firm strategies, away from homogeneity and predictability towards heterogeneity and flexibility (see Chapter 2 in this volume).

The revolution in manufacturing organisation which was required to achieve these new strategic ends was set in train by Toyota during the 1950s. The starting point was to challenge the view that inventories were an asset in production. It argued that not only did inventories require financing (a pecuniary cost) but more importantly they hid manufacturing inefficiencies - they were there 'just-in-case' anything were to go wrong. By buffering these inefficiencies, inventories allowed manufacturing to proceed with built-in flaws. Toyota developed a mechanism for highlighting the extent to which large volumes of work-in-progress encouraged waste. It measured the distance and time actually accruing during the process of production, and contrasted these with the minimum time and distance which was intrinsically required to manufacture the component/product in question. The difference between these two sets of measures reflected the extent of waste. The challenge was to reduce this differential and this was met through a series of organisational innovations which, when reinforcing each other, assumed the characteristics of a new manufacturing system [*Kaplinsky, 1994*].

The full account of this organisational agenda is not relevant here; but four central features of this form of production organisation are germane to the process of hospital reform described below:

(1) Single unit flow. Previously it had been customary for production to occur in 'lots'; a number of components/sub-assemblies were produced at a time and then passed in a group to the next point in production. If inventories were to be lowered, then it was necessary to work in single units (because piles of work-in-progress lock waiting-time into the production process) and then to pass these through the production process serially.

(2) Rapid changeover. Flexibility of production required the changing of machinery specifications; unless this changeover time could be reduced, flexible production would become prohibitively costly.

(3) Production pulling. Instead of pushing the work-in-progress through the plant - that is, each workpoint manufactured autonomously to the best of its potential, irrespective of whether the next point in the production line was able to utilise its output - the work-in-progress would be pulled. This meant that production should only occur when

final demand existed, but it also meant that each workpoint would only manufacture when the subsequent workpoint (its 'internal customer') had run out of work-in-progress. This not only significantly reduced inventories, but also enhanced flexibility since the factory would be making to order (with rapid response) rather than trying to satisfy customer needs from stock.

(4) Families of products and cellular production. It was necessary to differentiate between different groups of products and to dedicate separate mini-factories - 'cells' - to each 'family'. This was partly in the interests of reducing work-in-progress costs and partly as a mechanism of satisfying more discriminating and volatile consumer demand. In mass production factories had been organised on a functional basis, grouping like-pieces of equipment and like production skills together.

Thus although the Toyota approach to manufacturing organisation initially set out to systematically remove inventories from the shop-floor in order to reduce production costs, in the process it provided the capacity for flexible production.[2] Moreover, over time, instead of costs, product innovation and quality being traded-off, they came to be mutually reinforcing.

III. THE EVOLVING HEALTH CARE AGENDA IN SWEDEN

Sweden has historically had one of the highest rates of marginal taxes in the world, allowing for the social provision of a wide range of needs , including an effective health care system. But the tax-payers revolt sweeping through the OECD countries did not leave Sweden untouched, and the pressure on the state budget became severe during the late 1980s[3]. At the same time there was an increasing recognition that activities in the state sphere should also reflect the changing competitive conditions in the non-state sector and it should thus become more responsive to customer needs. As part of this debate, in 1992 the 'Stockholm Model' was introduced to govern the city's health provision. The key features of this system were:

(1) The purchasing and supply of health services were to be divorced. Instead of being given a core block of finance, standard payments were calculated for individual treatments (Diagnosis Related Groups, DRGs) and hospitals were to tender for their supply. This radically-changed incentive system meant not only that hospitals had to compete against each other on the basis of costs, but the 'success indicators' were significantly altered. Under the old system, large queues were seen as a strength and an indicator that more finance was required; under the DRG system, long queues had no intrinsic value.

(2) Patients in the Stockholm Region were given the opportunity to choose their hospital, subject to certain financial constraints. Thus patient satisfaction became an increasingly important component of a hospital's ability to thrive.

(3) Each hospital was required to generate and measure a new set of quality indicators. In the past hospitals had measured quality in narrowly technical terms, for example surgical outcomes and radiation doses. Now they were required in addition to perform on issues such as time taken to answer telephone calls, time waiting for appointments, length of waiting lists, etc.

The change to the Stockholm Model proximates closely to the change in market conditions facing the manufacturing sector. A supply-pushed system focusing on a single indicator of success had been substituted by a more diverse set of objectives, in which in addition to cost-effectiveness, customer satisfaction was critical. From the perspective of the hospital system, therefore, this was equivalent to the change in firm-strategy outlined above; the question was how was the hospital sector to respond to these changes, in other words how was its 'manufacturing strategy' to alter?

One obvious possibility was to cut costs all round, but this was unlikely to allow simultaneously for the newly-specified quality objectives to be met. The relevance of the organisational changes occurring in manufacturing - in which instead of higher quality and cost being traded-off (as in mass production), they were mutually reinforcing - became increasingly evident to the senior management of Sweden's largest and most prestigious teaching hospital, the Karolinska Hospital in Stockholm.

IV. ORGANISATIONAL CHANGE IN THE KAROLINSKA HOSPITAL

The Karolinska Hospital (hereafter KH) has an international reputation for medical excellence. It has approximately 1,100 beds, 4,100 employees and a budget in 1993 of just under Kr2bn (ECU207m). Traditionally it was organised in a functional manner, equivalent to the mass production form of organisation described above - 47 largely-clinical departments were headed by predominantly medical specialists. These largely autonomous departments met infrequently and only saw the CEO twice yearly, to discuss budgets which were negotiated on the basis of 'need' (and buttressed by long waiting lists). In 1991 a new CEO (Jan Lindsten) was appointed. He has previously been the Chief Physician and thus commanded respect from his professional peers; Lindsten became the architect of much of the organisational change in the KH.

One of his first decisions was to compose an Advisory Board which, for the first time, included representatives from industry, amongst whom were the CEOs of two of Sweden's largest manufacturing companies, Volvo and Aga. This provided an early window into the organisational changes sweeping through the manufacturing sector. Lindsten's first major step was to attack the autonomy of these 47 departments, and after considerable struggle, these were reduced to 11 clusters. This made it easier to coordinate and to introduce new ideas, and Lindsten met with them every two weeks. An important feature of these clusters is that only about half were headed by doctors, a unique arrangement in the European hospital sector.

Both the introduction of the Stockholm Model in 1992 and the public discussion which made it clear that hospitals would be forced to both cut costs and improve quality (broadly defined) forced Lindsten to look beyond these clusters. To some extent the DRG system was forcing change autonomously, since each department was having to earn revenue through the competitive sale of its services, and they were thus identifying areas for cost-cutting. But, partly though contact with his Board, Lindsten had become aware of the organisational changes being introduced in industry. He had also been made aware of the activities of the Boston Consulting Group (BCG) which had developed a particular route to organisational change across a range of sectors. This was called 'Time Based Management' (TBM) and although marketed as a distinctive approach to production, was essentially built upon the principles developed by Toyota in Japan.[4] In normal circumstances the fees charged by a premium consulting firm such as BCG would have made it infeasible for a public sector hospital to utilise their services. But Lindsten was fortunate to find a pot of public money (under the 'Working Life Fund', designed to reduce absenteeism) to fund a significant part of their participation, which began in early 1992.[5] This initiative to restructure internal organisation had three objectives - to save costs, to improve quality and to enhance employee morale.

Identifying Wasted Time and Resources

It began with a four week diagnostic study, identifying the potential for the introduction of TBM techniques, including process-flow analyses and interviews with staff and patients.[6] Thereafter, it was extended through seven clusters in three stages (Figure 18.2), so that by 1994, only one medical cluster (cardiology) and three non-medical clusters (laboratories, cleaning/catering and radiology/technical services) had remained untouched. In each case the primary tool utilised by the BCG was to identify wasted time and effort and to utilise this as a tool for identifying inappropriate organisational structures.

Figure 18.2. : Phasing of Time Based Management Changes

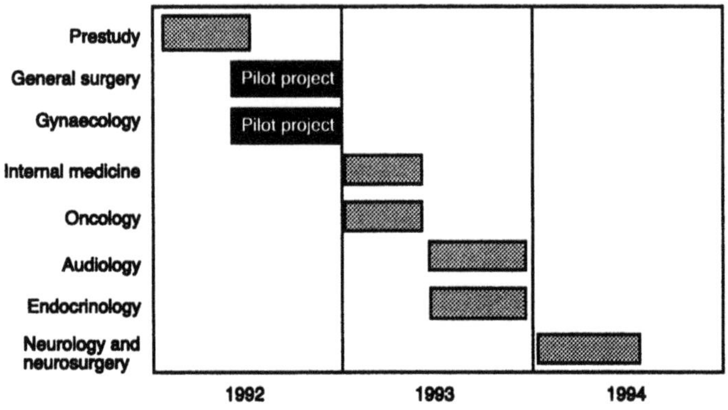

The BCG began with the surgery department since this was the first for which the DRGs had been calculated by the local health authority. A benchmark study of the surgical area had shown the possibilities for improvement (Table 18.1). The data on capacity utilisation was especially revealing, - 59 per cent of potential operating time was not being utilised.[7] Early stops to the working day accounted for 22 per cent of lost time, late starts for 28 per cent and changeovers between operations (bearing in mind the comparison with the Mayo Clinic shown in Table 18.1) for 54 per cent.. Three major factors accounted for this low level of utilisation. First, a breakdown of employee activities identified an imbalance between the previously autonomous functional groupings - whereas the anaesthetists and anaesthetic nurses were working intensively, the operating staff were relatively underutilised (Figure 18.3). Secondly, changeover procedures between operations were not optimised. And, third, operations were not organised by the speciality of surgery and this did not contribute to optimum theatre utilisation.

TABLE 18.1
BENCHMARKING OF KH OPERATING THEATRES

Key Indicator	Karolinska Hospital	Best Performer
Effective utilisation of operating theatre (%)	40	88 (Mayo Clinic, USA)
Time between operations (mins.)	59	12 (Mayo Clinic)
Bed utilisation (%)	87	98 (Sahlgrenska, Sweden)
Proportion day surgery (%)	20-30	50 (Potential)
Doctor and nurse time on patient care	20-30	60 (Henry Ford, USA)

Figure 18.3. : Use of Time in Operating Theatres

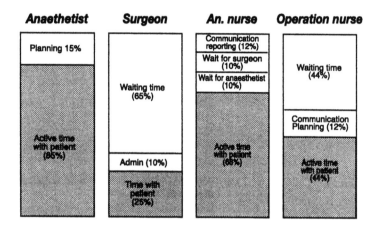

Thereafter a similar approach of identifying wasted time was adopted across the departments. Each area had special circumstances and showed up particular organisational weaknesses. For example, in the treatment of inguinal hernias, the investigation highlighted significant differences between wards (Table 18.2). In another example, an analysis of operations in a particular operating ward showed that 17.5 per cent of operations were cancelled: of these, less than one-third were because the patient did not show up or for medical reasons; the remainder were due to inadequate organisation.

TABLE 18.2
BENCHMARKING PERFORMANCE BETWEEN WARDS

	Day Surgery	Ward 1	Ward 2	Ward 3
Average age of patient (years)	50	67	68	64
In-patient days	0	3.5	2	1
Electro-cardiograph (%)	16	80	73	60
% patients with completed investigations at admission	100	10	36	80
Heart/lung X Ray	0	30	45	40
% planned operations cancelled	~0	14.8	17.5	3
Number of doctors treating patient	1	3	3	4
% referring doctors getting feedback from Karolinska Hospital	69	70	27	100

But, most powerful were the process-flow studies which showed the percentage of patient time which was 'dead', that is, which was spent waiting (Table 18.3). In some cases, this waiting-time was a positive feature (allowing doctors and patients to assess the extent of the problem or the impact of treatment), but in the majority of cases the medical staff recognised that these delays were sub-optimal. Similarly, although no data was collected, patients attending clinics at the hospital would frequently spend a great deal of their time waiting for treatment, or waiting between treatments.

TABLE 18.3
PERCENTAGE OF TOTAL TREATMENT TIME SPENT WAITING BY PATIENTS

Treatment	Total Time for Medical Care (days)	% Time in Treatment
Unprioritised prostrate gland	255	2
Claudicatio	180	6
Critical ischemi	90	23
Carotis	57	16
Tumor investigation	70	23
Inguinal hernia	183	2

The Organisational Response

As we have seen, the new forms of manufacturing organisation are built around the elimination of work-in-progress through an attack on wasted time. In the applications of these principles to the KH, two sets of wasted time were addressed. The first was the time spent by patients, in waiting for the initial treatment to start and between treatments - patients were thus treated as if they were work-in-progress. The second element of wasted time was that in the under-utilisation of resources, both of employees and facilities (particularly the operating theatres). In addressing these objectives, a number of key changes were introduced:

- The principles of 'families of products' (that is, group technology) were applied, both within the hospital framework as a whole and within individual departments. (This use of this group technology is most advanced in the Mayo Clinic in the USA, which is built around 12 'families'; a restructuring Danish hospital has chosen eight families). In this schema medical disciplines and hospital functions are grouped in clusters of illness. So far only three families have been identified in the KH - cardio/thorax, gastro and neuro (Figure 18.4) - and of these, only neuro (and to some extent cardio-thorax) have been effectively im-

Figure 18.4.: 'Families of Illness' in KH Reorganisation

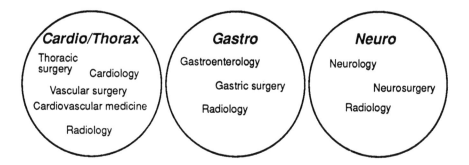

plemented so far.

This principles of group technology has also been used to considerable effect within the surgical area. Here it became clear that a source of considerable delay in changeover time was the separation of the theatres around the types of surgery involved (reflecting specific medical specialities). Following a detailed investigation of over 1,000 operations, it became clear that 67 per cent of all operations were predictable and took less than 60 minutes; others were both more specialised and less predictable. Thus the theatres were instead segmented into four groups, based upon the likely duration of the operation rather than the type of operation - the 'fast room', the 'medium room', the 'slow room' and the 'emergency room'. In endocrinology the application of group technology principles highlighted the fact that the 150 separate diagnoses fell into five groupings. In each of these areas, reorganisation occurred, with treatments being clustered on a multi-disciplinary basis.

- The breakdown of functional specialities was thus a necessary component of the application of group technology. In the surgical area, this meant that anaesthetists and surgeons - who used to work independently - are now coordinated on a daily basis. It also means that instead of wards being specialised by disciplines, they are shared with doctors moving to the patients.[8]

- The principles of rapid machine changeover were adopted to the surgical theatres, with an emphasis placed upon pre-operative preparation. Amongst other things, this meant that a new pre-operation anaesthetic out-patient clinic had to be opened. Throughout the hospital an emphasis

297

was placed upon the coordination of treatments and testing, with a particular emphasis on the completion of testing before patients were seen by doctors (this had been a major cause of delay for patients, and of cancelled/postponed operations for the hospital).

- The principles of 'production pulling' were satisfied through the application of the DRG system. Previously the KH had thrived on waiting lists (which had been seen as a strength, a sign of demand for its activities), but with the new Stockholm Model the treatments offered were more closely attuned to actual demand. The consequence was that the large 'inventories' locked up in waiting lists were rapidly depleted (see below).

- The TBM analysis had identified that many tests routinely conducted were unnecessary; in other cases they were unnecessarily intensive. Thus, of particular significance, a decision was taken to switch to the more intensive use of day-care operations wherever feasible.

V.   THE IMPACT OF ORGANISATIONAL CHANGE AT THE KAROLINSKA HOSPITAL

The three objectives underlying this reorganisation were cost-savings, quality improvements and an improvement in employee morale. Unfortunately, it is only recently that the KH has begun collecting the statistics which make detailed comparisons over time possible. However, the improvement in cost effectiveness has been significant. For example in the operating theatres, unit costs have fallen by approximately 20 per cent, in part because it has been possible to increase the volume of operations as a consequence of reducing changeover times, late starts and early finishes. These went up from 12,000 to 14,600 (30 per cent), but total costs fell by two per cent. (Two operating theatres were also closed down, so with additional throughput of patients, the potential realisable savings are in the order of 40 per cent). Additional cost savings were achieved in surgery (13 per cent), gynaecology (24 per cent per patient treatment) and the elimination of unnecessary tests (identified through the application of TBM principles). The total savings in this first phase of initial interventions was more than Kr35m per annum, four times the total cost of the resources put into the reorganisation. But these interventions only scratch the surface of potential impacts upon costs, both in terms of the depth of application of these new organisational principles and the spread of these organisational techniques throughout the hospital. Nevertheless, their impact on total hospital performance is already beginning to show, with unit patient costs falling in constant prices by five per cent in 1993 (Table 18.4).[9]

TABLE 18.4
IMPROVEMENT IN TOTAL HOSPITAL PERFORMANCE: COST PER PATIENT

	1992	1993	Change (%)
Number of beds	1,122	1,022	-9.1
Revenue (Kr1993'000)	2,069,263	1,963,259	-5.1
In-patients	47,303	46,959	-0.7
Out-patients	469,486	488,605	+4.1
Weight-adjusted patients*	1,667,064	1,674,893	+0.5
Productivity index	100	105.9	+5.9
Average length of stay (days)	5.54	5.33	-3.8

*Calculated to take account of differences between in- and out-patients

If these initial savings can be generalised throughout the hospital (and there is no reason why they cannot), it is estimated that the potential additional cost savings is likely to be in the region of Kr260m, equivalent in total to a 15 per cent cut in operating costs. These savings reflect the one-off benefits of a change in organisational structure, but ignore the potential impact of introducing continuous improvement programmes (see the contributions by Bessant and Kaplinsky in this volume). Moreover, these calculations only reflect the savings captured within the hospital. But there are a range of additional economy-wide savings which arise from the fact that patients spend less time waiting, both between treatments and once they have entered the hospital. They thus not only benefit in welfare terms, but are also likely to be absent less frequently from their places of employment.

But it is clear from Table 18.5 that non-traditional quality indicators (that is, outside of medical performance such as surgical outcomes) have also risen significantly.[10] And, although no figures are available to measure the impact upon staff morale, detailed discussion with a range of individuals throughout the hospital hierarchy, confirm that the new organisational practices are generally seen as improving the quality of working life.[11]

TABLE 18.5
SOME QUALITY INDICATORS

	Before Reorganisation	After Reorganisation
Time from referral to release (hernia) (weeks)	28	7
Time from referral to notice about out-patient visit	1 week - 5 months	< 1 week
Audiology waiting list*	22 months	12 months
Cancellations (%)	12	3
Coordination of testing** (%)	20	50

*With 25 per cent reduction in staff.
**This reduces the need for multiple visits

VI. SOME IMPORTANT ISSUES IN THE PROCESS OF ORGANISATIONAL CHANGE AT THE KAROLINSKA HOSPITAL

Although the process of organisational change at the KH has been successful in terms of cost reduction and quality enhancement, it is by no means unproblematic:

- The improvement in productivity has grave distributional implications. The ability to improve the utilisation of hospital resources (as for example in the more than 30 per cent increase in operations) depends upon the 'rationalisation' of the hospital system. This either means closing down one or more of these hospitals (Stockholm currently has eight hospitals, one every 3 kilometres) or reducing their capacity. So far the KH has not suffered from its improved performance since it has been able to eat into its waiting lists and has benefited from the transfer of an emergency ward from a smaller hospital. It will also benefit in the future from the transfer of a paediatric clinic from a smaller hospital. Nevertheless it is unlikely that these additional services will take-up all the improvement in capacity arising out of future changes and, more-over, the gains of the Karolinska have been at the expense of other hospitals. Thus, as in many other cases of technological change, there are difficult decisions to be made in the trade-off between employment,

300

access and operating costs. The inherently labour-intensive nature of hospital services (about 65 to 70 per cent of unit costs are labour), the sensitive nature of the services provided and the lobbying power of its medical staff are likely to further complicate the ability of society to reap the gains from organisational change.

- It is not clear how much of this improvement is due to the specific organisational changes introduced through the TBM system, and how much arise from the general introduction of the Stockholm Model's purchaser/supplier system. Because of the inability of the BCG and Lindsten to endogenise a process of organisational change (see below) and because the process trod on sensitive egos, many employees believe that the improvements result from the DRG system rather than from TBM, despite the fact that similar improvements are to be found in manufacturing enterprises which already operate in a market system. To the extent that it is the DRG-related organisational changes that have driven the improvement, this may not be a process free from difficulty. In the UK this system has led to very significant increases in managerial costs which threaten to outweigh the positive aspects arising from a cost-focus; it has also led to a health system which is less receptive to patient needs (unless they pay directly for their services, thus undermining the principles of socialised health). Moreover there are distortions which are built into the DRG system which may threaten its long-term future.[12]

- The process of introduction of these organisational changes through the BCG was complex. Many of the medical specialities felt that they were aware of the problems before they were identified by the time-based investigations, but that they neither had the funds nor the power to implement these changes. The BCG was associated with glossy publications, a Harvard Business School video ('I don't recognise myself or the Karolinska', observed one prominent specialist who had been filmed) and enormous razzmatazz. It thus led to resentment, sometimes because it showed up individual weaknesses, sometimes because of envy, but often because the hospital staff felt that their ideas had been appropriated. Whatever the reason, the fact is that the process of implementation has slowed down, and there is a widespread belief amongst management that the reorganisation should have been driven internally. There is thus virtually no evidence of any incipient processes of continuous improvement, and it is notable that the CEO who drove the changes through the hospital has resigned and has moved to a Danish hospital where he believes that it will be more possible to move to a more effective reorganisation based upon the same principles introduced into the KH.

VII. CONCLUSIONS

We have observed a complex set of organisational changes, both in the overall system of health care governing the hospital incentive system (proximating to 'firm strategies' in manufacturing) and in relation to the KH's internal organisation (proximating to 'manufacturing strategy'). It is clear that the benefits arising out of the first phase of organisational change have been substantial, but much is still to be achieved. KH is probably the most advanced example of this form of health care reorganisation in Europe, and its performance is only surpassed by a handful of American hospitals.

But what are the wider implications of its experience? Five stand out in importance:

(1) On the basis if this experience, it is clear that many of the principles of organisational change developed in the manufacturing sector are of generic relevance, not only to white-collar activities in manufacturing (through 'business process re-engineering'), but also to the service sector.

(2) As in the manufacturing sector, organisational change in services is primarily hindered by social processes rather than by technical constraints. This is reflected in part by the scepticism of some of the KH staff to TBM, the continuing opposition by some entrenched functional specialities (backed by law in Sweden, where Heads of departments are legally responsible for performance) and surfacing in comments such as 'we are working with human beings, not Volvo cars' and 'we are not working with machines ...'.

(3) The fact that little physical production occurs in the service sector may mean that these social obstacles to innovation may be more marked than in the manufacturing sector. The problematic nature of utilising market relations in this sector, also makes it difficult to introduce incentives to enforce organisational change. 'Profitability' and 'bankruptcy' are not very helpful concepts in the provision of social services.

(4) We have been able to identify a process of change in the hospital sector which provides the potential for an approximate 1 per cent increment to total GDP, even without taking into account the economic (and welfare) benefits arising from the fact that patients lose less time in their treatment. But health care delivery - understood as a cradle-to-grave process - is far wider than the hospital system, and other areas of care also lend themselves to reorganisation. The overall economic benefits of new principles of organisation in the total system will thus be considerably larger.

(5)   The observed improvements at the KH arise through the utilisation of new techniques of organisation and have been almost entirely disembodied in nature. Yet, in the long run (as is shown in the Japanese automobile industry)[12] changes in organisation provide the potential for utilising flexible information technologies effectively. There are thus likely to be significant further gains through the application of various computing systems through the health care cycle [*Pollak, 1985*].

NOTES

1.   In the first half of 1993, of 82 New York Times' articles addressing health care costs, access and quality, 79 related to costs [*Chelimsky, 1993*].
2.   The total market for automobiles in Japan only reached 250,000 - an optimal plant size in mass production - in 1959 [*Hoffman and Kaplinsky, 1988*].
3.   At over 10 per cent in 1993, Sweden's budgetary deficit is one of the highest in the OECD countries.
4.   The BCG system is outlined in Stalk and Hout [*1990*]; comparison with any of the texts of Japanese management practices [e.g., *Schonberger, 1992, Monden, 1993, Suzaki, 1987, and Bessant, 1991*] shows the broad similarity between these approaches.
5.   The total cost of the three phases of the BCG input exceeded Kr5m; in addition the Working Life Fund also provided Kr3.5m to cover the costs of hospital staff time.
6.   This involved 200 staff interviews, 30 interviews in the health care system, patient surveys, benchmark surveys in five hospitals, following 500 patients through hospital care and detailed analysis of over 1,000 operations.
7.   It would never be possible to have 100 per cent utilisation; the maximum feasible was around 85-90 per cent.
8.   The fact that the KH was spread over 13 buildings (rather than in one big complex) not only made it easier to separate these clusters, but also to realise space savings as productivity improved by closing buildings.
9.   Calculated in constant 1993 prices, the savings in total hospital operating costs in the first year (taking account of the different 'product mix' in the switch to out-patient surgery) was 5.9 per cent.
10.   The goals for the improvement in non-traditional quality indicators were: 1992 - each department was to develop its own indicators; but there was little response to this general exhortation; 1993 - (a) accessibility (for example, doctors answering telephone calls; waiting times for appointments; length of waiting lists (b) continuity - patient seeing same named doctor; 1994 - (a) more on emphasis on continuity, to include named nurse (b) greater documentation.
11.   Some respondents felt that they were working a little harder - 'a lot smarter and a little harder' - but even they were in favour of the changed practices.
12.   For example, many pregnant women suffer from Karpel's Tunnel syndrome. This used to be treated with a splint, but now that the department is paid for surgical interventions by the DRG system, it tends to be treated by operation.

In the intensive care unit, there is sometimes a reluctance of departments to treat some patients until they are put on respirators (which is generously rewarded in the DRG system).
13. See Hoffman and Kaplinsky [*1988*].

REFERENCES

Bessant, J. (1991), *Managing Advanced Manufacturing Technology*, London: Basil Blackwell.

Boston Consulting Group, (1993), 'Creating Cost Efficiency and Better Patient Service in a Changing Health Care Environment', Stockholm, mimeo.

Chelimsky, E. (1993), 'The Political Debate About Health Care: Are We Losing Sight of Quality?', Science, Vol. 262, 22 Oct., pp. 525-8.

Hoffman, R. and R. Kaplinsky (1988), *Driving Force: The Global Restructuring of Technology, Labor and Investment in the Automobile and Components Industries*, Boulder: Westview Press.

Kaplinsky, R. (1994), *Easternisation: The Spread of Japanese Management Techniques to Developing Coutnries*, London: Frank Cass.

Monden, Y. (1983), *Toyota Production System: Practical Approach to Production Management*, Atlanta: Industrial Engineering and Management Press.

Pollak, V. E, (1985), 'The Computer in Medicine: Its Application to Medical Practice, Quality Control, and Cost Containment', *Journal of the American Medical Association*, Vol. 253, No. 1, 4 Jan.

Schonberger, R. J. (1982), *Japanese Manufacturing Techniques: Nine Hidden Lessons in Simplicity*, New York: The Free Press.

Stalk, G. Jr., and T. M. Hout (1990), *Competing Against Time: How Time-Based Competition is Reshaping Global Markets*, New York: The Free Press.

Suzaki, K. (1987), *The New Manufacturing Challenge: Techniques for Continuous Improvement*, New York: The Free Press.

19

CHALLENGES TO PUBLIC POLICY:
A COMMENTARY

Bengt-Ake Lundvall

I.   INTRODUCTION

Let me first express my strong support for the general idea behind the overall project. It is well documented that not only public organisations but also private firms tend to operate with organisational routines which are inefficient. It is also increasingly recognised that public policy should be geared towards facilitating organisational as well as technical innovation and especially its diffusion to the whole population of firms.

Some years ago I made a study together with colleagues form Aalborg University of the specific Danish productivity paradox [*Naes-Gjerding et al., 1992*]. When interviewing a sample of 280 small and medium-sized enterprises we achieved results which strongly support the need for organisational change. We found that firms which had introduced information technology and which had registered adverse productivity effects indicated two single factors as the most important barriers to efficient introduction of IT;

* lack of organisational adaptation;
* insufficient human resource development.

As one result of this study new government programmes aimed at promoting organisational change were developed in close co-operation with the Industrial Federation of Denmark.

At the OECD we are now in the midst of a major effort to analyse the interaction between technology, productivity and employment as a response to a request emanating from the G7 meeting in Detroit which took place in April 1994. It is interesting to note that prominent among the issues raised was organisational change at the firm level and its impact on the demand for labour, including implications for the demand for skills. It becomes more and more obvious that analysis and policy that focus exclusively on technology and neglect organisational change are biased and misleading.

II. ORGANISATIONAL CHANGE AND STANDARD ECONOMICS

Let me at this point add some reflections on how mainstream economic theory treats the kind of issues which are on our agenda. There is little room left for bettering the organisation of firms according to standard economies. It is assumed that competition exterminates organisations which are sub-optimal in this respect. It is difficult to make such a model compatible with a real world where firms actually do use quite substantial resources to ameliorate the workings of their organisation. Either the money is well used or it is wasted and in both cases standard theory assuming rational behaviour and efficient organisation as the norm is mistaken.

The studies by John Bessant and Klaus Semlinger are about networking between firms. Neither of these phenomena, which most businessmen recognise as being of great strategic importance, well covered in standard textbooks on microeconomics. If firms do co-operate in the textbook world they do so only to collude and to exploit consumers.

These deviations between the approach of this book and standard economics should perhaps have been made more explicit. The kind of findings presented here are important and they should be used even as part of an effort to move towards a more realistic and relevant body of economic theory.

III. THE IMPORTANCE OF THE SYSTEMIC CONTEXT

The two chapters on industrial networks by Bessant and Semlinger as well as Raphael Kaplinsky's study on organisational reform in the health sector have in common a focus on organisational change and learning. In all three cases a somewhat more developed analysis of the 'systemic context' could have been more useful. While it might be justifiable to disregard the social and cultural context in standard economies where the focus is on exchange and allocation of given resources this is much less so when it comes to analyse learning and change. Learning and organisational change involve social interactions and the broader institutional set-up will affect the outcome of the process.

Can the UK and German experiences in building networks analysed by John Bessant and Klaus Semlinger (and the Swedish experience described by Kaplinsky) be successfully transferred to other countries? The relationship between academics and business will be different in the UK and Mediterranean countries, not allowing for the playing of the same kind of mediating role in the network formation process. The specific role played by university scholars in the UK case and by technical institutes in the

306

German case may, for instance, not be easily replicated in countries in Southern Europe.

In the Kaplinsky analysis of organisational change at Karolinska the professional self-perception of doctors and other hospital personnel would be important factors for realising organisation change. Such factors would differ typically between countries.

A well-known weakness with case studies is of course that generalisation of results is often difficult. Supplementing case studies with the development of broadly based indicators for organisational change, therefore, should be considered. Ideally such indicators should be developed in such a way that they allow comparisons to be made over time and across countries[1].

A general recommendation for further work would be thus, on the one hand, to develop the analysis of the systemic context and, on the other, to supplement qualitative case study work with analysis on the basis of new indicators.

IV. ON THE IMPORTANCE OF TRUST IN NETWORKS

The importance of trust is obvious in relation to all three studies. When considering how to stimulate the formation of networks Bessant and Semlinger refer to 'trust' as a fundamental factor. The more trust there is among a given set of actors, the easier it becomes to engage in demanding any long-term commitments. Within the Japanese *Keiretsu* we find a high degree of mutual trust in this sense. To a certain extent this might reflect a stabilising authoritarian tradition. In Sweden the Uppsala network school [*Håkansson, 1987; 1989*] has demonstrated that Swedish firms also enter into long-term relationships without too many difficulties. At the other extreme the US has developed a legal and contractual system that assumes that mutual trust is very limited, and firms seem to behave accordingly, bringing lawyers to the table when inter-firm conflict arises. A better understanding of the real basis for such differences is very important for any policy aiming at creating network.

V. HEALTH CARE REORGANISATION AND QUALITY CONTROL

The reorganisation of the Swedish hospital, Karolinska, analysed by Kaplinsky, is extremely interesting for many reasons. The idea that new organisational forms developed in the automobile sector should be applicable to a publicly owned hospital is provocative. According to the analysis it appears that both patients and personnel derive benefits from the new system. It might be useful however, to give some attention to the long-term impact of the reform on the trust relationships between 'doctors and patients'. Do the new ways of doing things undermine the professional pride and, indirectly, the professional ethics of doctors? In manufacturing, quality mishaps are costly. In the health sector the overall quality of services is critically dependent on the trust patients can have in doctors and hospitals. The trade-off curve between efficiency and quality is steep. Again different national traditions among health care personnel might be more or less resistant to the temptation to weaken quality control when faced with the demand for higher productivity.

Another point raised by Kaplinsky is the long-term impact on employment in the health sector. In a less complex or more dynamically growing economy resource savings should be unequivocally welcomed since resources would be put to other more efficient uses. Given that many European governments are now considering how to promote labour-intensive activities in the private service sector, the issue is worth considering. Is it realistic, however, to have a highly productive, professional and well-paid staff in the public sector coexisting with a private service sector that is low-productive and that pays much lower wages?

VI. CONCLUSION

Case studies of organisational change are useful in inspiring policy developments where the focus is on diffusing better-practice within and between countries. To avoid simplistic copying and naive imitation it is important to realise that organisational change intervenes in social structures that vary between regions and countries. A more explicit specification of the systematic context is therefore necessary.

NOTE

1. The innovation surveys pursued by Eurostat in co-operation with the OECD do include questions which might be helpful in this context.

REFERENCES

Håkansson, H. (1987), *Industrial/Technological Development, A Network Approach*, Kent: Croom Helm.

Håkansson, H. (1989), *Corporate Technological Behaviour, Co-operation and Networks*, 1989, Worcester: Billing & Sons Ltd.

Naes-Gjerding, A.N., Johnson, B., Kallehauge, L., Lundvall, B.A. and P.T. Madsen (1992), *The Productivity Mystery*, Copenhagen: DJØF Publishing.

PART VI:
PERSPECTIVES

There is a growing recognition that the path to renewed competitiveness lies in the adoption of new forms of organisation, even through the appreciation of the detailed implications for corporate strategic orientation and for government and Community-level policies is not always well developed. This final Part follows on from the earlier case studies and considers the conclusions drawn from these in a wider policy context.

In a view from the USA, Nathan Rosenberg shows the growing emergence of relevant policy debate, even though this is submerged in wider discussion of trade policy and support for high technology. Yet, as in Europe, the USA does not yet appear to be adequately focused on the importance of these organisational issues in industrial restructuring. Luc Soete's own research in Europe confirms the existence of the 'productivity paradox' which we have identified, and reinforces the importance of these organisational issues in the challenge to revive European competitiveness. In the final chapter, the editors of this volume reflect briefly on some of the wider issues raised by this case-study material, and point to the implications for policy formulation at the local, national and supra-national levels.

20

PERSPECTIVES: A VIEW FROM THE USA

Nathan Rosenberg

It is not obvious what role an American ought to be playing at a European Union conference devoted to the question of organisational innovation as a way of improving European competitiveness. Which of several possible hats ought he to wear? Should an American describe organisational arrangements in the United States that might serve as models to be considered for European adoption? Or should he commiserate with his European cousins by providing yet further evidence of how the Japanese seem to organise their economic lives so much better than we do? While mulling over these alternatives, I read of the 'World Competitiveness Report', published in September 1994 by the World Economic Forum. The report provided a ranking of the competitiveness of 41 countries by use of no less than 381 criteria. On the specific issue of the effect of government policies on competitiveness, the report ranked The United States among the top ten, a ranking that, I can assure you, would elicit gales of derisive laughter in many American circles. But, perhaps more seriously for a European audience, none of the top ten countries was a member of the European Union, whereas four of the bottom ten are members of that Union.

What I propose to do, therefore, is to look at the current policy debate in the United States, with special attention to issues of government policies as they relate to the questions of competitiveness and organisation. What the particular relevance of these observations may have to the European scene is something that I am happy to leave to Europeans to decide.

America is currently in the midst of a rather painful, often divisive debate over the appropriate policy responses to a changing international environment. There is, first, the issue of the decline in American dominance of high technology markets. For 25 years or so after the end of the Second World War, many people in the United States came to regard as 'natural' what was, in fact, a most unnatural state of affairs: an unchallenged American dominance of high tech markets while the rest of the industrial world was recovering from the most devastating war in history.

I am sorry to say that this is not a very well-informed debate, at least among the policy-makers in Washington, DC. It is often acrimonious, full of populist rhetoric and, in particular, coloured by intemperate and ill-informed 'Japan bashing'. America's trade deficit with the Japanese tends to be explained in highly simplistic terms, dominated by the depiction of Japan as an unfair trader. Relatively little is said of the underlying macroeconomic determinants of the trade imbalance, and there are hardly any references to America's drastic departures from its own free trade rhetoric, such as 'voluntary export quotas' - a voluntary export quota being, of course, a quota that is *not* voluntary.

The second, more recent element in the policy debate has been associated with an otherwise extremely happy event: the end of the cold war. A bit of historical perspective may be useful here, because it is often not widely appreciated how much international events, beginning with the outbreak of the Second World War, have moved economic and social policy in the United States from its pre-war moorings.

Perhaps much of what I want to say can be encapsulated in a single historical observation. In 1940, the last year in which the federal budget was not yet dominated by the Second World War, the federal government's R&D budget for the Department of Agriculture exceeded that of the combined armed services! Which is to say that the Second World War, together with the cold war that succeeded it, created an entirely new situation in terms of the role that the federal government played as a result of the sea change in its spending commitments.

Ever since the outbreak of the Second World War the federal government has come to play a dominating role in total R&D spending in the United States. A transforming event, perhaps ironically, was the gigantic Manhattan Project, a 'crash programme' whose success resulted in the early end of the war in the Pacific, with the explosion of the atomic bomb. As the hot war slipped into a cold war, the federal government maintained a massive research commitment to nuclear power for both military and peaceful purposes. Similarly, the military and strategic importance of aircraft led to huge post-war subsidies to innovation in the aircraft industry and to a special commitment to the development of the jet engine that was introduced in the closing months of the war. In the case of the computer, all of the early financial support for an electronic computer came from military budgets. The first successful electronic digital computer, the so-called ENIAC (Electronic Numerical Integrator, Analyzer, and Computer), emerged at the University of Pennsylvania shortly after the end of the war. Research was financed by a contract with the Army Ballistic Research Laboratory at Aberdeen, Maryland, which needed an enhanced computer capability to assist in ballistic research.

The transistor story was different in that, unlike the two innovations just mentioned, it was financed privately, at AT&T's Bell Labs, and not publicly. The main impetus toward its development, announced in December 1947, was the desire to improve long distance telephone transmission. However, the Department of Defense was quick to understand that miniaturisation and increased reliability of electrical circuits would also play an important role in the improvement of military hardware. It was widely realised that further improvements in this technology would find a large and ready market in military procurement contracts. Thus, when the integrated circuit was introduced after 1960, purchases were overwhelmingly dominated, for several year, by the military. The essential points here is that the impact of the military upon technological change was not exercised only through large R&D budgets but also through the awareness, in the private sector, that very large military procurement contracts were likely to be captured by firms that could generate the appropriate new technologies.

Closely associated with the role played by the military in some of the main high tech innovations of the second half of the century was the dramatic impact of federal financial support for university research, especially research of a more fundamental nature. The flowering of American universities as world class centres of scientific research was a post-war phenomenon. Since the end of the war the federal government became, by far, the main patron of university research. This expressed itself through several agencies of government including, initially, the Office of Naval Research and, later, the National Science Foundation and, much more important in recent years, the National Institutes of Health. But, in addition, the Department of Defence came to support university research at quite basic research levels in a variety of fields which were thought to be of potential relevance for military purposes. This included many rather low visibility programmes such as the Joint Services Electronics Program at a number of the foremost research universities, as well as the new field of computer science which was heavily supported by the Department of Defence.

The end of the cold war and the increasing emphasis on international competitiveness is leading to a broad reconsideration of the role of American universities. On the one hand, the strong rationale that the cold war provided for huge libations of financial support to university research has substantially weakened. On the other hand, universities are coming to be regarded increasingly as weapons in the international competitiveness battle. American universities can not patent the results of research that was supported by federal funds. Engineering Research Centers, established at a number of universities with National Science Foundation funding, are encouraged to look for commercial applications and to enter into collaborative arrangements with private industry. Congress in fiscal year 1994 required that the

NSF allocate 60 per cent of its budget to support 'strategic projects'. There is great concern that a major university commitment to economic 'relevance' will, in the long run, not only seriously compromise the quality of university research but also fail to provide a rationale comparable to the earlier rationale of national security.

One of the greatest concerns that currently dominates the American policy debate is the low rate of productivity growth that has characterised the economy for the past quarter century. Low productivity growth, it is coming to be increasingly realised, translates into the very slow improvement in real wages that has been experienced since the early 1970s.

In some respects the poor productivity performance can be attributed to demographic phenomena. The past couple decades - again going back to the early 1970s - saw a huge growth in the labour force, as members of the 'baby boom' years entered the labour market and the female labour force partici- pation rate continued its climb. An associated feature was a less experienced labour force, one that was not well prepared to adapt readily to the ongoing structural changes and altered skill requirements that have been generated by technological change and the growing importation of labour-intensive manufactured products. As a result there is an increasing focus on the need to improve the educational system and the ways in which that should be accomplished. More attention is now being given to the need for better vocational training. There is a good deal of recent interest, for example, in the German system.

When one looks at productivity growth by sector, one factor stands out. Productivity growth in the manufacturing sector - at least as it is conven- tionally measured by government agencies - is far higher than in the service sectors, but the service sectors now constitute more than 70 per cent of the American labour force and the manufacturing sector less than 18 per cent. The appropriate conclusion is beginning to be drawn but, so far, only from more thoughtful observers, that much greater attention needs to be given to ways of raising productivity in service employment. The recent proposals for health care reform may be regarded as, at least partially, a reflection of this new awareness. I should like to stress my belief that there are potentially huge productivity payoffs from organisational innovation in the service sector, and that the subject is well deserving of a high priority for future research.

The unsatisfactory productivity performance is leading to a realisation that is reluctantly, but gradually, coming to be accepted: that improvements in technology are far from being a sufficient condition for productivity growth. This realisation has been helped along by a number of 'horror stories', such as that of General Motors during the 1980s. GM spent many tens of billions of dollars installing sophisticated robotics and other highly automated equipment, but failed to halt a steady deterioration in its position in the car market. There is now a growing sense that technological factors have been overemphasised at the expense of a number of other factors that are crucial to the successful commercialisation of new technologies. More voices are now advancing the position that government technology policy has excessively emphasised the 'big breakthrough' mentality, at the expense of the smaller, incremental improvements that may ultimately determine success or failure in the market-place.

A healthy by-product of the failure to achieve relatively easy technological 'fixes' for poor economic performance has been an increasing willingness to address organisational issues. So far this discussion has been limited to only a few issues, especially the question of optimal size of firms and the associated questions of the economic desirability of mergers and the possible relaxation of the anti-trust laws to permit more co-operative activities among competing firms.

One of the most conspicuous features of the recent discussion of size of firms is an increasing attention to the virtues of small new 'start-up' firms as carriers of successful new technologies. Associated with this has been an increasing tendency to regard very large firms as bureaucratic behemoths with rigid decision-making procedures and limited capability for assessing new trends in the market place and adapting quickly to them. The recent difficulties of firms such as General Motors and IBM of course lend some credibility to this new perspective. The management 'guru' literature that fifteen years ago celebrated the virtues of the largest firms have increasingly become 'cheerleaders' for start-up firms struggling, with venture capitalist support, to bring new and superior products to the market-place.

There is no doubt that a distinctive organisational difference between the US, on the one hand, and both Europe and Japan on the other, has been the prominent role played by new start-up firms as carriers of new technology. This has been especially true of electronics technologies in the post-war period, particularly in the related fields of semiconductors and computers (mini, micro and super). That role is currently especially prominent in the newly-emerging biotechnology industry. It is worth emphasising that the prominence of small firms has been closely connected with the important role of the venture capital industry, on the one hand, and the openness of the American university system, on the other.

Although there is little explicit discussion at the policy level in the United States of the need for significant organisational change, there is widespread recognition of two things that would seem to point forcefully in that direction. First the failure, already mentioned, of large firms to improve their competitive position merely through vast expenditures on new technology. But secondly there is now widespread acknowledgement that there is much that is admirable in the operation of Japanese firm, although there is widespread disagreement over what accounts for these admirable features. Even when there is some agreement, as in the benefits that flow from long-term employment and the greater element of trust that characterises interfirm relations, there is considerable disagreement on the transferability of the conditions that make these benefits possible. There is great admiration for the absence, in Japan, of the sort of 'trench warfare' that seems to characterise much of US industrial relations, especially in the mass production industries. There is a growing awareness that long-term employment security has a great deal to do with the willingness of Japanese firms to make significant investments in the training of their employees. It also appears to play an important role in the Japanese flexibility of work assignment, the lack of rigid job descriptions, and the relative ease of introducing new technologies.

A closing comment on the case studies. The concern with organisational innovation is, in my view, a focus of major importance and potential value. I applaud it and regret that these issues are not yet receiving similar attention in the US. What I miss in this discussion, at least so far, is an examination of how new organisational forms will enable the European firm to become a more effective innovator with respect to new technology. There is a strong focus in the case studies on ways in which organisational modifications can render the firm a more effective operator in catering to the diversity of *existing* demand, and with *existing* technology. Thus, while I have been critical of the excessive American preoccupation with new technology, it also seems to me that the European discussion has been insufficiently attentive to new technology and to how new organisational forms might improve the ability of European firms to play a greater leadership position in introducing new technology. My reading of the case studies is that they exhibit a valuable concern with how organisational change can make possible a much more effective exploitation of existing technology, without showing much interest in how new organisational forms might place Europe at the forefront of technological change. Unless this bigger issue is addressed more energetically, I believe that Europe's longer-term future is destined to be one of second rank economic status. And I should also admit candidly to a concern on my part that some of you have already accepted this second class status as inevitable. My own view is that it is by no means inevitable and certainly not desirable, but I would not want to presume, as an American, to pronounce on how Europeans ought to go about defining their own future.

21

ORGANISATIONAL INNOVATION: A EUROPEAN PERSPECTIVE

Luc Soete

INTRODUCTION

In these couple of pages of reflections on the 'European perspective' of organisational innovation, three sets of issues will be briefly discussed. First, and corroborating the analysis by Coriat, one can, I believe, talk about a research 'paradox' today. Whether such paradoxical evidence is sufficient to argue that organisational innovation is the missing link, is an interesting research question, and one which many of the chapters in this book are devoted to. However, as far as I am concerned there are many competing explanations. Second, and following on from the previous point, once we believe that organisational innovation is indeed the crucial missing element, how does one go about studying it? Is the case study approach indeed the most appropriate one? Can 'organisational change best-practice' cases be transferred across sectors, organisations, plants? Or do we need more generalisable information and indicators of organisational change, which we can subject to the whole toolbox of statistical techniques? Third and inescapably, what are the policy implications of all this? Should policy makers force firms to change organisationally? What can governments actually contribute in this whole area?

I.   PARADOXES AND 'MISSING LINKS'

Europe's technology and research situation has been described in the Commission's White Paper on *Growth, Competitiveness and Employment* as suffering from a deficit with respect to R&D efforts (particularly in terms of business enterprise performed R&D), the valorisation of research results and uncoordinated, fragmented S&T policies in member countries.

An alternative way of putting this deficit is, as Coriat points out in his chapter, in terms of a research 'paradox': despite continuous efforts in supporting R&D in member countries both nationally and at the European level, European growth and competitiveness, particularly in high tech sectors, has not improved and compared to the US and Japan even deteriorated[1]. How to explain this apparent paradox? Does it just relate to ineffective or inefficient RTD policies? Or does it relate to the setting of wrong policy goals?

Clearly, the overall 'pervasiveness' of some new technologies, such as information technology, implies what could be called *flexibility in uses*. The latter limits practically by definition the process by which 'routines' are set up to ease learning processes. In other words, some new technologies such as information technologies bring about far more hazardous and coordination problems in learning practices than other less pervasive technological innovations. This coordination and learning problem as illustrated in some of the chapters in this volume is one of the main reasons for the often disappointing productivity gains associated with the introduction and use of new information technology at the level of individual organisations. While that evidence has also been recognised at the macro-level and been referred to as the 'Solow-paradox', it has not really filtered through at the policy, and in particular the research policy level.

Pervasiveness also means indeed a shift in the particular role of the various actors in the technology generation and diffusion process. Thus, the pervasiveness of information technology has led to a significant reinforcement of the contributions and role of *intermediaries* (banks, specialised services, telecommunications, networks, and so on.) in the transfer and diffusion process of technological know-how. At the same time, the internal organisational response in terms of its flexibility and readiness to adapt itself has become an essential feature of effective use and adaptation of the technology to the organisation's own needs.

Both features point towards a somewhat reduced importance of the role and contribution of the 'hard' technology producers and suppliers. It is this latter feature that has so far been insufficiently recognised in an European RTD policy setting. From this perspective the study of organisational innovation represents indeed an essential complementary research element.

II. HOW TO GO ABOUT IT?

Studies on organisational innovation have an obvious tendency to focus on particular cases which illustrate successful organisational innovation. It is then assumed that such innovations can be transferred to other sectors, firms or organisations. The approach has to some extent much in common with the old 'best practice' technology or productivity plant studies popular in the 1960s and 1970s, and which have been instrumental in the rapid diffusing of best practice technology management practices.

The more fundamental question that can be raised, though, is whether the study of organisational innovations is so generalisable. In so far as organisational innovations involve unique combinations of human learning, crucially dependent on individual adjustments to particular new situations, each case of organisational innovation appears, to some extent, to be unique. The challenge therefore appears twofold: what can we learn from individual case studies, and is there scope for some taxonomic regrouping of cases of organisational innovation?

Den Hertog and de Sitter in the old tradition of socio-technical research have investigated in much detail the possibilities to learn from individual case studies. Obviously, as the number of case studies of organisational change and innovation further increases, the overall knowledge field expands and the question about the generalisability of such case studies can be addressed with examples, exceptions, and so on. At the same time the scope for developing particular taxomonies increases. Personally, I wonder whether, given the rich panoply of cases studied in this area, it is not time yet to try to develop more systematically success and failure studies of organisational innovation.

The notion of 'best practice' is to some extent antinomic to the concept of organisational innovation. The latter concept starts indeed from the idea that no single best practice technique exists; what one could hope therefore from pairwise studies of best and worst practice studies, is the identification of some key factors. Whether the latter can be quantified and transformed into an organisational innovation 'indicator' is at this stage probably an aim too far removed from the practical, 'advising' purpose of much of present-day research in this area. I would sympathise, though, with any attempt in this direction, if only to make the subject more popular with policy-makers.

III. ON THE ROLE OF PUBLIC POLICY

Having convinced policy-makers and politicians of the importance of organisational innovation for overall European competitiveness the most fundamental challenge to researchers in this area is probably to come up with some relatively simple proposals about what governments can do about it. Clearly if organisational innovation is the missing link, one would like to have some idea about what can be done to enhance such innovation in firms. Traditional concepts such as market failure do not help the policy debate here very far. If indeed, for example, small firms do suffer from lack of information on the particular way in which they should respond and adjust to the new opportunities offered by new technologies, how may government agencies assist. Through setting up or funding various technology intermediaries/consultants? What if those firms are not interested? Should they be forced to listen?

An interesting view might consist of focusing on areas in which governments are themselves directly involved and which have suffered from low productivity growth, despite heavy investments in new technology. This could cover both manufacturing and service sectors, but it will be clear that the latter, as illustrated in the health case analysed by Kaplinsky, offers probably the largest number of new insights and scope for policy action.

The research agenda in this area is, however, far from final. The study of organisational innovation, despite its long historical tradition rooted in many European research groups and traditions, is still in its infancy.

NOTES

1. The recent European Science and Technology Indicators report presents more evidence on the poor productivity performance of the most R&D intensive sectors in Europe.

22

CONCLUSIONS

Lars Erik Andreasen, Benjamin Coriat, Friso den Hertog and Raphael Kaplinsky

I.   ORGANISATIONAL RESTRUCTURING: THE MISSING LINK IN EUROPEAN COMPETITIVENESS

The European economy is at an abyss. On the one side lies the challenge of price competition in which the cheap labour available in the first and second tier newly industrialising countries poses a continual threat to the maintenance of real wages. On the other side the challenge is posed by the highly innovative East Asian and North American economies which have managed to shrink innovation cycles, to sustain product quality and differentiation, and simultaneously to reduce production costs. In the context of an increasingly open global trading system, inaction is clearly impossible. It is also unlikely that the member states will be willing to target a systematic policy of wage reduction as their response to the growing pressures of global competition. Furthermore, a growing trend towards inequality (as evidenced in North America) is also unlikely to be acceptable to member states.

This means that Europe, too, has to enter the path of rapid and sustained innovation in order to protect both consumer and producer interests, and to renew its global competitiveness. Competitiveness in this context should be seen as the sustained increase of standards of living, in a context favouring employment growth and normatively acceptable patterns of income distribution. But in an increasingly open global economy, the achievement of these objectives is necessarily constrained by the trade account, and for this reason an important dimension of competitiveness is to be found in the ability of the European economy to confront these external competitive challenges. On the other hand, competitiveness cannot be reduced to meeting the challenge of global rivals since there are important domains of economic activity which are largely determined by factors internal to Europe.

As is evidenced both by the macro economic analysis of Chapter 1 and the individual case studies which are presented in subsequent chapters, the decline in European competitiveness cannot be ascribed to the failure to invest in technology, in terms of R&D expenditure, investment in new production technologies or in assisting 'national champions' in their technological endeavours. Instead, we can witness what we have termed the 'productivity paradox'. Many of the classical instruments of 'technology' are in place, often in quantities which are superior to those of many of our major global competitors. Yet our relative performance has declined over the past decade and looks likely to continue unless there is a major change in direction.

The existence of this productivity paradox is explained by what we have termed the 'missing link'. By this we refer to the inability of European producers to translate their impressive technological investments into marketable goods and services with adequate alacrity, differentiation and quality, and at competitive prices. The source of this missing link is to be found in a cluster of organisational innovations. Thus, as the White Paper on *Growth, Competitiveness and Employment* concludes:

> Between 75 per cent and 95 per cent of firms' total wage and salary bill is now accounted for by functions linked to organization rather than to direct production, for example information technology, engineering, training, accounting, marketing and research. *Organizational capacity* is thus one of the key components of a firm's competitiveness (emphasis in original).
>
> ...This type of investment is becoming the key element in bringing about growth that is durable, creates skilled jobs and is economical in the use of resources. European Commission [1994, p 76]

It is notable that the recognition of this 'missing link' follows in part from the striking success of the Japanese economy and is increasingly reflected, as Nathan Rosenberg points out (Chapter 20) in the debate on industrial restructuring which is occurring in the USA.

II. OPENING THE BLACK-BOX: THE SKELETON OF ORGANISATIONAL CHANGE

We are now witnessing a fundamental change in industrial paradigm, one reflecting a transition from the principles of mass production to those required for the achievement of flexible production. The organisational principles and procedures which now underlie the bulk of economic activity follow from past commitments to mass production - to the standardisation of product, the specialisation of task, to economies of scale and to a competitive framework narrowly constructed on the basis of price. These competitive attributes have now been supplanted by a new competition in which variety is to the fore, in which product innovation and quality supplement price competition and in which instead of the labour force being seen as a cost to be minimised, it is now recognised as the key competitive asset. It is this change in industrial paradigm which necessitates the adoption of the new organisational procedures discussed in this volume.

As can be seen from the many case-studies presented in earlier chapters, as well as from comparative international experience, there are important areas of market failure in the diffusion of these new organisational techniques. But for the design of appropriate policy responses, it is necessary to open up the 'black box' of organisational change in order to identify the policy-levers; a blunt and unfocused commitment to 'organisational change' is unlikely to provide the desired rewards.

In Chapter 2 we provide a lens for prying into this cluster of organisational techniques. Three spheres of activity are identified as requiring organisational reform. The first occurs within production itself; the second in the process of research and development; and the third in the management of human resources. In each of these three spheres, new organisational techniques are being introduced which fundamentally affect the way in which work is being undertaken. But there is an additional feature to the new organisational techniques which needs to be addressed for a successful outcome to emerge. A critical component of these changes is their systemic nature [*Kaplinsky, 1988*]. This means that successful organisational innovation necessarily requires a process of integration.

Three levels of integration have been identified. The first is that between the different functions within each of the spheres (production, R&D and human resource management). The introduction of cellular production in Zilverstad (Chapter 6), Baxi (Chapter 13) and the Karolinska Hospital (Chapter 18), as well as the integration of human resource management in four Dutch companies (Chapter 11) and product development in Renault (Chapter 8) are cases in point. The second requires integration between new organisational practices in each of these spheres - for example, between design and production, as is evidenced in a variety of the case-studies including Swatch (Chapter 4) and SGS-Thomson (Chapter 9). The third level of integration arises between the operating enterprise and its external environment. Here the experience of Peugeot with its suppliers, as well as the networks described in the UK (Chapter 16) and Germany (Chapter 17) show the critical role to be played by new forms of integrative inter-firm linkages.

III. PUTTING FLESH ON THE SKELETON: ORGANISATIONAL CHANGE IN PRACTICE

The various case studies presented in this volume confirm the importance of these organisational challenges. In particular they confirm that the successful adoption of these practices provides substantial rewards and reinforce competitiveness. This is associated with enhanced profitability and growth - for example Oticon (Chapter 14), Baxi (Chapter 13) and Zilverstad (Chapter 6). But it also improves market shares (for example, Peugeot and Renault, Chapters 5 and 8) and assists European enterprises in coping with competition from the USA (SGS-Thomson, Chapter 9) and the Far East (Swatch, Chapter 4 and Zilverstad, Chapter 6). These rewards are not confined to the corporate bottom-line and there is wide-spread evidence that working conditions have improved considerably (for example as reflected in career development in the four Dutch firms described in Chapter 11) and permits the payment of relatively high wages (Baxi, Chapter 13).

The case studies also emphasise the critical importance of integration, particularly in relation to the development of new linkages with the outside world. This emphasises that competitive production in modern capitalist economies is as much about co-operation as it is about competition. But in addition to confirming the importance of organisational change for the resumption of European competitiveness, and for the need for these organisational reforms to be integrated in a systemic framework, the case-studies identify six particular features to the change process which are briefly worthy of note.

Setting Organisational Innovations in Context

Clearly, however important the diffusion of organisational changes may be at the enterprise and inter-enterprise levels, they comprise only part of an appropriate policy agenda. As the White Paper on *Growth, Competitiveness and Employment* makes clear, Europe also needs to respond to the competitive challenge by reviving the rate of investment, by refashioning the external trade regime, by investing in infrastructure, by expanding education and training, and by specific measures designed to reverse the growth of unemployment (which threatens the social framework facilitating growth).

Attention also needs to be paid to market structures. Alexis Jaquemin points out that the progress of organisational change may be undermined and/distorted by market structures (Chapter 3). And in the introduction of cellular production techniques to the hospital sector in Sweden (Chapter 18), it is still not clear how much of a role - or indeed whether this role was negative or positive - was played by the simultaneous introduction of quasi-market relations to the provision of health services. The structure of the labour market - that is, that in the economy at large rather than that within firms (which is subject to enterprise-level decisions) - is another important area where the success of organisational reform is contingent upon complementary domains of policy making and economic organisation.

Yet, it is important not to lose sight of the central importance which organisational change plays as a necessary condition for the resumption of European competitiveness. Nathan Rosenberg points to the 'debacle of General Motors', and the lessons which have to be learnt from this (Chapter 20). By this he means that merely reviving the rate of investment, or more particularly the commitment of specific investments in high technology, without first making the necessary organisational reforms described in this volume may at best lead to an unchanged rate of deterioration in competitiveness, and at worst may even increase the rate of relative decline. The recent experience of EC support for high-tech in the Third Framework Programme, as shown in the introductory chapter, provides a closer and even more important lesson of the limits of policy interventions which do not pay adequate attention to the organisational challenge.

The Use of Organisational Rents

As Giovanni Dosi makes clear, organisational innovation can be seen in a classically Schumpeterian framework as providing a source of temporary protection from the pressures of competition (Chapter 10). There are two elements to the generation of these rents which are illuminated by these various case-studies - the way in which they are being utilised by the enterprise, and the distribution of rents through the chain of inter-enterprise links ('relational rents').

Consider first the case of the intra-enterprise utilisation of organisational rents. The more dynamic firms whose experience is described in earlier chapters see these rents as being the source of future growth. For these firms these innovations represent a major source of profits with which to fund continued growth and profitability. The firms have thus adopted a positive and proactive response to the agenda of organisational change. On the contrary, those firms which fail to see the opportunities which are opened up by organisational change, respond defensively and reactively; invariably they adopt a variety of 'cargo-cult' approach towards a succession of organisational fixes such as TQC, JIT and now business process engineering which are soon discarded as they run up against vested interests within and without the firms.

This distinction between a positive proactive and negative reactive approach to the challenge of organisational change closely parallels the wider policy discussion around flexibility (and indeed the environmental impact of production). On the one hand, flexibility is seen as a positive attribute, providing the opportunity to generate Schumpeterian rents and hence to sustain the growth of competitiveness (as we have defined it in Chapter 1); this is indeed the approach adopted by the White Paper on *Growth, Competitiveness and Employment*, as well as by some of the progressive firms and trade unions. On the other hand, flexibility is seen as a method for short-term cost-cutting, in part through the employment of lowly-paid part-time workers. In all these cases it is important to move the innovating agenda from a reactive, cost-cutting focus to a proactive anticipatory search for new forms of innovative rents. At this point of industrial history organisational changes are not only the most easily accessible innovative rents, but are a necessary requirement for the reaping of rents through new generations of technology (see below).

The second rent-related issue raised by the diffusion of organisational change, relates to the distribution of relational rents. Running through virtually all of the case-studies in this volume is the critical importance of restructuring the enterprises' links with the external environment. In most of these cases, these inter-enterprise links are confined to the spheres of production (for example, Peugeot's relationships with its suppliers, Chapter 5) and R&D (SGS-Thomson's alliance with Phillips, IBM and Siemens, Chapter 9); but new links with the outside world are becoming increasingly important also in the sphere of human resource development (for example, Baxi's links with the local college of further education, Chapter 13). But perhaps the most fully-developed examples of the gains to be achieved from inter-enterprise linkages are to evidenced in respect to the network of SME's in Baden-Württemberg (Chapter 17), and the UK network for continuous improvement (Chapter 16).

It is through these new forms of inter-enterprise links that a large measure of the organisational rents are to be found, particularly in the medium term once firms have restructured their own internal operations. This throws the focus of attention on the distribution of these relational rents. Crudely speaking, it is possible to distinguish two patterns here. At the one end of the spectrum, a single link in the chain of innovation and production is able to appropriate the bulk of these rents through its market power and/or its critical role in the production chain; usually this occurs when production or marketing and purchasing are dominated by large, oligopolistic firms (vertical linkages in the case of production, horizontal linkages in the case of marketing/purchasing). At the other extreme, these new inter-enterprise linkages are much more closely imbedded in a framework of relations of trust; the distribution of the organisational rents is much more equal through the production chain, and the dominance of single large firms tends to be lower with SMEs more prominent in production.

Which of these two distributional patterns of relational rents prevails is contingent upon a number of factors, including the national context and the particular social imbeddedness of production, the sector under consideration, and the balance of production held by SMEs. A priori whilst there may be normative reasons to favour a more equal distribution of rent, the economic case for one or other pattern of trust relations can not be made at this stage of the research process.

The Social Imbeddedness of Organisational Change

This importance of trust in inter-firm relations is only one dimension in which social relations can be seen as central to the process of organisational reform. But they are pervasive and are pivotal to the new procedures which are being introduced. Indeed, just as electronics and fibre optics lie at the core of the information technology revolution, so it can be said that social relations are at the base of organisational innovation. It is for this reason that the Baxi case is so interesting since it represents one experiment to encourage participation in technological change through participation in ownership (Chapter 13). The four Dutch case studies on personnel management also address the challenge of participation by linking personal career development with better knowledge flows in the firm (Chapter 11), whilst the case of Oticon (Chapter 14) represents an alternative path through the sweeping away of internal hierarchies and functional specialisations.

Since social imbeddedness is thus at the core of organisational innovation, the diffusion of this form of technological change thus poses particular problems of market failure. One particular problem which arises is when the process of change occurs in labour-intensive organisations; in this case, the impact of change is frequently pervasive, affecting virtually all employees and (in the case where organisational change improves labour productivity) having severe impacts upon the level of employment. When this involves highly-skilled personnel, or those in socially critical areas such as health (Chapter 18), the barriers to diffusion may be particularly substantial.

A further important consequence of the social imbeddedness of organisational change is that it may be highly locationally specific. Lundvall observes of the Swedish hospital that not only do the organisational innovations occur within the particular context of Sweden, but there is a danger that the changes in work organisation and the incentive system may undermine the extra-market commitment of social sphere workers to their patients (Chapter 19). This locational specificity may also have an impact upon the policy instruments which are most appropriate to foster innovation, and which may limit the process of learning from comparative innovatory experience (see below).

Technology as a Complement to Organisational Change

As we have seen in Chapter 1 and elsewhere, there is extensive experience that new forms of embodied technology - especially those utilising microelectronic controls which provide an enhanced capacity for flexible production - cannot be utilised effectively without a prior process of organisational change, involving integration within and between the three spheres of operation of the enterprise. Moreover, there is also extensive evidence that particularly in the early stages of the transition to flexible production, new forms of organisation provide the capacity for substantial gains in performance, and often make it unnecessary to invest in complex and costly new embodied technologies.

However, it does not follow from this that the commitment to new technologies should be forsaken; merely that the phasing of their introduction should occur within a context in which organisational change plays a central role. Thus, we can see from a number of the case-studies, that the successful utilisation of both new techniques of organisation and new forms of organisation depends upon their interplay in the cycle of innovation. In the case of Renault's Twingo design, the heavyweight-teams had access to sophisticated CAD systems (Chapter 8); in SGS-Thomson, high levels of investment in new technologies were a necessary complement to the development of the 'lab manufacture' and the inter-firm technological alliances (Chapter 9); and in the process of organisational reform in the health sector, the utilisation of new forms of surgery facilitated the introduction of out-patient operating theatres and will surely be followed by sophisticated database systems which hold comprehensive personal medical histories.

Organisational Change and Employment

The introduction of new forms of organisation has a comprehensive impact upon employment, both in relation to its quality and quantity. With respect to the nature of work, the potential lies to significantly enhance the non-material returns to employment. The new organisational reforms require that employers invest more substantively in their labour forces, that jobs become less fragmented and that work is conducted in a less isolated framework. Whilst the Japanese experience shows that this need not translate into a pattern of working conditions that is likely to be socially acceptable in Europe, it does provide the potential for an improvement in these conditions. Of the case studies involved in this volume only one explicitly addressed this issue - the examination of change in the Swedish hospital (Chapter 18) - and confirmed the general hypothesis that it was associated with an enhancement of work-satisfaction.

With regard to the quantum of employment, the new forms of organisational which are diffusing generally increase labour productivity; as we have seen, there is consequently reason to believe that there will be significant obstacles to their diffusion, particularly in the labour intensive service sectors. But as with earlier rounds of radical technological change, this displacement of labour at a particular point in the production chain does not necessarily mean that the overall employment impact will be negative. From the perspective of the individual firm, early adoption of these organisational techniques may enhance market share and hence lead to a sustained (and perhaps even enhanced) level of employment, but for the economic system as a whole, there may also be positive employment effects. As Nathan Rosenberg points out, for example (Chapter 20), despite the cheapening of health care costs as a consequence of organisational change, it may be possible to meet a wider range of needs. Organisational reform may also have the effect of reducing the costs of investment (by increasing its productivity), and may hence lead to an increase in productive capacity. Thus the medium- and long-term consequences of organisational reform may not only be to enhance European industry's competitiveness and improve consumer welfare, but also to contribute to the solution of Europe's unemployment crisis.

The Role of Organisational Research

The case studies also illustrate the importance of organisational research and the diffusion of organisational knowledge and experience in this area. New views on organisation have to be validated in practice and have to be analysed and compared in order to compile a body of knowledge which could be utilised by a new generation of managers and professionals within firms. This kind of research should be imbedded in practice and should be directed to achieve a rapid process of diffusion. This research process can be reviewed as a kind of 'R&D for organisational innovation'. But just as in the new protocols for more conventional 'hard technology' R&D, it is required to be:

- concurrent, that is, undertaking research on organisational change whilst the new forms of organisational innovation are being introduced;
- networked, drawing firms and institutions together to exchange experiences; and
- multidisciplinary, involving disciplines such as economics, sociology, psychology, information technology and so on.

It is possible to characterise this as 'action research'. The idea underlying this concept of research is to shorten the innovatory cycle. The intent is similar to the process of concurrent engineering utilised so successfully in the development of the Renault Twingo (Chapter 8) and involves an active collaboration between the observers and the implementers of organisational reform. In terms of the case studies reviewed in this document, examples of action research can be found in the case of the UK network on continuous improvement (Chapter 16), and the role played by the academic community in the changes at Zilverstad (Chapter 6). Whilst this form of research has much in its favour, it does provide the possibility that the 'external observers' will be so compromised by their participation in the process of adoption, that they will be unable to provide the detached analysis which is required in the medium and long term if organisational change is to proceed effectively. We are still too early in the action research development cycle to determine whether these strengths outweigh the weaknesses or whether new forms of organising action research may lead to better outcomes[1]

But real learning cannot be based on stories of 'best practice' and indeed the search for 'best practice' is illusory; the well-known phrase used in total quality management - 'best is the enemy of better' - is illuminating in this regard.. Moreover, failures and mistakes have proven to be an important source of learning. Thus Luc Soete reminds us in this respect of the importance of paired studies (Chapter 21), comparing successful and unsuccessful cases of adoption.

Finally, R&D on organisational innovation is not starting from scratch. National programmes have been established in a number of European countries to deal with these issues. They vary in focus and methodology, but have generally played a critical role in raising awareness for organisation as a critical input to foster international competitiveness. Here reference can be made to the German Federal and Länder programmes on Work and Technology, the French programme on Technology, Work and Employment, the Swedish Organisational Learning Programme, the Dutch programme on Technology, Work and Organisation, and the British programme on Information and Communications Technology. The countries of the European Union also count a substantial number of high quality research institutes in this multidisciplinary field of study. These national institutes and initiatives form an excellent platform for the exchange of knowledge and experience across national boundaries. The combination of these forces is extremely important method for raising awareness of the importance of organisation in Europe's quest for enhanced competitiveness. But the principles of subsidiarity can be applied here, not the least in relation to the fostering of organisational change in less industrialised member states.

IV. CONCLUSIONS

There are clearly a large number of lessons which can be leant from this emerging process of organisational reform in European industry. We would like to limit ourselves here to a few brief conclusions on the implications for public policy.

First, given the productivity paradox identified in Chapter 1, there is clearly a need to foster a rapid diffusion of organisational change in European industry in order to facilitate the revival of European competitiveness. There are two possible approaches to this sub-optimal pattern of diffusion. On the one hand, this may be due to problems of market structure - as Jaquemin points out, this may influence the pace and nature of organisational change (Chapter 3). This being the case, the appropriate form of policy intervention is that which involves the elimination of these market distortions. On the other hand, it may be that even if markets do operate in a quasi-perfect manner, there are critical areas of market failure which are suggestive of a role for public policy. There are no a priori grounds for arguing an exclusive case for either of these impediments to diffusion. The optimal policy response is likely to involve a mix of both market-oriented and market-correcting interventions, but without further detailed research it is not possible to fill in this policy detail with any precision.

Second, as the Baden-Württemberg and the UK continuous improvement network cases indicate (Chapters 16 and 17), an appropriate 'policy response' means neither an exclusive role for the state, nor that support should be in a financial form. There is widespread experience which shows that there is extensive scope for joint public/private initiatives, with the tertiary research and education sector often playing a critical role. Moreover, this programme of public support is arguably most effective when undertaken on an 'in-kind' and supportive framework, with the firms investing considerable resources themselves in the adoption of new forms of organisation.

Third, the adoption of new forms of organisation in industry often requires the detailed participation of the tertiary sector, particularly that of producer (often termed 'business') services. Whilst this segment of the service sector is relatively well-extended in Europe, it nevertheless remains sub-optimally developed and may require public support. As the experience of the UK shows, this support may be most effectively given by promoting the demand for these services (through financial subsidies).

Finally, the optimal location of this public support will vary and in most case will require response at a large number of levels. In the case of Baden-Württemberg, it was the local government which played a critical role (Chapter 17); in other cases (as in the UK network, Chapter 16), the appropriate form of support is that provided by the national government. But in other cases such as when high-tech industries are involved (SGS-Thomson, Chapter 9), it may be that the optimal arena is at the Community level. There is a further reason, particularly relevant with respect to organisational change, why support at the Community level may be relevant. This is because there is a very significant diversity of experience with respect to the types of organisational techniques which can be utilised and the social frameworks within which they are imbedded. Taking advantage of this extraordinary diversity almost certainly requires coordination at the supra-national level, building on regional and national programmes. The synergies which arise from this coordination will add value to each of these levels of support for organisational restructuring. At the same time, the limits imposed on diffusion by the socially imbedded nature of these innovations also presses for a supra-national programme of support. The time is thus ripe for a major initiative at the European level.

In conclusion, therefore, it is clear that European industry is at a vital crossroad. The path to resumed competitiveness lies in the high road of innovation and proactive flexibility rather than in the low road of reactive cost-cutting and competition through lower wages (often mediated through changes in the exchange rate, thus contributing further to destabilisation). Organisational change is a key to the resumption of competitiveness, but is a costly process, subject to significant social obstacles and various forms of market failure. A policy response is thus urgent and is required at a range of levels, including at the level of the Community. Without urgent action, there is every danger that the European economy will continue to suffer from a crisis of competitiveness with a consequent decline in living standards, a growth in inequality and unemployment, and an exacerbation of social tensions.

NOTE

1. Some attempts have been made to define indicators, but clearly greater attention needs to be given to this issue. See Greenan *et al.* [*1993*].

REFERENCES

European Commission (1994), *White Paper on Growth, Competitiveness and Employment*, Brussels-Luxembourg: ECSC-EC-EAEC.

Greenan, N., Guellec, D., Broussaudier, G. and L. Miotti (1993), 'Innovation organisationnelle, dynamique technologique et performance des enterprises', Document de Travail, Direction des Etudes et de la Statistique, Paris: Institut National de la Statistique et des Etudes Economiques.

Kaplinsky, R. (1994), *Easternisation: The Spread of Japanese Management Techniques to Developing Countries*, London: Frank Cass.

For Product Safety Concerns and Information please contact our EU
representative GPSR@taylorandfrancis.com
Taylor & Francis Verlag GmbH, Kaufingerstraße 24, 80331 München, Germany

www.ingramcontent.com/pod-product-compliance
Ingram Content Group UK Ltd.
Pitfield, Milton Keynes, MK11 3LW, UK
UKHW021834240425
457818UK00006B/191

* 9 7 8 0 7 1 4 6 4 6 3 0 5 *